THE
THEATER PROPS
HANDBOOK

THE
THEATER PROPS
HANDBOOK

A Comprehensive Guide to
Theater Properties,
Materials, and Construction

THURSTON JAMES

Betterway Publications, Inc.
White Hall, Virginia

Published by Betterway Publications, Inc.
Box 86
White Hall, VA 22987

Cover Design by David Wagner
Cover Photos Courtesy of University of Virginia Department of Drama

The cover photos, demonstrating theater properties in use, are production photos of the Virginia Players and Heritage Repertory Theatre, producing organizations of the University of Virginia's Department of Drama. Grateful acknowledgment is made to LaVahn G. Hoh and Martin A. Beekman of the University of Virginia Department of Drama for providing access to the photographic resources of the Virginia Players and Heritage Repertory Theatre. Productions represented on the front cover are: top, *Dracula* and *The Devil's Disciple;* center, *You Can't Take It With You, A Midsummer Night's Dream, Edward II,* and *Twelfth Night;* bottom, *Oh What a Lovely War* and *Tiny Alice.* Photos on the back cover are from *Vanities, The Prisoner of Second Avenue, The Inspector General,* and *As You Like It.*

Typography by Typecasting

Every precaution has been taken in preparing *The Theater Props Handbook* to make these projects as safe and successful as possible. However, neither Betterway Publications nor the author assume any responsibility for any damages or injuries incurred in connection with the use of this manual.

Library of Congress Cataloging-in-Publication Data

James, Thurston
    The theater props handbook.

    Includes index.
    1. Stage props—Design and construction. I. Title.
PN2091.S8.J34   1987   792'.025   87–15924
ISBN 0-932620-88-4
ISBN 0-932620-86-8 (pbk.)

Printed in the United States of America

0 9 8 7 6 5 4 3 2 1

CONTENTS

APOLOGIA . . . . **ix**
"A Very Broad-Based Subject" ix
A Definition of Properties x
  A Moving Van of Personal Property
A Definition of a Prop Man xiii
A Picture Morgue xiv
  The History of My Picture Morgue

ANIMAL FORMS **1**
Dummy Figures 1
Moths and Butterflies 2
An Owl 3
  Sculpting the Body
  Making the Legs and Talons
  Obtaining the Feathers
  Applying the Feathers
A Baked Peacock 8
Restoring a Natural Pelt (Cheetah) 11
Building a Prop Pelt (Sheep) 13
Scarecrow 14
A Barbecued Lamb 18
A Turtle 21

ARCHAEOLOGICAL RELICS **26**
Arrowheads 26
Bone Tools 26
An Ancient Pottery Urn 27
Brass and Copper Relic Jewelry 27

BARBED WIRE **28**

BLOOD **30**
Making a Heart 31
A Blood Knife 33

BOOKS **35**
"A Book Is a Book" 35
Familiar Books 36
"Antique" Replicas 36
  The Book Cover
  Binding the Book
  The Character Cover
Examples of Hand-Made Character Books . 40
Lightweight Books 42
Fake Dust Jackets 44

CONFETTI **46**

**CONSTRUCTION
TECHNIQUES** **47**
Epoxy Putty 47
  Modeling with Epoxy Putty
  Bonding with Epoxy Putty
Ethafoam 50
  Cutting Ethafoam into Half Round Molding
  Painting Ethafoam
Invisible Knot 52
Making a Butter Churn 53
  Setting the Pitch on the Saw Blade
  Making the Jig for Cutting the Tapers
  Using the Jig to Cut the Beveled Taper
  Making the End Plugs
PVC Pipe 59
  Bending a Shepherd's Crook
Sculpting Urethane Foam 61
  The Band Saw as a Sculpting Tool
  Sculpting a Space Gun
  Sculpting a Urethane Dog
Machine Tooling Urethane Foam 67
  Turning a Large Goose Egg
  A Drill Press Lathe
  Sculpting Foam Balusters
  Sculpting a Beehive
Some Tips on Sewing 73
  A Drapery Table
  Straight Cuts on Fabrics
  Pulling a Thread
  Sewing a Straight Hem

CONTAINERS **78**
Faking a Beer Can Label 78
Making a Vile Vial 79
Russian Tea Glasses 82
    Making Two Russian Tea Glasses
Rustic Jugs from Wine Bottles 83

ELECTRICITY OF
LOW-VOLTAGE LAMPS **87**
Physics of Electricity 87
    Series Battery Connections
    Parallel Battery Connections
    Parallel and Series Battery Connections
        Compared
    Series–Parallel Battery Connections
    The Power Supply Package
    Some Electronic Definitions
    Series Load Connections
    Parallel Load Connections
    Series–Parallel Load Connections
    Physics of Electricity — Summary
Converting a Lamp to Battery Operation . . 95
    The Top End
    Converting the Bottom End of the Lamp
A Dimmer-Controlled Flashlight 97
A Dimmer-Controlled Oil Lamp 98

EYEGLASSES **99**
Binocular Replicas for the Stage 99
Eyeglasses 101
    A Short History of Eyeglasses
Building a Pair of "Granny Glasses" 102
Building a Monocle 103
Lorgnette 105

FIRE **107**
Blazing Fire Flames 107
    The Plastic Sheet
    Moving the Plastic
    Lighting the Plastic Sheet
Simulating Fires 109
    A Flickering Log Fire
    Making a Camp Fire
    A Smoldering Fireplace
    A Firebrand Torch
Smoke Effects 118
    Barbecue Grill
    Flash Pot Substitute

FOOD **120**
Providing Edible Prop Food 120
Making Beverages for the Stage 121
Artificial Food 121
    Bread
    The Greatest Compliment
    Candy:
        Chocolates
        Peppermint Sticks
    Cauliflower
    Cheese
    Making a Chicken Drumstick
    Making a Hamburger
    Making a sandwich
    Fruits and Vegetables:
        Lettuce
    Making a Slice of Pie
    Sausages
    Tropical Fruit Cocktails
    Strawberries

FOOTLIGHTS **139**

GLUES AND ADHESIVES . . **141**
Animal Glue and Its Successors 141
Elvanol 142
FEV 143
Flex-Glue 144
    An Introduction to Flex-Glue
    Applications and Aliases
    Making a Leather Texture
    Making Skin, Membranes, and Tissue
    An Embedding Material
    A Paint Binder
    Shatter-Resistant Skin
    Rough Textures
Hot Glue 152
    Non-Adhesive Applications of Hot Glue:
        Hot Glue Candle Drippings
        Doughnuts and Danish
        Hot Glue Ornamentation
        Casting with Hot Glue

GRAMOPHONE **159**

ICE CUBES **165**

JUNK ART— FOUND OBJECTS 168
Support Your Local Scavenger 168
The Use of Found Objects 169

LAMP PARTS 173

OLD-TIME PHOTOS PROCESSED ON A BLUEPRINTER 178
Everything You Never Wanted to Know About Brownline 179

PLANT FORMS 182
A Landscape Hedge 182
Topiary Bushes 184
Foliage Flameproofing and Preserving 186
A Bale of Alfalfa 188
Dressing a Hay Cart 189
Making Stylized Plant Foliage 192
A Sapling Tree 195

REHEARSAL FURNITURE .. 196
The Problem of Rehearsal Furniture 196
Rehearsal Furniture 197
The Rehearsal Chair 198
The Rehearsal Sofa 204
The Rehearsal Cube 205
The Rehearsal Bench 208

RUNNING WATER 210
Gravity-Fed Water Supply 210
Running Water—Under Pressure 211
A Recirculating Electric Pump 211
Rain Effects 213

STAGE MONEY 214
Coins 214
Paper Money 216
Do-It-Yourself Stage Money 217
Foreign Currency 218

SIMULATING STAINED GLASS 219
Laying Out the Window 219
Make Your Own Leading Paste 220
Leading the Lines 221
Staining the Plastic Panel 223
Making a Polyester Window Pane 224

TEXTURES 226
Distressing Wood 226
Torch and Brush Weathering Technique .. 227
Marbleizing 229
Glare Reduction 232
  Reynolds Wrap?
  The Use of White on Stage
  The Problem of Light-Colored Furniture
  Softening Glare with Nylon Net
  Other Methods of Glare Reduction

WEAPONS 236
Toy-Store Plastic Replica Pistols 236
Stage Firearms 236
  Building a Shotgun
Thompson Sub-Machine Gun 242
  Making the Gun Stock
  Painting a Gun-Metal Finish
  A Property Master's Dreams
  Simulating Machine Gun Fire with a Strobe Light
Swords 251

WRITING MATERIALS 253
A Historical Overview 253
  Parchment
  Paper
Simulating Parchment 254
Simulating Early Hand-Made Paper 255
Pens 256
Pencils 256
Making an Inkwell Set 256

APPENDIX 259
Glossary 259
Where to Get Your Supplies 264

INDEX 269

APOLOGIA

"A Very Broad-Based Subject"

The scene takes place backstage in a large university theater. There is no setting on the stage and all of the masking has been flown up to high trim. The stage, however, is not bare. Tables have been assembled, decorated, and filled with several kinds of finger foods. A restaurant counter from a recent show has been pressed into service as a wet bar, fully stocked now with authentic beverages. Rugs, sofas, and easy chairs, pulled from the caged storage area, are arranged in informal groupings. The scene is peopled with 30 or 40 members of the theater faculty, staff, students, and their friends. The event is a retirement party for one of the department's faculty directors, and it seems to show the signs of a successful celebration. All those in attendance have taken advantage of what the scene has to offer. Small gatherings are clustered around the furniture, hands have been filled and refilled with drinks and toothpicked tidbits. A congenial din fills the air as the participants vie for control of their conversation groups. A good time is being had by all.

The PROPERTIES MASTER *is standing at the fringe of one group, nursing a Coke. He spies a* THEATER MANAGER *from the south end of the campus, he waves to draw attention, and the two old friends meet shaking hands.*

THEATER MANAGER Well, well, I haven't seen you in a long time. How are you doing?

PROP MASTER Doin' good, real good. As often as we see each other, you'd think we worked in different cities instead of on the same campus.

THEATER MANAGER Are they keeping you busy?

PROP MASTER Sure, sure. Busy enough. Keepin' out of trouble.

THEATER MANAGER There's one thing about your job I've always envied — it's never boring.

There's always something new coming your way in the prop shop.

PROP MASTER That's true. But I've got a project going now that's making my work even more interesting. I've been putting together a book on properties.

(A GRADUATE STUDENT, *a Ph.D. candidate from the moving picture division, joins the two men in their conversation. Having slightly exceeded his limit, he seems to be feeling no pain.)*

GRAD STUDENT Whatcha doin' with that Coke? They've got beer over there. Want me to get you a Coors? *(He familiarly pokes the stomach of the* PROPERTIES MASTER *with his finger)*

PROP MASTER Naw, that's O.K., I feel like havin' a Coke right now.

THEATER MANAGER *(to the* PROPERTIES MASTER*)* You were saying, you're writing a book.

GRAD STUDENT You're writing a book? I didn't know you were writing a book!

THEATER MANAGER I've not seen many books on properties. It's a tough subject to cover. There are so many things that ought to be included. Actually, I guess you would have to include everything! Everything is a potential prop.

PROP MASTER That's true. *(He smiles a little tentatively)* It's a very broad-based subject.

THEATER MANAGER Books have been written on nearly every phase of technical theater. Costuming has been thoroughly covered, scenic painting, theater lighting, sound, stage management — it's surprising that in all of theater literature, the subject of properties has been so slighted.

GRAD STUDENT I'm not surprised. Intelligent people don't try to do impossible things.

PROP MASTER I may not be able to do a completely comprehensive job, but I'm enjoying the project, and I'll see where it goes.

GRAD STUDENT Comprehensive! Humph. *(aside)* It would be a lifetime work for a team of — *(pointedly)* young men.

THEATER MANAGER What audience? What group will you be writing for?

PROP MASTER I'm trying to make the text basic enough for inexperienced people to follow. I'm not assuming that the reader will have a lot of technical background.

THEATER MANAGER So. It will be a beginner's handbook.

PROP MASTER No, no, a lot more than that. I think that even experienced prop men will be able to profit from it. I've picked up a lot of tricks . . . and techniques that they may not be aware of.

GRAD STUDENT Sounds like you're trying to be "all things to all men." That can be a rather dangerous position to take.

PROP MASTER I want to keep the approach uncomplicated, without being simplistic. Does that make sense?

THEATER MANAGER: It does to me. *(The GRADUATE*

STUDENT *frowns and shakes his head)* Where are you beginning? What subjects do you feel must be covered? Do you have any priorities?

PROP MASTER So far I'm just taking things as they come through my shop. If they're interesting and unusual, I'm photographing them and writing them up.

GRAD STUDENT And all of this without an outline? *(Muttering, barely audible, barely coherent)* A hodge-podge of scattered data, with no direction.

PROP MASTER In a couple of years of working like this, I should have a good cross section of property problems and documented solutions.

THEATER MANAGER You're in an excellent position to know what kinds of problems are encountered, and how frequently they crop up. I say, give it a try. You'll soon know the truth of the matter.

PROP MASTER I've been working on it for a while. I'm not discouraged yet.

GRAD STUDENT Well, sir, I'll give you this: You've got guts! An untried author, writing on an impossibly large subject, with only the barest idea of how to proceed. You are really going to need some good luck. *(He exits laughing)*

PROP MASTER *(mildly amused)* Who was that masked man? I wanted to thank him.

A Definition of Properties

The term "properties" is extremely general. It includes everything in the world — past, present, and sometimes even future.

Most writers of stagecraft and design textbooks define *properties* by grouping them into categories according to their size and purpose.

They refer to such terms as "set props," "trim props," and "hand props." I am no different! I will follow this tradition; but first, in the interest of interest, I offer a definition in the form of an analogy.

A Moving Van of Personal Property

When a person (let's call him George) buys or rents a house, he selects one that reflects his tastes

in architecture and his lifestyle, one that is in keeping with his economic class, one that he can be comfortable in. These unfurnished bare walls, when translated into stagecraft terminology, are called *scenery*. The walls, floor, stairs, railings, the fireplace (that George loves so), the coved ceiling, cornice moldings, wainscoting, pillars, beams, and anything built in, are all considered to be part of the scenery.

When the moving van arrives on the site, George and his family begin to fill this scenic shell with their possessions. These things are called *properties* or *props*. The properties that George owns and surrounds himself with are what makes his home different from his brother's or his father's, and are what makes the neighbors envious of him.

The accumulation of personal property that he has collected and surrounded himself with is a reflection of his personality, whether he likes it or not. Sometimes people live in such a clutter of things that a single moving van is insufficient to truck in their belongings. But, few or many, these monuments to individuality are known in the theater as *props*.

Of course a stage setting representing a hotel room, a café interior, or a railway station cannot have this personal touch of reflecting the personalities of those occupying the space, but no matter. A moving van *did* come up to the doorway and these properties were unloaded, under the direction of *someone*, and this someone dressed the walls which were left bare by the plasterers, finish carpenters, and painters.

This "moving van" illustration gives a pretty good general idea of what the term "properties" entails. This analogy breaks down a little bit in today's economy, where most homes are partly furnished before the buyers move in. The lighting fixtures, wall-to-wall carpeting, and the draperies are already installed in the house; and yet in the theater, they are the responsibility of the properties master.

The setting shown below, designed by Kermit Heckert for *When You Comin' Back, Red Ryder?* graphically demonstrates the effect of adding "properties" to "scenery." Compare this with the production photo on the next page. The atmosphere provided by the properties gives this setting its personality.

The *traditional* definition takes this "moving van" full of stuff, and breaks it down into groupings of props, like this:

Set props   Any items that sit on the stage and would show up on a floor plan. This classification includes things like tables, sofas, rugs, podiums, rocks, and lampposts.

Trim props   Items that you might find hanging on the walls of a setting. Curtains, draperies, wall sconces, pictures, signs, and bulletin boards are representative examples.

Set dressings   Items that are on the set because the character in the play would most certainly have them in his possession and as a part of his environment, but which are not used as a part of stage business.

Hand props   Objects called for by the script, or by the director, to be handled and used in the business of the play.

Personal props   Any hand props for which the custodial responsibility has been transferred, by mutual consent, from the prop crew head to the actor. This class of props covers items such as wallets, combs, pocket watches, jewelry, eyeglasses, and possibly dress swords and canes. The reasoning is that the property, due to its nature, belongs with the costume, and the actor takes the responsibility for the item and cares for it as he cares for his costume.

Greens   Any plants, trees, shrubs, hedges, and bushes, whether real or artificial, not built by standard scenic construction methods, are the responsibility of the property department.

Manual sound effects   Any sound effects not produced from a record or tape, and not provided by an orchestra, are provided by the properties department. This grouping covers sound effects such as gun shots, door slams, offstage crashes, doorbells, buzzers, thunder, chimes, horses and wagons, and noises of all kinds that are to be generated "live."

Now I'll allow that I did not get all of these sound effects and trees and rocks and lampposts out of a moving van, but I still like the analogy as a general concept of what a prop is.

A Definition of a Prop Man

A properties man goes about supplying the hundreds of specialty items a production may need. There are two ways he can do his job.

1. Obtain the genuine articles. In metropolitan areas, which house large populations within a compact space, "seek and ye shall find." Antique shops and thrift shops and flea markets abound. Listings of rental houses occupy considerable space in the Yellow Pages. Small shops cater to the special wants of esoteric minorities of this population. You can find shops that specialize in brass beds, vintage firearms, juke boxes, stuffed animals, needlepoint, musical instruments...the list is endless. Anything can be found if you know where to look. Occult shops can be found to supply the needs of witches, at a time when many of us are certain that witches do not even exist.

A properties master who is particularly good at this system — and there is an art to it — is an expert at sources. He knows where to go and find everything. Not *anything,* but *everything.* His mind works like a catalogue. He travels his city extensively, and he remembers what he sees and where he saw it. He keeps little black books and what he cannot remember he writes down. He knows these specialty shops and what they specialize in. This "source" system is expensive because hard-to-find items are likely to command a steep price. However, the "source" method is very reasonable in terms of man-hours. A properties master who knows his business can find things quickly in a city he is familiar with, and he doesn't spin his wheels needlessly searching.

2. Make reproductions of unusual items. A properties master who relies on his own abilities to construct replicas of most of the props he needs must be an expert at techniques. A prop builder must be a jack of all trades, and hopefully master of enough of them to get by. He must be a seamstress, welder, carpenter, upholsterer, electrician, taxidermist, and chef — this list, too, is almost endless. He must know the techniques of building anything. He doesn't need the big city, except to procure the materials he needs for construction. His motto is "Show me a picture and I'll make you a copy!" He needs research materials; he needs a picture file.

The properties builder spends relatively small amounts of money on materials. His expense is felt in terms of time. It takes longer to build a gramophone than to buy one, but if labor is not a consideration, and if in the bargain you can pass along to someone the techniques of property construction, then the time is not so outrageously expensive.

An ideal properties master, of course, must have the best qualities of both of these extreme examples. He is aware of sources, maintains a stock of frequently-used items, uses good judgment as to what needs to be built, and knows how to go about constructing it.

A Picture Morgue

Designers need reference material. This is a fact and it is not something to be ashamed of. No one can memorize all of the details of the world around them, and no one is expected to.

Prop builders need research data too. Any time you set about making a prop, and you are not working from a designer's working drawings, it is of utmost importance that you (1) find some reference material, and (2) know exactly what this object looks like. Here, the prop builder takes on some of the responsibility of the designer. Even if you are planning simply to make a stylized caricature of some item, you still need reference material which depicts the real features of the object, so you can be sure of precisely what to exaggerate. The designer or prop builder who refuses to search out and be guided by reference data is being foolish—and presumptuous.

Reference materials come in many forms and from many places. The best research you can get is three-dimensional. A scale model is ideal if you can get one, or you may use a real object for reference. The most common (but not the best) resource is a picture or photo of the item. Your local library would be an obvious first place to look for pictures, but, alas, it has its shortcomings too. I am not going to talk against libraries here. I will say, however, that you might be disillusioned in an academic library. Picture books there are a rare commodity. I have been known to spend up to two hours in a prestigious library, without finding a picture any better than I might have found at home, in my own encyclopedia.

Actually, encyclopedias are a marginal source of pictures. They are organized alphabetically, and they cover an awful lot of subjects, but the pictures are usually in black and white, and they are typically small. On the other hand, encyclopedias are convenient...so they have their special value as reference sources. I have accumulated four sets of old encyclopedias (from thrift shops and garage sales) and keep them in a cabinet in the UCLA prop room, ready for use when other sources fail.

Another way of making pictures available for ready reference is to start saving and filing pictures in your own "morgue." This is not an easy way to obtain reference material (in fact, it is a lot of trouble), but I strongly recommend that you begin to save interesting pictures as you run across them. Perhaps you have already experienced the frustration of the following thought process:

"Oh, I recently saw a photo like that...Wait, let me think...Oh, it would have been exactly right...I think I kept it for a while...Oh, where is it?...Well, I guess I threw it away."

Every designer (costume, scenery, lighting) and every prop builder should begin, early in his theater career, to build a picture morgue. At first your file will be a sort of personal journal, but if you are patient and organized and diligent, this journal will grow into a resource that you will find indispensible and your colleagues will covet.

The History of My Picture Morgue

I have one heck of a picture file, and I can remember how it began. Twenty years ago, before I had channeled my theater interests into the line of properties, I got my hands on some very cheap volumes from an incomplete set of encyclopedias at a thrift shop. In the back of my head was the vague notion that someday I would clip out and store some of the pictures, for my own reference.

About the same time I was nagged by the feeling that I was wasting too much time watching television—so I salved my conscience by doing the creative act of tearing out pages, while watching television, and storing them in a cardboard box. Everything of any interest was saved; the idea of selectivity or censorship was rejected. I collected kings, insects, Nebraska farm equipment, unusual musical instruments, famous men with beards, Roman ruins, statues, animals, and capitals of foreign cities. These grew into a very confused mixture of pictures until I began to evolve a system of loose organization. I found some file folders and put *things* into one folder. This turned out to be a large category, and I made plans to subdivide it later.

Animals, birds, and insects made up another large category—a grouping that I had no strong interest in but that might be useful in making up a scrapbook for my father, who does have a passing interest.

Places—towns, buildings, ruins, and architectural features—made up another thick folder.

The kings, bearded men, and people went into still another.

The idea of putting the various files into scrapbooks seemed like a good one, so, as I searched for more encyclopedias, I began collecting scrapbooks for the day when I might have time for pasting. I continued collecting odd encyclopedia volumes, being careful not to collect duplicates. (If I had two volumes by different publishers on the same letter, that was O.K. If that resulted in two pictures of a flying squirrel, at least there were two poses of him flying.)

I was quick to notice that children's encyclopedias have more pictures in them than the more scholarly editions. So I picked up some Golden Book volumes and a complete set of *Picture Encyclopedia for Young Readers*.

After about two years of pursuing this project off and on, as a hobby, I was ready to make the first of the scrapbooks. I'd spend a week of idle time on the project, then put it away for a month, work another two days, and lay off for two months. The work was ongoing, but sporadic. My folders were even stored in the attic for a long while.

I had enough columns and capitals to make your head swim. I could show you Ionic, Doric, echinus, Corinthian, Byzantine, and Romanesque. In the bridge section, I could show you the difference between suspension, cantilever, pedestal, and trestle. And I had at ready reference what several of the leading authorities had to say on the subject.

While I was holding this small scrapbook I was inspired to compile a picture dictionary containing every "thing" in the world. Sure, it would take some time, and certainly it would be a thankless task, but what was I to do with my evening hours? Watch television?

It came to my attention that magazines have good pictures in them. One of the best illustrated magazines for "things" was *The National Geographic*. And thrift shops had them, and they were cheap.

I started cutting up *National Geographic* magazines. I found that when you tear off the front and back covers and remove the staples with a pair of pliers, the pages almost fall apart.

National Geographics were so ideal a source for my picture file that I intensified my search for back issues. I kept a checklist in my wallet, so there would be no chance of collecting duplicates.

As time marched on, I ran into some *Life* magazines and a big stack of *Look*. The tearing and clipping of pages continued, and I found that a large folder of personalities was accumulating. These magazines were yielding more social comments and fashions and politics than pictures of *things*. The best source of "item" pictures was the ads, so I began paying a lot of attention to the ads.

One evening (it was raining, as I recall) I decided that it was time to start the sorting process and see where I stood with my "things" file. In my cardboard box was a three-and-a-half-inch accumulation of tidily clipped pictures. I began to arrange them in piles by categories—on tables, counters, chair seats, the floor, even on the piano keyboard. *The elephants with palanquins go here, the fishing boats go there . . . no, wait, there are too many boats and ships; I'll put them all together and subdivide them later. Here is a poison dart blowgun—should that go under "darts" or "blowguns"? Well, I'll put it under weapons, and keep down the number of stacks.* And so it went into the night. Soon it was two o'clock and I'd only gone through about two inches of my stack. I was getting tired, but I could not go to bed with this mess all over the room—my wife would kill me! *I could stop and put everything in more folders, but it would take so long to spread them out again...and when would I be motivated to go through this again? Besides, I had such a good start. No! No turning back; I must plunge ahead.* And so I did.

My stacks of categories, even the number of categories, were too numerous to fit into the scrapbooks I'd collected. I needed a good system for keeping the file which was, by then, pretty valuable to me. The pictures were in manila file folders and the folders were in a strong cardboard box. The idea of loose pictures in folders didn't appeal to me. I could imagine them getting dog-eared or lost. *Maybe they should be in a loose-leaf notebook, or maybe I could glue them to stiff cardboard.* Nothing seemed right. I finally got large envelopes for storage till I could come up with some really good system. That could come later.

I continued to stay on the lookout for good picture sources. I found that the *Smithsonian,* the *American Heritage Magazine, Horizon,* and *Gourmet* were valuable in collecting and searching for photos.

In 1976, I began work at UCLA as the properties master for the Theater Arts department, and since my file was organized well enough to find things in, I brought it to the job and began to show it off. Everyone agreed it was ''interesting'' and ''very nice'' and ''might even be usable,'' if we ever needed a picture of a boot jack, or a chastity belt, or Japanese contour farming. About this time we were doing an original production called *Pipe Dream* (a drama, not the musical you might be familiar with). We needed an Indian peace pipe, one that could be taken apart (stolen diamonds were to be hidden inside it). I went to my file and looked under the heading ''Pipes,'' where I found an Indian peace pipe! Elated with the ease of my research, I smilingly presented it to the director for his approval. My peace pipe was made of wood, and somehow he had envisioned a terra cotta pipe. So, one of the students was sent to the campus research library. She came back with a book devoted to ceremonial pipes of the North American Indians, with illustrations showing pipes of wood, bamboo, sandstone, and terra cotta.

Do you think my picture file and I were in any way crushed? You bet! Here, after all this time and work, I had one picture — and the library, about a block away, had whole books on the same subject.

But my file has had its successes, too. As the morgue developed it became more valuable. In 1976 my picture morgue was comfortably housed in two cardboard boxes. I got a filing cabinet and transferred the material into two of its drawers. Now, ten years later, this file has grown to fill all eight drawers of two filing cabinets. The faculty and MFA (Master of Fine Arts) graduate designers regularly come to the file and use its contents as a first resource since it's so handy. Not only is the file convenient, but frequently a search ends there, not out of compromise, but because the ideal picture has been located.

I hope that this narrative has moved you to at least consider making your own picture morgue. Do it.

ANIMAL FORMS

Dummy Figures

A dummy form (either man or beast) will show up as a "dummy" on stage, if you do not put as much special attention into its skeletal form as you do its more obvious outward features. No matter how well dressed and how realistic the makeup, a dummy will be a distraction if the anatomy lying under the cosmetics is not accurate. The skeleton must have the required shape, weight, and articulation, if you want the dressing that you pile onto the form to stand a chance of appearing realistic.

A skeleton of wood, such as is assembled for a marionette or a mannequin, is ideal in the making of a human dummy.

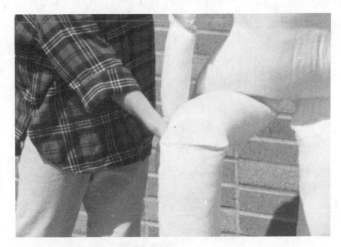

Stuffing a suit of clothes with wads of padding might make a scarecrow but it does not make an acceptable human dummy form.

    Stuffing a suit of long underwear with padding, however, does "flesh out" a passable form —especially if the knee, hip, elbow, and shoulder joints are sewn to allow for a hinging action.

Stops added to the front of each joint help to restrict the amount and direction of motion.

Moths and Butterflies

It is not every play that will call for a butterfly collection. However, for our production of *Tango,* the director asked for dressings that would suggest a character's interest in taxidermy, archaeology, and entomology. We decided to make the character a part-time butterfly collector. The paraphernalia of collecting was sought—a but-

Once our case was completed, we were ready to begin hunting for display specimens. But it was January, and butterflies were out of season, so we had to make our own. We consulted a children's encyclopedia in our picture morgue and

terfly net, a table full of bottles, pins, cotton, and a display case. Now the easy way to obtain a butterfly display is to contact someone who has one and borrow it. If you cannot find such a collector, or such a collector is found but refuses to lend his prized display, then you have some construction work ahead.

A display case is rather straightforward in its construction. Run a long 1″ × 2″ through the table saw, making a groove ⅜″ deep, ¼″ from one edge. (The saw we used was just the right width so that a ⅛″ sheet of Plexiglas would slide into the groove.)

    This 1″ × 2″ should then be cut into segments of appropriate length and assembled like a picture frame. (Our case was 16″ × 24″.) The "frame" is then reinforced with a backing of Masonite. The pinboard is made of a very thin sheet of Styrofoam with a velour covering glued to it.

found some nice big colored pictures of moths and butterflies. I don't suppose a butterfly purist would have a moth in his collection, but with aesthetic distance helping us out we didn't think the audience would be likely to notice.

Snip along the outline of one of the most colorful specimens with a pair of scissors.

Make a body by forming a little roll of masking tape with the adhesive side out.

Roll the body of the cutout picture around the tape to give it a dimensional form.

The advantage a collection of this sort has over one of real butterflies that you might catch in a flowered field is that the manufactured collection

Bend the wings to take them out of a flat plane. Stick a pin through the masking tape and mount the butterfly on the display board.

does not have to be composed mostly of monarchs. Some specimens can be bigger than life size, and the rarest species can be easily included.

An Owl

Making a bird is like making any other animal. Start with a quick study of the anatomy, sculpt the body shape, and then begin to clothe it.

Making the owl's body is not a difficult sculpting job. The really important details — the

"owlish" features — are added as the actual feathers are applied. The sculpted form is just a general body shape. While doing the carving keep some reference material before you. We used both an owl figurine and a picture book on owls.

Sculpting the Body

Carve two pieces of urethane foam into the shape of an owl's body and head. Urethane foam can be shaped very easily with a wood rasp and / or coarse sandpaper.

Attach the head with a sharpened dowel. Push the dowel down through the head and into the body. Join the head to the body at an angle.

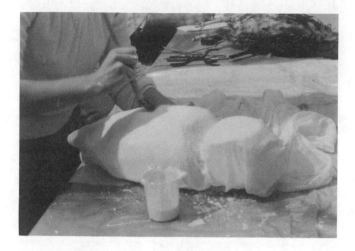

All the pictures seem to agree that this is characteristic of owls.

It is a good idea to give the body a coating of cheesecloth and glue for three reasons.

1) It secures the head to the body.

2) It makes a tough outer skin so the foam is not so fragile.

3) It gives a firm footing for the feathers, which are about to be glued on.

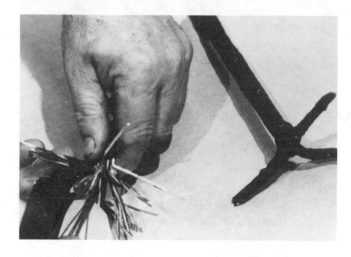

Making the Legs and Talons

Make the legs and talons for your owl from pieces of multiwire telephone cable taped to three wire coat hanger segments that have been bent into "L" shapes. To form the talons, tape one-third of the telephone wires to the short bottom edge of each hanger wire. After all of the toes are taped, they can be formed into hooked claws with a pair of pliers.

Use an ice pick to jab some pilot holes into the body where the legs should go, probably about three-quarters of the way down the owl's body. Check with your reference picture for the appropriate location. The taped wires can be forced into the foam body where you have made the ice-pick holes. Glue a coating of cheesecloth onto the legs (but not onto the talons) to give them some bulk and to secure them firmly to the owl's body. Set the owl aside to dry overnight.

Give the owl a coat of brown paint. As you feather the bird, you should try to leave no areas uncovered by the feathers. If any of the body shows through the feathers, it is best that it not be white.

Obtaining the Feathers

You can use chicken or turkey feathers to dress the owl. If you live in an agricultural area, the barnyard might be your easiest and best source.

However, in Los Angeles (and probably other large cities), there is a listing in the Yellow Pages under the heading "Feathers." Feathers are available either from craft stores or from wholesale suppliers. Crafts stores sell colored feathers in small packages for use in flower arrangements, decorations, jewelry, etc.

Wholesalers deal in sterilized feathers for use in pillows. They also dye them and sell them in bulk to the folks who repackage them for the craft stores. If you buy wholesale, you must buy by the pound, but the cost is a tiny fraction of the marked-up prices of the smaller packages. At this writing a pound of dyed turkey feathers costs four dollars. Even if you must purchase in minimum one-pound lots, do it. You'll have more than enough feathers for ten owls, but it's the cheapest way to go.

Get one pound each of the 3″ and the 9″ turkey feathers. Get some that have been dyed brown. (Note that the lower half of a 3″ feather is covered with a fuzzy down which is not desirable for this project and should be cut away.) You could also use a pound of brown 5″ pigeon feathers for the wings and neck.

Applying the Feathers

Begin feathering the owl by working the front of the bird. Start low down in the tail area and apply layer after layer of small feathers, using hot glue to adhere them. Overlap the rows so that each new row covers the glued tips of the preceding row. If you lay the feathers on with a certain amount of care, the feathered area will have a realistic look.

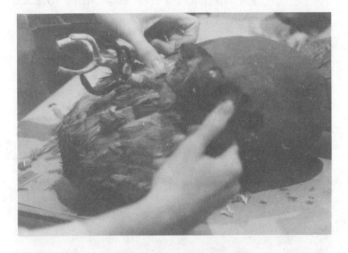

There is a natural curl to almost all bird feathers. Some are "right-handed" and some are "left-handed." This photo shows the difference very clearly.

Pay attention to the natural warp of the feather as you are selecting the larger feathers for the tail and wings.

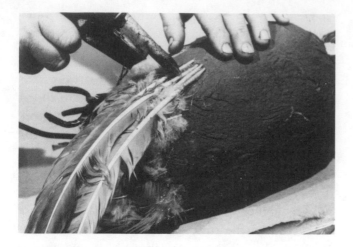

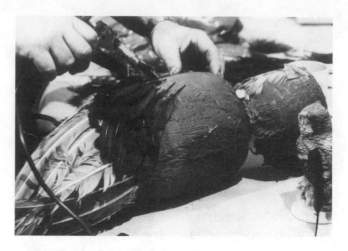

Hot-glue several 9″ feathers on each side of the owl for the tail. Keep your reference pictures before you as you glue on these important owlish details.

Brown 5″ pigeon feathers are used to dress the wings. Use right-handed feathers only for the right wing, left-handed feathers for the left wing. As before, lay them on a row at a time, so each new row overlaps and covers the glued ends of the last.

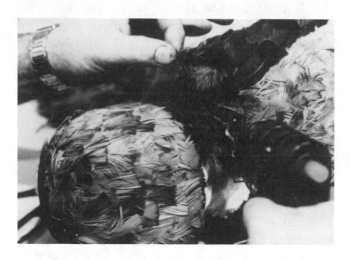

Continue using the same technique of feather application to cover the head and face of the owl. Sort through your 3″ turkey feathers and you will find that some are smaller than others. These smaller ones will be about an inch long when you have cut away the fuzzy end.

Cut some of the pigeon feathers in half. (While cutting can be done with a pair of scissors, I have found that gently pressing the point of a mat knife through the shaft of the feather is easier.) Use these smaller pieces to make a collar for the owl.

Building a ruff or collar around the owl's neck will both accentuate the head and smooth out the seam between the head and body.

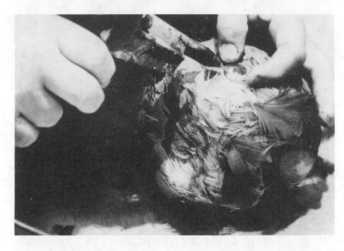

Facial features are very important. The details of an owl's face are what make it distinctly an owl, instead of an eagle or a hawk. Cut some feathers with scissors to make the characteristic "horned" projections that look like alert ears. Apply these with hot glue.

Make a beak from a piece of pine. You can shape it by whittling with a knife or by using a disc sander. Figure out what size the beak should be, and then make it at least twice as long. Attach the beak securely by forcing its extra length into the foam face.

The eyes are an especially important feature in defining an owl's appearance. We were able to purchase plastic owl eyes from a crafts supply store; but if these are not available to you, buttons make an acceptable substitute. Or you could use marbles, surrounding each with a link of a plastic jewelry chain.

The lightweight feather-covered foam owl is strong enough to stand on its own two claws, which can be bent to grasp its perch.

A Baked Peacock

Fantasy props can be a lot of fun. I have, on two occasions, "baked" peacocks for the dining pleasure of royalty. With the aid of the following recipe, you too will be able to cater to the whims of a king.

The construction of this peacock is much like that of the owl in the preceding section, except that there are fewer feathers and a lot more skin.

Begin by sketching a proud-necked peacock on two blocks of urethane foam, one for the body and one for the head and neck. Remember that the bird will be squatting low in the baking pan. He will have no practical feet, as these must be tucked up and pointed to the rear to make "drumsticks." Use a band saw to cut out the sketched pattern, and round off the edges with a wood rasp.

The combined effects of hot glue, a wooden dowel, and a cheesecloth skin will make a secure joint between the neck and the body. Drive a sharpened 3/8″ dowel through the "meatiest" part of both neck and body. Pull the joint apart slightly, squirt a fair-sized stream of hot glue into the crack and quickly reclose the gap. (The hot glue would be sufficient without the dowel but for its tendency to melt the foam.)

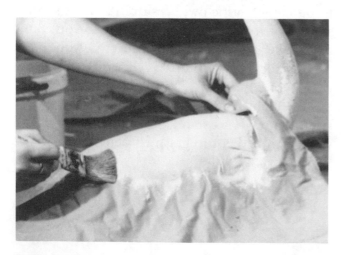

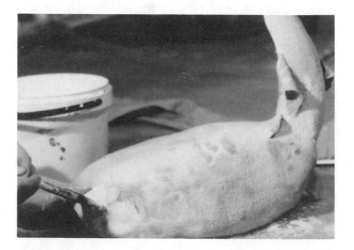

Make a "skin" for the peacock with flannel and flex-glue. The flannel will not only protect the fragile foam surface, it will also provide a perfect

textured base for making roasted "flesh." (See the section on barbecued lamb for further details on this "flesh-making" process.)

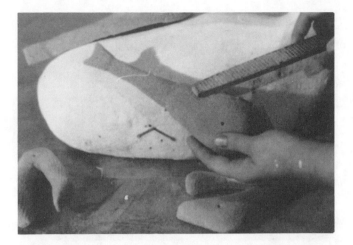

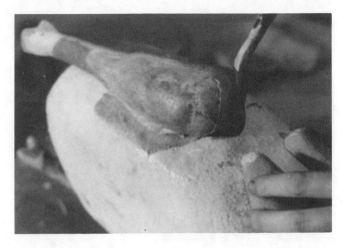

Form the wings and drumsticks out of urethane foam. Using nails instead of a dowel, hot-glue these appendages to the body as you secured the neck.

Use dyes and inks of yellow, orange, and brown to produce the look of roasted flesh. Liberally wet the entire surface of the bird with a fresh coat of flex-glue. Apply the color onto this wetted surface. Sometimes the lighter colors can be applied directly from the bottle. They can be blended

Make each joint secure with an application of flex-glue and flannel "skin" to the limbs.

into the flex-glue very easily with a brush and more glue.

Darker colors should be blended into some flex-glue and applied more carefully. (More comprehensive details on making flesh tones can be found in the section on flex-glue.)

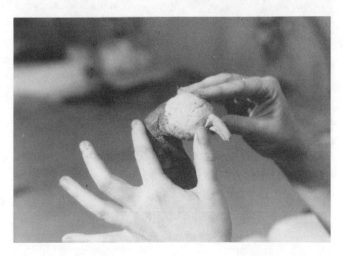

All of the details of the head and face should be sculpted from A–B epoxy putty. Coat the whole head with putty, feathering the edges smoothly.

Make the beak with two short "ropes" of putty.

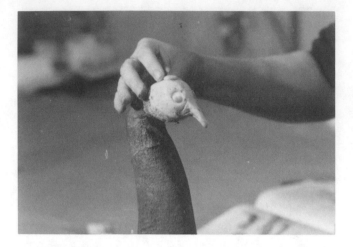

Press some eyes into the soft putty. We used ''teddy bear'' eyes for a cartoon look, but you might want to use glass beads if your bird is to appear less comical.

Make a small ball of putty and press it into the crown to serve as a base for the decorative cockscomb which is to come.

Use hot glue to attach small blue and green feathers to the neck of the bird. We used 3″ turkey feathers which had been dyed and cut down to the size we needed. Dress the bird with feathers from his breast clear up to his face. (See the section on making an owl for a discussion of the sources of feathers and instructions for cutting and applying them.)

Make the comb by hot-gluing green sequins to green florist's wire. Drill small holes through the hardened putty which makes up the crown. Set these wires in the holes, and then push them in to their proper depth. Use hot glue to secure them there.

Paint the face of the bird with green acrylic paint.

Make a double row of shortened tail feathers. The length of these feathers is up to you. We cut ours so they would not be much higher than the head, but yours could be twice this tall and still be realistic. Stick these feathers into a small base of urethane foam, and hot glue the foam tail piece to the bird's rear end.

Snuggle the finished peacock into a nest of garnish (our garnish consisted of crabapples, plums, and sprigs of parsley, dill, and licorice). Be sure the garnish hides the foam tail piece from view. And make way for the kings!

Restoring a Natural Pelt (Cheetah)

Our prop room once received a donation of a cheetah pelt. This skin had been removed by a professional, and its teeth and claws were intact, but its head had been crushed in storage and was badly misshapen.

Having no experience in taxidermy, we phoned several taxidermists in the Los Angeles area for advice on how to soften the hardened skin and reshape the head. The taxidermists were all frustratingly evasive; none would give advice over the phone. (Well, you can't really blame them. They're in business to make a living, and you can't make a living giving free advice on the phone.)

We put on our do-it-yourself hats and tried rubbing an assortment of preparations—mink oil, neat's-foot oil, and leather balm—into the skin side of the pelt to soften it. We succeeded in softening our fingers, but not the hardened animal skin.

A friend who works with puppets learned of our plight and suggested that we use...water! He had some experience straightening leather

shadow puppets that arrived from India badly curled. He said that he had been successful softening these leather puppets by laying them between layers of wet newspapers. He cautioned us, however, not to leave the skin soaking too many days, as that would cause it to rot.

Well, why not? We decided to try.

We shoved a wet sponge into the cheetah's head. We wrapped the whole head in aluminum foil and left it overnight.

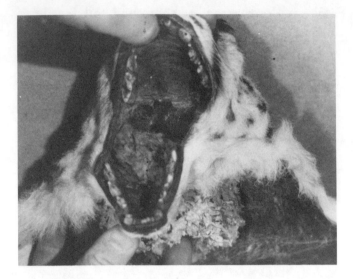 

The next day we checked progress and were pleased to find that the hide was softening. The jaw hinge began to flex a little, and the crown of the head was becoming pliable. And sure enough, the moist skin was beginning to smell. The odor was not too offensive, so we put the sponge back in place and re-wrapped the head for another day of soaking.

The next morning, a few pokes with a finger confirmed that the skin was ripe for shaping. (One whiff verified that it was ripe in more ways than one.) The head could be pushed into shape, but it was so soft that it would not stay in place. The head cavity had to be stuffed with something —rags, newspapers, or the like. We opted for Plasticine, which we felt would give us greatest control.

We made eyes for the cheetah from green glass beads. These were poked into the clay, and then the eyelids were pulled back into place, around the beads.

One negative side effect of the soaking process became apparent while the skin was soft and damp: the fur began to loosen. Small wads came out while the head was being worked. As the head dried out, the fur tightened up again. The odor disappeared after the skin dried, too.

Our cheetah has seen use as set dressing several times since its repair.

Building a Prop Pelt (Sheep)

In the opening scene of *St. Joan*, Shaw calls for a village street scene, with all of the inherent activities of the townspeople. In our production, the director wanted the street to include a tannery, and he called on us to build some animal skins for it.

A woolly sort of pelt can be cut from a white shag rug.

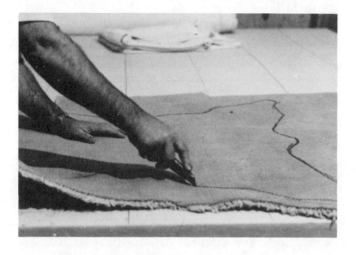

The pelts were mounted so the shag side was facing upstage, away from the audience, so most of the discussion in this section will be concerned with making the backing of the rug look like an untanned skin. The "fur" side of the pelt looks O.K., especially since no one gets a very good look at it.

Treat the rug backing with flex-glue and dyes, as outlined in the section on flex-glue, to give it the look of rawhide. Use brown and orange dyes to achieve the proper color. The flex-glue treatment will close the pores of the rug's jute backing and will provide a semi-gloss texture.

A piece of business required the tanner to busy himself scraping fat from the stretched hides. Our next step, then, will be to make the pelt appear to be covered with fat.

The construction of this "fatty skin" is begun by peeling a dried coating from the inside of an old flex-glue bucket.

Cut the dried glue into strips and wet them with an application of fresh flex-glue. Work the strips into the back of the pelt.

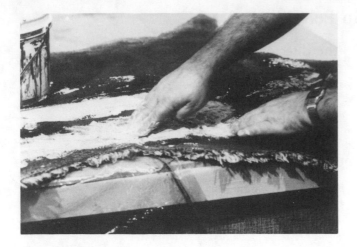

As the coatings from the bucket begin to soften, pull them apart. This action will make uneven edges and get rid of the scissored-edge appearance. Further working with the fingers helps to disintegrate the dried flex-glue and work it into a controllable pulp.

Elvanol glue congeals when it comes in contact with flameproofing fluid. The reaction of these two substances is usually considered a disadvantage, but in this case we will be able to use the reaction to our advantage.

Apply a heavy coat of flameproofing to the "pelt." Gently pour Elvanol onto the flameproofing solution. It will coagulate almost immediately. The blobs that appear can be manipulated with a brush. When all this dries, it will have a convincing semblance of fatty tissue.

Scarecrow

A scarecrow is a kind of dummy, and although there is not a set of jointed "bones" making up the skeleton, the framework under the scarecrow's clothing is very important in determining how the clothing is going to hang.

The farmer fills out his scarecrow form by stuffing him with straw. The potential fire hazard inherent to straw is dangerous in a theater, and it can be largely eliminated by building up the frame with foam rubber padding.

Construct a simple wooden frame of 2″ × 2″ rails. Add a little meat to these "bones" by slipping some arm-sized rubber pipe insulation over the horizontal rail. Wrap a long strip of rug padding around the frame to form shoulders and a chest. Wrap another strip of padding into a head shape.

Cover the padded head with a musiin sack with drawstrings, and pull the drawstrings tight.

A power sander (the kind meant to be used on wood) can be used to distress the scarecrow's clothing, making it look worn out.

A plastic gallon container shoved into the trouser leg offers resistance and helps control the effect of the sander. The hole produced by this method has a bleached look as a result of the cloth becoming threadbare.

A ragged look at the cuffs and pockets can be quickly accomplished with a disk sander and is a more realistic tatter than can be made with scissors.

We stuffed some straw into the neck and arm holes to make it appear that the whole figure was stuffed with straw.

As we moved our scarecrow on and off stage, however, much of the straw fell out of the arms, leaving a trail of straw stubble. The following system was devised to prevent this shedding.

Lay out some 2″ wide masking tape, sticky side up, and place an orderly arrangement of straw on it.

Wrap the prepared strip of tape around a PVC pipe.

Prepare a second tape strip, but this time arrange the straw in a criss-cross pattern. Wrap this strip

around the first to give the straw a more helter-skelter appearance.

Here is a photo of our finished scarecrow. His floppy hat adds the comfortable air of a working-class straw man.

A Barbecued Lamb

Our production of Shaw's *Saint Joan* brought a request for a barbecue spit on which to "cook" a meal for the troops in the field. (No, it isn't in the script, but the director wanted it.) It would be used to cook a medium-sized animal—

To repeat this construction, begin by sketching and cutting two ¼" plywood sections which will form the left and right halves of the body. Check closely with your reference picture as you make this sketch. This shape defines the important

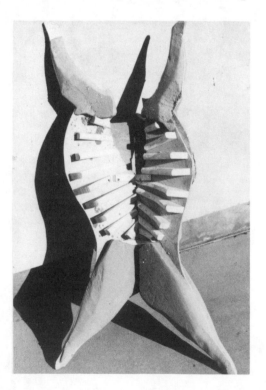

a pig, a sheep, a goat, or a deer. A rabbit would be too small; a bear would be too big. We decided on a sheep and went to our picture morgue for reference material.

We found this photo, which had been torn out of a *National Geographic* magazine. It shows sheep being cooked over an open pit barbecue in Argentina. We mounted the photo on cardboard and kept it in front of us as the construction of our roast sheep got under way.

lines of the sculpture. The two pieces of plywood should be joined with bent metal straps so that they are kept at a rigid angle. The angle should suggest that the carcass had been forced open and split at the backbone.

Using a band saw, cut some ribs (9 or 10 for each side) from scrap ¾" plywood, and round off the square edges with a disk sander. Nail these in place as shown. Sculpt four legs from urethane foam and glue them to the plywood form, to add some dimension. (Contact cement works well on urethane foam.) Shape the legs as accurately as you can, using sandpaper as a sculpting tool. This is not a difficult sculpting job; the silhouette is already there from the plywood outline, and all you are doing now is adding thickness.

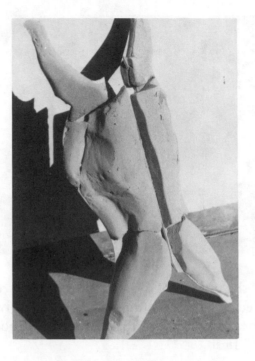

In the same fashion, glue a slab of urethane foam to the back of the plywood and shape it with a wood rasp or coarse sandpaper.

Fill in the rib cavity using papier-mâché. Make a pulp from newspaper strips and wallpaper paste or white glue, and bridge in between the ribs with the mixture. You can also use the papier-mâché pulp to repair gaps or imperfections in the urethane foam.

Run a rod lengthwise through the foam about where the backbone would be. This rod, when

it is removed later, will make it easier to insert the roasting spit.

Apply a "skin" of flannel using flex-glue as a binder. Flannel can be stretched and will conform to the shape of your carcass without many seams. The combination of flex-glue and flannel gives a good simulation of animal hide. Use flex-glue liberally both to attach the flannel and to give it a texture coating.

When you get to the edges of the rib cage, double the flannel over to simulate a flap of skin. This flap will look like charred fat when color is applied.

Wrap the flannel completely around the legs. Trim the skin close to the doubled flannel around the rib cage.

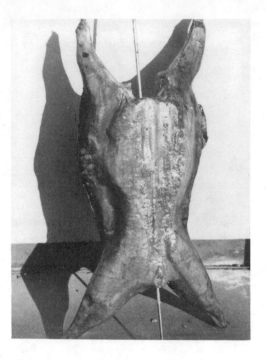

Cover the interior of the rib cage with cheesecloth applied with flex-glue. Cheesecloth gives a rougher texture, approximating the look of cooked flesh.

The texture of roasted fat can be achieved by building up several coats of flex-glue and pushing the glue into rivulets with a small brush.

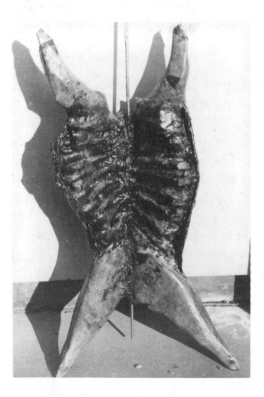

Color the barbecued sheep with dyes as the final coating of flex-glue is being applied. Texture the "skin" of the roast by using orange dyes with blotches of brown brushed into the wet flex-glue (the color should imitate that of a Thanksgiving turkey). Those areas which represent cut flesh — the innards, neck, and leg ends — should be colored with red dye and two tones of brown until the color of well-done steak is achieved.

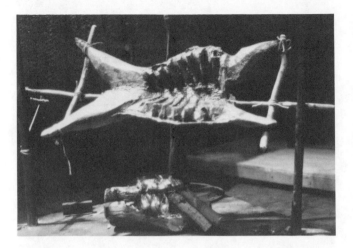

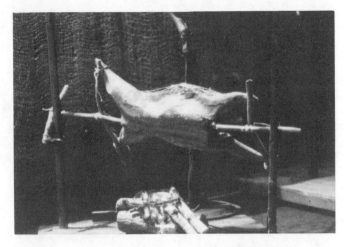

Remove the rod and skewer the carcass with a spit or roasting stick. Spreaders are then lashed to the spit and to the legs of the carcass.

The unit is now ready to be suspended over the fire.

A Turtle

I was once asked to build a ''stand-in'' turtle for a television program. A live turtle was to appear in most of the shots, including all of the closeups. But for the dangerous ''stunt'' scenes, the ''double'' was to be brought in. Part of the stunt business called for the turtle to be hurled through the air, land in the roadway, and be crushed by the wheels of an oncoming truck.

The script called for a land turtle. I worked from research material consisting of Polaroid photos of the live turtle I was duplicating, pictures of turtles from my picture morgue, and a sea turtle that had been preserved by a taxider-

mist. The only significant differences between the live land turtle and the stuffed sea turtle were the size (the sea turtle was larger) and the shape of the legs. Even the shell coloring of the two species was similar, so I could rely heavily on the sea turtle for reference.

The body could have been sculpted from any of several rigid plastic foam materials. I chose a product called Falcon Foam (a bead foam made from styrene) because I had a piece on hand that was the right size. To make a turtle as described here, select a piece of foam of the appropriate size and proceed with the following instructions.

Take a close look at the back of the turtle's shell in your reference picture. Draw this outline on the top of your block of foam.

Next, examine the end view of your reference picture. Ignore the legs and tail; fix your attention on the shape of the shell. Sketch this view on the end of the foam block.

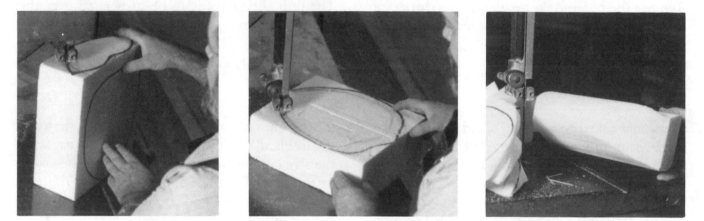

Cut these outlines on a band saw, and you will have a rough approximation of the turtle's shell.

Make your first cut by standing the block on end and following the outline you have drawn. This cut will remove the outline you drew on the face of the block, but that's no problem. Reassemble the block of foam by using toothpicks to hold the scraps you just cut away back in place.

Make a second cut following the outline you made on the flat surface of the block.

When your second cut has been made, pull out the toothpicks and remove the scraps of foam. The large central portion of the foam block will be roughly the shape of the turtle shell. (See the section on sculpting rigid urethane foam for a more detailed explanation of how to use the band saw as a sculpting tool.)

 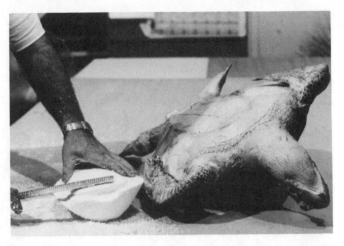

Use a wood rasp to finish shaping the foam. Take a close look at the shell of your model or reference picture. You will see a gradual taper down to the tail, and a ridge down the middle of the shell (the backbone lies inside the turtle's shell along this ridge). Add these details with the wood rasp. Be sure to keep a high hump at the shoulder of the shell where the head and neck will be attached. At this stage the edge of your turtle's shell will be thin and somewhat fragile. The coating of body putty which we will be adding soon will give it strength.

Use the end of the rasp as a gouge to hollow out some holes where the head and legs will go. These holes should be about 2″ deep. They need

Examine the underside of the turtle in your reference picture or model, and carve the visible features into the foam. On a real turtle, the belly is a separate shell and is joined to the back shell by tough flesh at the sides. Carve in the dropped edge where the two shells meet.

not be tight-fitting; if they are a bit oversize we will fill them in with a sort of "flesh" in a later step.

Mix up a quantity of Bondo (enough to yield two or three lumps the size of golf balls) according to the instructions on the can. Coat the entire surface of the shell with this plastic filler. When this material dries, it will give your turtle the hard shell finish it needs. You can also use the Bondo to fill in and correct any errors you may have made in the carving stage—but be careful to not obscure the shell details you have carved into the form.

When you have finished coating one side of the shell and the Bondo has begun to set, turn the shell over and work on the other side. The rim

around the circumference of the shell should be strengthened, so use a liberal application of the plastic filler to build it up.

As soon as the Bondo becomes firm (10–15 minutes), you can begin to carve it and smooth it. Body filler can be shaped quickly and easily in a semi-cured condition, although you are likely to find your tools becoming clogged with the soft filings.

Keep referring to your pictures or model while you shape the plastic filler. You will be able to refine the shape of your turtle shell considerably as you smooth the putty finish.

If while you are shaping the shell you should accidentally file through to the foam plastic underneath, you need only apply another coat of Bondo to make a repair.

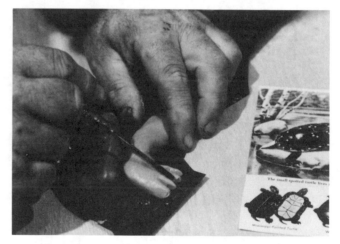

The head and feet should be built up from two-part (A–B) epoxy putty. Work the epoxy as if you were modeling with clay.

Make the neck of the turtle long enough to fit into the depression made while you were shaping the foam block. Try the neck in place; you can remove it and trim it or re-shape it until you have the right amount of neck projecting from the shell. Use black glass beads for the eyes. Poke small holes in the proper places with a pencil point and embed the eyes in these sockets. Using a dull knife blade, make an indentation on the underside of the head to suggest a mouth.

Just before the epoxy putty has hardened, use the dull knife blade to press a "diamondback" scale pattern on the top of the head.

If you are making a land turtle, the front feet should resemble little stubby hands. Those of a sea turtle are webbed and resemble flippers. (Consult your reference material for the exact shape.)

The hind feet are set at right angles, and have visible ankles. Keep the leg portions of the feet just long enough to fill the holes you made in the shell. As the putty begins to set use a screw driver to create a scale pattern on the upper portion of all four legs.

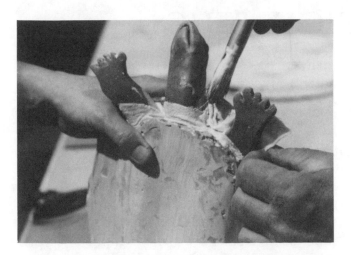

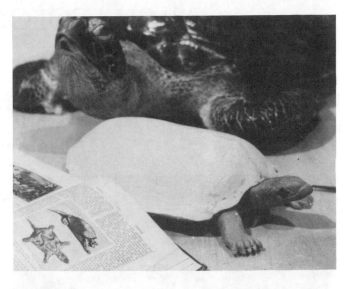

Join the appendages to the shell with a ''flesh'' made of flex-glue and flannel, as follows. Liberally wet the holes in the shell with flex-glue, and then insert the neck and legs into their sockets. Soak some small flannel strips in flex-glue, and press them into the crevices where the neck and legs don't quite fill the holes. Poke the flannel tightly in place with a knife or pencil point. Then apply one final smooth coat of glue and flannel over the joints. When this coating of flannel and flex-glue is painted it will pass for turtle skin even on close inspection.

Use the Bondo again, this time as the ''filler'' it was designed to be, and fill in any pits or imperfections in the shell. When the putty is dry sand it with medium-grit sandpaper. You can re-putty and re-sand until the shell is as smooth as you want it.

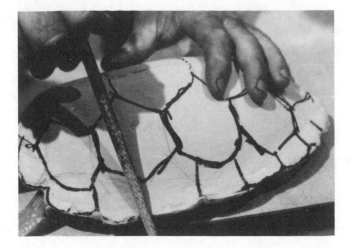

Use a felt pen to sketch the diamond pattern on the back of the turtle. This pattern will indicate where you should make light indentations around the edge of the shell. A rat-tail file and sandpaper can be used to achieve this scalloped edge.

Paint each diamond shape individually by wet-blending it in tones of brown, ochre, and olive. Re-define the pattern with a fresh coat of raw umber. Finally, if you want the shell to have the glossy sheen typical of domestic turtles, coat the entire shell with varnish or lacquer.

ARCHAEOLOGICAL RELICS

The Mound Builders by Lanford Wilson takes place in the headquarters of an archaeologist. The script calls for the setting to be dressed with many boxes of prehistoric tools and weapons of ancient Mississippi.

Arrowheads

The arrowheads and spearheads shown here were modeled from a photograph we found in our picture morgue. These points were shaped from pine, using a band saw. The "chipped" look is achieved by repeatedly touching the arrowhead to the edge of a disk sander. Use a coating of shellac to hide the wood grain.

Coat the arrowheads with gray and tan scenic paint. Then after the paint has dried dip each piece into a thin wash of raw umber to accentuate the rough edges and to give it the look of having been buried for centuries.

Bone Tools

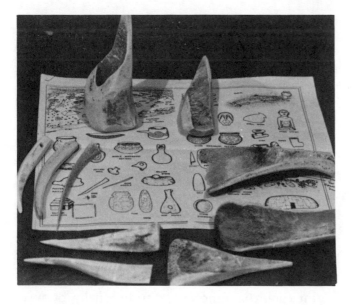

"Prehistoric" tools—such as awls, scrapers, and needles—can be made from real bone.

Obtain a couple of large soup bones from a butcher, and boil them for two or three hours to remove all of the meat and marrow. Make a cut with the band saw along the length of the bone, and let your imagination dictate the prehistoric tool suggested by the shape of the cut bone. Convert this fantasy into reality by smoothing and refining the shape on a sander. (Even the girls who were working on this project claimed they began to feel like cavemen.)

An Ancient Pottery Urn

A trip to our art department produced this pottery bowl that some student had turned, fired, and abandoned. It was given to us; we brought it back to the prop room and abused it with a hammer.

We then hot-glued the shards back together, as if they were pieces of a jigsaw puzzle. To add a look of authenticity, one piece was left out as if it had been "lost."

Brass and Copper Relic Jewelry

Make ancient brass and copper relics by distressing metallic costume jewelry. Rubbing Bondo into the metal pieces and chains will make them appear crusted and corroded. Color can be enhanced by spraying the "relics" with copper and brass aerosol spray paints. Tarnish and more advanced corrosion can be suggested by rubbing green and black dye onto the encrusted jewelry.

An identification tag should be attached to every relic unearthed at an archaeological excavation.

It is possible that we were overly imaginative in our choice of identification numbers.

BARBED WIRE

A locked gate provides some security, but it is security of a vulnerable kind. When you dress the top of the gate with barbed wire, you have a gate that fairly screams "keep out!" Although barbed wire is frequently associated with the Old West, it does not get its only theatrical use in Westerns. Barbed wire can be used to advantage in any setting where you want to put out the "un-welcome mat" and convey the notion of "restricted area."

Real barbed wire is dangerous—both to the flesh and to the actors' costumes. The barb on the wire presented here is made of real wire; but it is softer than steel, coated with rubber, and lacking sharp points. Making barbed wire by this method is quick and easy, and the result will be convincing in its appearance.

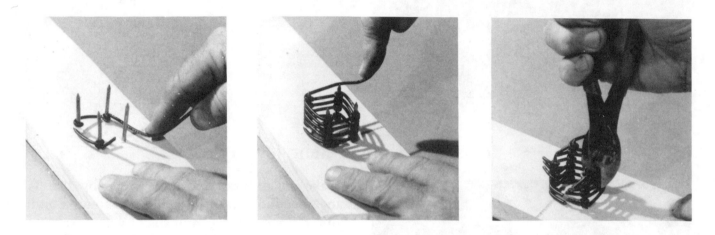

With a pencil and ruler, draw a square with 1¼" sides on a piece of ¾" board. Drive an eight-penny nail into each corner. Drive the nails into the board so that the points protrude all the way through.

Wrap #12 or #14 TW copper wire (electric wire used in home construction) around this spiked jig as shown. Wrap the wire around one nail, go on to the next nail and wrap once around it, go on to the next, and so forth. Keep wrapping the wire in this fashion and spiraling it upward until you reach the points of the nails and there is no room for more wire.

Use a pair of diagonal cutters to snip the wire into individual barbs. Clip the wires straight down, midway between each pair of nails. You should be able to run your wire eight times around the nails and thus produce 32 barbs.

If you repeat this operation over and over, it won't be long before you have a box full of "safe" barbs. We required 300′ of barbed wire with the barbs 4″ apart, so we needed to make 900 of of these little barbs.

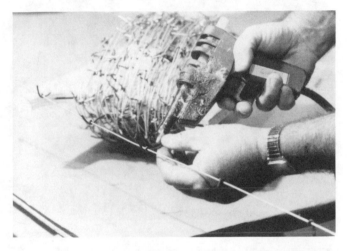

The barbs just slip onto the main wire; then a quick twist locks each in place.

A dab of hot glue on the main wire will keep the barb from sliding out of position.

BLOOD

In these days of explicit, R-rated violence, more and more stage presentations are calling for bloody scenes to be depicted realistically. A restrained suggestion is no longer sufficient.

There is no clear delineation as to which of the production departments is responsible for the production's "blood." Small quantities might be provided by the makeup department. More lavish bloodletting might require the services of the prop department's special effects staff. In either case, the costume department is sure to have an interest, since many formulations of stage blood will stain clothing.

The formula given here for stage blood is realistic in appearance, non-toxic, washable, and non-staining — and not sticky and uncomfortable as you might have supposed.

These are the only ingredients in our recipe for stage blood:

    White corn syrup
    Red food color
    Blue food color
    Liquid dishwashing detergent

Use a whole 16-ounce bottle of corn syrup. The syrup has a heavy body and is easily washable — a good combination for stage blood. Add about a tablespoon of red food color to the syrup. Food coloring in this concentration is not likely to stain, though it would be wise to make a test on the fabric you are using. (If you use the whole bottle of food color to tint your corn syrup, don't be surprised when your stage blood leaves a stain.) Add two or three drops of blue food color to darken the blood a little and take away the orange tint.

A few tablespoons of liquid detergent will retard drying and will make the blood mixture easier to remove.

Making a Heart

Motivated by envy, the beautiful but evil queen summons the castle huntsman to inform him that she requires the heart of the lovely Snow White... ''And you must bring it to me in this box as a token.'' Bloody business for a children's story!

We didn't build this heart for *Snow White*, but rather to prove the king's death in *Macbeth*. You'll find other theatrical uses.

As always when you build a prop, begin with reference material. We used *Gray's Anatomy* to guide us in the construction. We chose to use a sponge and a chamois skin to give what we imagined to be realistic texture and absorption characteristics. Our research showed that the human heart is about the size of a fist, so we cut a sponge to the shape of a heart about that size.

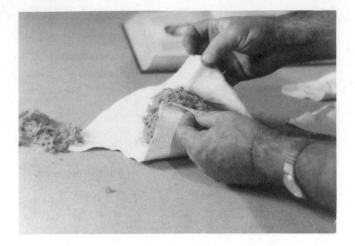

Cut a piece of chamois large enough to cover the sponge. Before you begin stitching, try wrapping the sponge several ways, to determine the best fit—one that will require the shortest seam and the fewest stitches. Sew the chamois with ordinary needle and thread.

Tuck and sew the excess skin on both sides to form large arteries and veins. Cut a short length of ⅝″ dowel to fit deep into the "aorta." This chunk of wood should not show; its purpose is to keep the hole open.

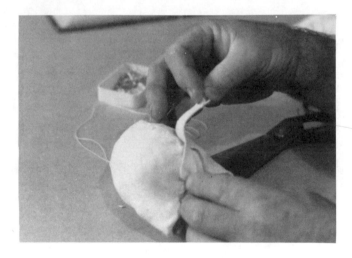

The sutured seams will have an unrealistic appearance, but you can hide most of the seams by sewing flaps of chamois over the stitches. Leave the flaps ragged to suggest hacked flesh and torn membranes.

You can make the heart more grimly realistic by dipping it in a mixture of stage blood.

A Blood Knife

This knife leaves a trail of stage blood as it is drawn over a performer's skin. The principal feature of the knife is the tube which runs through the blade, issuing from the handle where it is connected to a rubber syringe, and terminating at the end where it fits through a hole in the blade near the tip.

The knife blade—about ⅛" thick—must be made of soft aluminum so it can easily be worked with hand tools. Not only must the blade be shaped, but a groove must be worked into the length of its back edge to accommodate the tube, and finally a hole must be drilled through the width of the blade to allow the blood to run out along the cutting edge.

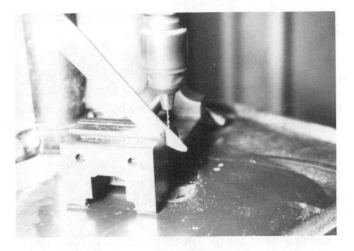

First decide whether your knife is to be a butcher knife, a hunting knife, a dagger, etc. Then design the shape of the blade—draw it on a piece of soft aluminum and cut the outline on a band saw. ⅛" aluminum can be cut without trouble on a band saw fitted with a skip tooth blade.

Clamp the aluminum in a small vise and drill a hole diagonally into the narrow edge of the blade, all the way through its width. A ³⁄₃₂" drill will cut its way through the edge of a piece of ⅛" aluminum for this short distance without penetrating the flat side of the blade, if you are very careful. However, a drill press is absolutely essential in this step, to keep the drill tracking straight.

Use a fine-toothed file to cut a groove or channel along the back edge of the blade. Use both a triangle and a small round machinist's file to make this groove. File for a while with the sharp edge of the triangle file, and then switch to the round file to make the groove deeper; then go back to the triangle file. This is a very slow process requiring a good deal of patience, but be assured that persistence will pay off—repeated filing will eventually produce the desired groove.

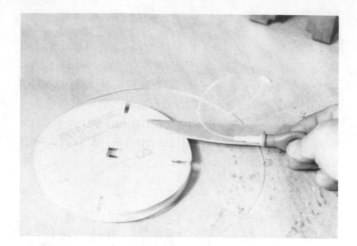

A ³⁄₃₂″ polyethylene tube (obtainable from a medical supplier) will slide into the hole and fit tightly into the groove that you have made along the aluminum blade. Firmly secure the tube with spray adhesive. Connect a small rubber syringe to the other end of the tube. The ring at the mouth of the syringe should be tight-fitting but removable, so the syringe can be filled with stage blood. For this application, it may be necessary to modify the recipe for stage blood given earlier; thinning the blood with a little water will make it easier to force the blood through the narrow tube.

The knife handle must be hollow in order to house the syringe. It must also be flexible, so that pressure applied to the handle squeezes the syringe bulb and forces the blood mixture out of the hole in the edge of the blade.

BOOKS

"A Book Is a Book"

The scene takes place backstage during a technical rehearsal. The stage is dimly lit by colored work lights. There is a warm glow of light from a shaded lamp over the prop table. The PROP CREW HEAD *and an* ACTOR *are UR near the prop table, waiting idly while the* LIGHTING DESIGNER *and his crew are setting and recording light cues.*

The ACTOR, *who is playing the role of a preacher, looks past a tormentor at the halted action on stage.*

ACTOR Boy, these technical rehearsals are long. We've been here for two hours and they still haven't come to my entrance in scene one.

PROP CREW HEAD Yeah, but this is typical. I've been working through three productions here; they're all alike.

ACTOR I don't care if it *is* typical. It's a terrible waste of my time.

PROP CREW HEAD Humph! Where have you got to go?

STAGE MANAGER *(from offstage right)* Shhhh.

ACTOR Yes, yes, shush. *(under his breath)* We must remain, but we must remain silent. *(to* PROP CREW HEAD*)* It seems like they could set these light cues without having all of us standing around.

PROP CREW HEAD They're just trying to make you look good.

ACTOR Oh, I know. And I appreciate it. But *they* don't stand around watching while *I'm* preparing for the performance, and I wish I didn't have to stand around and watch *them*.

PROP CREW HEAD You don't want to share the experience, eh?

ACTOR *(a little laugh)* That's right. *(A sigh of resignation—changing the subject)* On my entrance, I'm to be carrying a Bible. Do you have it ready?

PROP CREW HEAD Sure, it's there on the prop table.

ACTOR *(Walking to the table, searching)* You mean—this dictionary?

PROP CREW HEAD You and I know it's a dictionary. But you're an actor. You can make the audience think it's a Bible.

STAGE MANAGER *(offstage)* Hey! Hey, you guys back there, knock it off. Hold it down.

ACTOR Oh, be fair. I'm standing here in the dark and I can tell—it's a *Webster's Collegiate Dictionary*.

PROP CREW HEAD *(pointedly)* Well, I think it's going to have to do.

ACTOR Every person in that audience will have one of these blue dictionaries on his desk at home. If I carry this on they'll be thinking, "Here comes an illiterate preacher. He can't spell, so he's obliged to carry his own dictionary with him."

STAGE MANAGER *(Coming into view from his position DR; he is wearing a headset and carrying a clipboard)* What's going on here? If you're going to have a fistfight, you ought to at least have the decency to take it into the greenroom.

ACTOR Here, look what this idiot is giving me to use for a Bible.

STAGE MANAGER It looks like a dictionary.

PROP CREW HEAD Aw, a book's a book.

ACTOR No, you mean a *dictionary* is a *dictionary*. I think you've selected a rather poor quote to use in support of your argument.

PROP CREW HEAD Well then, ''You can't judge a book by its cover.'' How's that?

STAGE MANAGER Whoever said that must have been referring to novels. Why don't you put the dictionary away, and try to find us a Bible.

PROP CREW HEAD Because it's not necessary, and we can't afford it. I'm going to take this up with the technical director. *(He exits)*

ACTOR I'm going to discuss this with the director. *(He exits)*

STAGE MANAGER *(left alone)* Terrific! And I'll go tell my mother! Maybe among the three of them, they can bring some maturity to this discussion.

Familiar Books

We are so intimately familiar with some books that it's true we can recognize them as we might recognize an old friend. You can identify and distinguish between a ledger and an appointment book, even though they may be about the same size and color. It would be very difficult to disguise a Sears catalog and successfully pass it off as a metropolitan phone book. And it is no trick at all to distinguish between a *World Book Encyclopedia* and a volume put out by Funk and Wagnalls. Books have personalities.

Usually you will be able to find the books you need for a production at a used book store or from your local bookseller. Antique books are another matter — they are generally out of print.

''Antique'' Replicas

Period books were usually what would be considered oversized today, and they were sometimes two to three inches thick. Medieval books were usually made of coarse paper or sheepskin parchment. Victorian books sometimes used finer quality linen paper or vellum. You should give some thought to the selection of an appropriate paper for your book. There are a wide range of oversized papers you can select from — newsprint, bond, sketch paper, construction paper. We once made an ''ancient'' book on alchemy, using industrial paper toweling.

A bookbinder might find reason to raise his eyebrows at the methods described on the following pages; the crudeness and lack of refinement might make him laugh. But the heck with him. If you follow these instructions, you will be building a book unlike anything on his shelves — your book will be uniquely designed to fit the needs of your production, and it will be durable as well.

After the paper has been selected, cut it to the required size. Assemble, straighten, and clamp the paper so that the edge that will be bound can be glued.

During the clamping and gluing process it is helpful to flank the ''pages'' with two pieces of ¼″ or ⅛″ Masonite, cut to the approximate size of the pages. Clamping will keep the pages from slipping out of alignment while the glue is applied. Tight clamping will also control the amount of glue that can seep in between the pages.

Coat one edge of the pages with flex-glue, and set the unit aside to dry overnight.

The Book Cover

Five pieces are needed to make up a book cover: a spine and two binding strips (these three make up the binding), and two cover flaps, front and back. Cut these pieces from Masonite or very heavy cardboard. Cut them to overhang the pages by ¼″ on the unbound sides. The five cover sections should therefore be dimensioned as follows:

Spine (1): Height is ½″ more than page height; width is thickness of the pages.

Binding strips (2): Height is ½″ more than page height; width is ⅝″.

Cover flaps (2): Height is ½″ more than page height; width is page width plus ¼″ (for the overhang) minus ½″ (to accommodate the binding strip and a hinging clearance).

Join the five cover pieces, attaching them with flex-glue to muslin or canvas. The cloth will then serve as the main hinge. Leave ⅛″ space between the binding strips and the cover flaps to allow for the hinging action.

Folding the cloth over the top and bottom edges of the front and back flaps adds considerably to the cover's strength. Glue down all of the loose edges and set the unit aside to dry.

Binding the Book

After the pages and the cover have dried, you can assemble and sew them into book form.

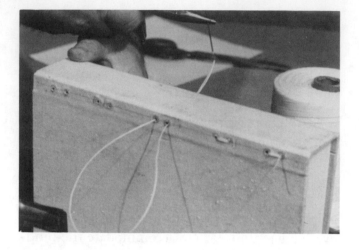

Carefully fit the cover over the pages and again clamp to prevent slippage. The clamps should go onto the binding strips gently but firmly—that is to say, don't clamp so tightly that the binding strips break. While the book is thus clamped, drill several pairs of small holes clear through the binding strips and the pages. Keep the clamps in place while you sew through the pairs of holes. Use a large needle and nylon string. After you have sewn through all of the holes and tied off the strings, you can remove the clamps. You now have a well-constructed, durable book ready to receive its "character" covering.

The Character Cover

Select the material to be used for the final cover. Some materials worth considering are vinyl up-holstering, leatherette, cloth, or the leather-like material described in the section on flex-glue.

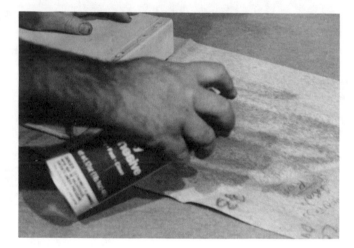

Lay the covered book open on a table. Cut the covering material about 2" larger than the dimensions of the open book cover. Permanently attach the cover material to the cover flaps. Liberally spray both the cover material and the cover flaps with rubber adhesive, and after the glue has become tacky, with the book closed, press the glued surfaces together.

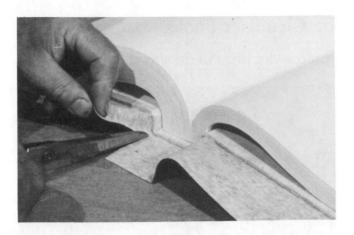

Cut two incisions in the cover material at the top of the book as shown, making a flap. Apply glue

to this flap and tuck it into the spine. Repeat this procedure at the bottom of the book.

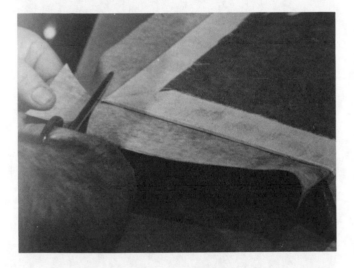

At each corner cut a "V" shape in the cover material to remove the excess material and thus al-

low for a smoother fit in the corners. Glue down all six edges, and your cover will be complete.

The job can be finished by gluing a sheet of paper over the inside surface of each cover flap. The endpapers should be the same size as the book pages, but they should be a heavier weight.

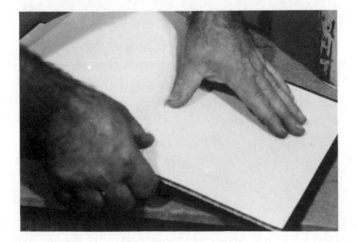

Examples of Hand-Made Character Books

The books on this page were all made by the process described in the preceding text.

The rich quality of this book was achieved by covering it with a patterned vinyl upholstering material.

The use of a leather-like covering material gave these books an ancient appearance.

The clasp on this book was made by sewing a leather wrist watch band to the covers.

A Victorian look can be achieved by applying patterned lace to the cover with flex-glue. The lace is totally sealed with repeated applications of the glue. Here color has been rubbed into the texture of the lace.

This captain's log (which is meant to look as though it has recently been fished out of the watery depths) is actually a UCLA campus phone directory. We put it together as a prop for *Thunder Rock*. Each page was wiped with a thin umber wash which darkened and crinkled the paper. An imitation leather cover was glued on and aged with shoe polish.

A book of personal poetry (made for a production of Ibsen's *The Wild Duck*) was made of onionskin typing paper bound with a ribbon threaded through punched holes. The cover is posterboard covered with leatherette.

This book had to have its pages cored with a mat knife for a scene in *Harvey* in which a bottle is hidden in a bookcase.

Lightweight Books

Let's talk about making books lighter. There is an advantage to making a bookcase weigh less. Books weigh, on the average, about 15 pounds per foot of shelf space. Sets of encyclopedias and law books weigh even more — 25 pounds per foot.

Shifting this weight during a scene change is an unnecessary strain. A row of faked books weighs only four pounds per foot. The whole secret to making books lighter? Remove the pages!

Many hardbound books with sewn bindings require just two cuts on the inside up the spine to remove all the pages from the cover.

Others, such as case-bound books and books that have been rebound, are constructed so that the spine is integral to the book and cannot be cut out. With such a book, fold the covers back and run the pages through a band saw, as shown. (This is an unorthodox use for the band saw, but there is no more danger, either to the operator or to the band saw blade, than when a piece of pine is cut.)

But once the pages are gone, a book loses its shape. Its structural integrity will have been re-

moved. One way of countering this is to insert a rib, out of sight, behind a group of books.

Before the books are hollowed out, select a group that forms a visually interesting arrangement and number them to aid in restoring their sequence. Cut a piece of 1″ × 3″ pine equal to the length of the row of books, and mark the board as shown to indicate the front edges of the closed covers.

Use the band saw to slot the $1'' \times 3''$ at these markings. These slots will receive the front edges of the cover flaps. This wooden rib will restore the shape of the book covers and make the group of books a single durable unit.

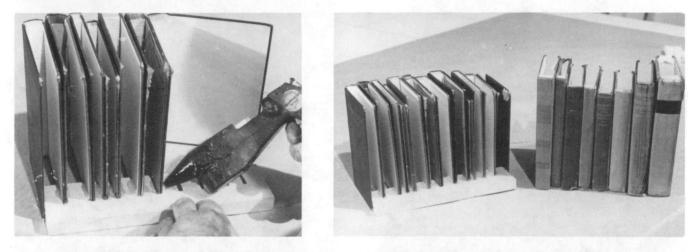

Glue each cover into place. Hot glue will work well for this operation.

If the bookcase is in a position where the audience does not have a good view of it, the construction can be simpler. Run each book through the band saw, cutting it down to a 1″ strip. A 1″ book weighs a lot less than a 7″ book.

The bookshelf need not be full depth, either. If it is sufficiently dark behind the books, a shelf 2″ deep will suffice.

You can reassemble individual books by replacing the removed paged with a hollow three-sided pine frame. The weight reduction is not as great as is achieved with the notched-rib method, but it is still significant.

Faked books do not necessarily have to be arranged in neat rows. These books were purposely assembled in a disorderly fashion to look more "used" on the bookshelf.

This set of books was assembled on a slant. It was intended to go at the end of a book row.

Fake Dust Jackets

A design for *The Big Knife* required us to dress a bookshelf with "new" books, when all we had on hand were Nancy Drew mysteries, grade-school textbooks, and *Reader's Digest* condensations. We solved this problem by making fake jackets for these old books from magazine ads. When finished, they appeared convincingly like the dust jackets of new books.

The advertisements in the accompanying photos were cut from *Esquire, Fortune,* and *Seventeen;* but any magazine with large pictures will do. Tear the pages out and cut them to book size. If a book is taller than any of your magazine pages, there is no reason why you can't splice two or more pictures together in order to cover it. You can tape the ads to the books' front and back covers with masking tape; these surfaces should

never be seen by the audience. Once the books are properly in place, only the decorated spines will be visible.

Here are the raw materials: some old books and some old magazines with large interesting type.

Cut the magazine page to the size of the book so that the words fit over the book binding. Note in the photo that the "Supersports" article has been combined with a "Toni" ad to cover one large book, and the word "Fashion" has been spliced together with a "Hanes" ad on another.

Tape the magazine page to the the front and back covers of the book. If you use tape instead of glue, the "dust jackets" can be removed and the books reused for a later production.

On the finished shelf of books we added a book with a real dust jacket to each end where the sides might be visible.

CONFETTI

You can get confetti from a party shop, if there is such a shop in your city. Toy stores sometimes stock small packages which they sell for a modest sum, but these packages only contain a cupful or so of confetti. If you need a great quantity—a gallon or more—the cost leaves the realm of modesty and becomes indecent.

Confetti in quantity can be made with a band saw from a thick telephone directory or a Sears catalog. This confetti will be larger than the store-bought variety, but for use in a proscenium theater the larger size has the advantage of greater visibility. And the larger size makes the confetti easier to sweep up, no matter where it is used.

Rip the front and back covers from a phone book. The covers are like thin cardboard and are too heavy to be used in the confetti. Use the band saw to make a series of cuts across the book, each cut beginning at the spine and moving across the full width to the outside edge. These cuts should be about ½″ apart. The glued binding on the spine will help to hold the strips together in manageable little booklets.

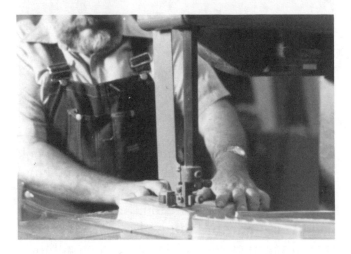

Paper can be cut safely on a band saw if it is kept in a tightly controlled stack such as a phone book provides. Be careful to observe the usual safety rules when using the band saw. Avoid the temptation to hold the book too close to the cuts; you don't want to get your fingers too near the blade.

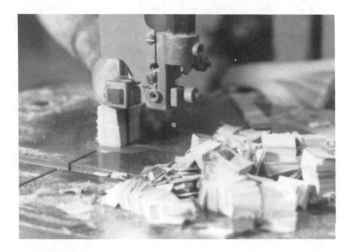

Run the long strips through the band saw again, this time lengthwise. Keep the edge with the glued binding on your left (if you are right-handed) as you make these cuts. Each cut brings the binding closer to the blade, and the last cut removes the spine, which should be discarded.

Once the confetti is fluffed up, the yield from a metropolitan phone book will be about a gallon.

CONSTRUCTION TECHNIQUES

Epoxy Putty

This plastic putty made of epoxy resin is marketed by several manufacturers as a bonding agent for metals of all kinds.

Epoxy resin has some properties which make it the only logical solution to certain production problems. It is:

1. Tenacious. It has excellent bonding qualities for all kinds of surfaces (properly cleaned), no matter how dense or smooth.

2. Strong. Epoxy resin reinforced with Fiberglas is stronger than steel.

3. Very hard when cured. It is abrasion-resistant. It can be filed and machine sanded, but it is resistant to hand sanding.

4. Physically stable. It will not shrink.

5. Non-conductive. It can serve as an electrical insulator.

6. Resistant to both acid and alkali.

7. Heat resistant. It is not affected by temperatures in the 200–300°F. range.

It is also:

8. A little on the expensive side.

When you use epoxy putty in prop construction, you may not be concerned with all the attractive properties listed above. I use epoxy putty for three main reasons:

1. It is convenient. The putty is easy to mix and use.

2. It has a very low viscosity. A fresh batch has a consistency similar to that of Plasticine clay.

3. It sticks to a wide range of materials.

The instructions that come with packages of putty are chiefly devoted to cleaning metal surfaces to assure the best bond. The product we are most familiar with includes no information regarding the health hazards associated with the product. In fact the curing agent for epoxy is more hazardous than the catalyst used in polyester resins, so obviously some precautions are in order. Use these chemicals only with adequate ventilation and after using them clean your hands thoroughly.

Epoxy putty is sold in the form of two sticks, designated ''A'' and ''B.'' These two parts must be hand-mixed to produce a putty possessing all of the aforementioned characteristics. Under-mixing causes an uneven cure and invites failure with what should be an excellent product.

Although the putty is somewhat expensive (the brand we use costs $6 for a pair of 8" sticks), it can be used economically if you are careful to not cut more than you need. If you need a ¼" slice, that's all you should cut. Make sure you use equal portions of the ''A'' stick and the ''B'' stick. This product has a good shelf life; the unused portions will keep for well over a year if they are rewrapped.

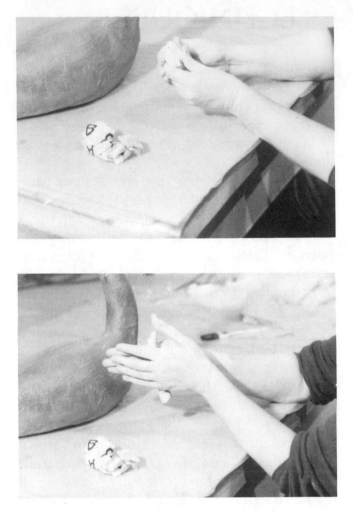

Kneading the two parts together is the obvious way to mix the putty, but this is slow and laborious. Your hands will get tired before the putty is properly mixed. I've developed the following technique for mixing the putty. It's not particularly clever, but it does the job thoroughly.

Roll the putty between your hands as if you were a kindergartener rolling out a clay snake. Then fold the ends over and roll out another snake.

Working the putty this way also makes it more flexible and easier to model. It will remain workable for about 45 minutes. Epoxy putty hardens gradually. It will slowly stiffen during the 45-minute period. If you continue to knead the unused portion in your hand, you can retard curing and keep that portion workable. The putty, in

Continue to fold and roll, fold and roll, until the putty becomes uniform in color with no visible streaks.

the final stages of its malleability, can be smoothed to a high polish with a finger or modeling tool moistened with water. *Do not moisten your fingers by licking them.*

The examples on the next page may trigger your imagination and suggest some uses for epoxy putty in prop construction.

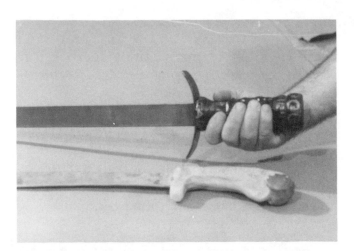

Modeling with Epoxy Putty

These sword handles were sculpted of epoxy putty. Even an inexperienced sculptor should be able to turn out a small form like this in an hour.

The bowl of this pipe was extended with epoxy putty to make it appear longer and grander.

Turn to the section in this book on animal forms, and examine the photos detailing construction of the turtle and the peacock. Epoxy putty was used to fashion the feet of the turtle and the peacock's head—two more good examples of small permanent forms sculpted from this putty.

Bonding with Epoxy Putty

"Aladdin's Magic Ring" was made by attaching two pen-light bulbs to a small key ring with epoxy putty. Wires were run up Aladdin's sleeve and to a battery pack at his belt to make the ring light up.

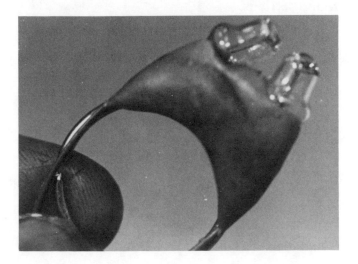

Ethafoam

Ethafoam is Dow Chemical Co.'s tradename for flexible polyethylene foam. The foam is made in several forms, but the shape most useful in prop building is the cylindrical variety which is used commercially as an insulating sealer. This material is solid but flexible, and the smaller diameters are sold in rolls.

Ethafoam can be purchased in diameters from ½″ to about 4″. The foam is sold by the foot, but its selling price is based on weight. The ½″

Nail the tunnel to a sheet of ¼″ plywood of a size that will fit comfortably on your band saw table. Run the jig into the saw a few inches, so that the blade is running dead center down the middle of the tunnel. Now clamp the plywood securely to the band saw table.

Ethafoam is therefore relatively inexpensive, whereas the cost can become a serious consideration with 3″ and 4″ Ethafoam.

Theater craftsmen have found many uses for this product, but it is used most widely in the theater as a flexible half-round molding. A flexible molding is handy for adding dimensional details to curved or free-form objects such as planters, lamp bases, and round table tops.

Cutting Ethafoam into Half Round Molding

In order to use Ethafoam as a molding, the round stock must be split down the middle. You can construct a wooden jig for yourself which will allow you to split the foam rod quickly and accurately. Make a channel or, better yet, a square tunnel of plywood about 18″ long. Make the height and width of the tunnel equal to the diameter of the Ethafoam you wish to split. The fit must be tight enough to hold the foam centered in the jig, yet loose enough for the material to slide freely and smoothly through the tunnel.

As you push the Ethafoam into and through the tunnel, the band saw blade passes through its center, splitting the foam into two half-round sections.

Our prop room has six jigs like this, one for each diameter of Ethafoam that we keep in stock.

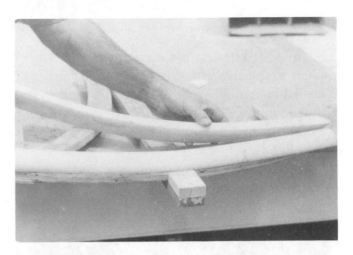

When you use the Ethafoam half-rounds, glue them securely with contact cement. This stylized

chandelier was given a rounded appearance by applying Ethafoam to a plywood cutout.

The 2″ half-round molding at the bottom of this twelve-sided cupola was made of a length of split Ethafoam which was cemented to the wooden frame.

You will no doubt find many uses for this versatile product. The section in this book on foods

explains how it can be used to simulate sausages and sweet rolls.

Painting Ethafoam

The one big drawback to polyethylene is that it is one of those materials to which nothing will stick. The only way you can paint Ethafoam is to treat the surface of the plastic first. One method is to coat the Ethafoam with muslin and glue; another is to cover it completely with masking tape. Either way, you are providing a surface to which paint will adhere. A quick pass of a pro-

pane torch over the plastic surface will roughen the Ethafoam sufficiently to allow a good paint bond. Last year a student building an Ethafoam bumper for a small golf cart tried using spray adhesive as an undercoating, and it worked very well. The spray adhesive sticks to the foam plastic, and the paint has no trouble clinging to the thin coat of adhesive.

Invisible Knot

The invisible knot can be used anywhere that repeated wrappings of cord are required, either as a lashed fastening (such as might be used in the construction of a primitive hut) or as a whipped decoration (such as might be found on a knife or sword handle).

An ordinary knot shows up as an obvious ball of cord. If two pieces of cord are used to make a wrapping, then two knots will probably show. One knot might be hidden in the wraps of the succeeding lashings, but the final knot will surely remain visible.

The selling feature of the invisible knot is that the wad of cord and its attendant loose ends are tucked inside the wrappings and thus are entirely hidden from view.

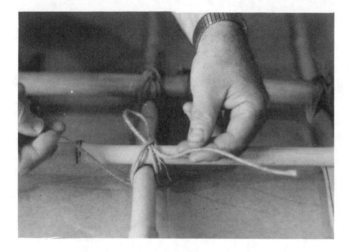

Before you begin lashing the cord, make a loop with it and leave about 8″ of loose line in the short end of the loop. Begin to wrap the necessary lashing or whipping, being sure to always leave the loop partially exposed.

When the wrapping is completed to your satisfaction, tuck the end of the cord through the loop.

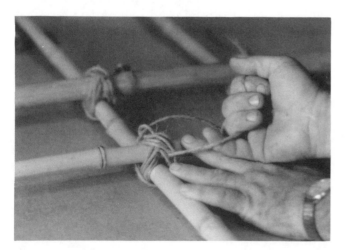

As the 8″ loose line is pulled, the loop will close, pulling the end of the cord deep into the interior of the lashing.

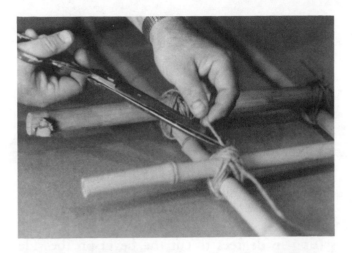

Clip both ends of the line away and the fastening will be completely hidden.

Although this is not a true knot, experience has shown that it is very secure and has no tendency to come loose.

Making a Butter Churn

The technique demonstrated here can be adapted to solve the construction problems encountered in making any multi-faceted object with tapering sides. This construction plan can be applied not only to this butter churn but to such tapered articles as foot stools, planters, waste baskets, lampposts, columns, and so forth.

The joints between the faces on a structure of this kind form a compound miter, and keeping a close fit can be tricky.

Much of this section will be devoted to setting the correct pitch on the saw blade and to an understanding of the making of the jig (or guide) that is to be used to help you cut the tapered and beveled side pieces of the churn. The rest of the job is the comparatively uncomplicated matter of joining the pieces together.

Setting the Pitch on the Saw Blade

Begin your churn by determining three dimensions: The height of the churn and the width across the top and bottom. These dimensions will determine the steepness of the taper.

It will help you to understand this technique if you will draw two circles, a larger one to represent the bottom of the churn and a smaller one to reflect the size of the top of the churn.

In the accompanying photo, the large circle was drawn with a 7″ radius, and the smaller one with a 4″ radius.

Next decide how many sides or faces you want your churn to have. We decided our churn would have six sides, but this choice is arbitrary, and

any number of faces (within reason) could have been chosen without complicating the construction process.

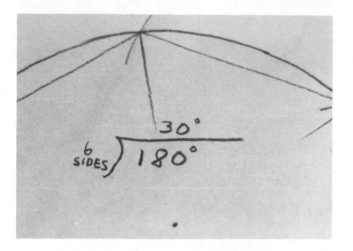

A rule for calculating the bevel cuts has been devised and it is simple. You take the number of sides your churn will have and divide that number into 180°. (We divided 6 into 180° and got 30°. Had we chosen eight sides, we would have divided 8 into 180° and gotten 27½°; had we chosen twelve sides, 180° ÷ 12 would have given us 15°.) This quotient gives you the pitch setting in degrees to cut the bevel on the side pieces of the churn. In the case of this hexagon, adjust the dial on your table saw to a pitch setting which reads 30°.

If you want to test the soundness of this formula, construct regular hexagons inside the circles you drew earlier. Draw in radius lines to the points of the hexagons. The angle formed from the radius to a side of the hexagon will be 60°. Use a bevel gauge to copy and transfer one of the radius-to-side angles to your table saw. Tilt the saw until the angle between the blade and the table conforms exactly to the angle of the bevel gauge

(60°). Look at the dial on your saw that indicates blade pitch. It will read 30°! The pitch indicator on a table saw refers to the fence of the saw rather than to the table bed; it always gives the complement of the desired angle. When you are making a square cut (90°) on a board, the pitch setting will read 0°. A six-sided figure will have miters measuring 60° but the saw is to be set at 30°.

Making the Jig for Cutting the Tapers

The next step is to make the jig, or guide, mentioned earlier. Using a tape rule, measure one side of each of the polygons (both the large one and the small one) that you drew in the preceding step. These measurements are used as you make one further drawing on butcher paper— a full-scale plan of one side of the churn. The being made in the accompanying photos has sides that are 4″ wide at the top and 7″ wide at the bottom, a difference of 3″. This difference will show up as a 1½″ taper on each side. (In practice, once you are familiar with the principle involved, you will be able to construct the jig without making such a drawing.)

Construct the jig by joining two pieces of wood in the shape of an ''L,'' as shown in the photo above. Put two notches in the short leg of the ''L.'' The first notch represents the 1½″ taper, and can be transferred directly from the drawing. The second notch is 1½″ beyond the first notch —a total of 3″ from the edge of the long leg.

The long leg of the jig must be as long as, or perhaps a little longer than, the height of the churn. We had determined that ours would be 28″ high.

Prepare six side pieces for the churn by cutting wood rectangles 7″ wide (the width at the base) by 28″ long (the height of the churn). These boards will be cut to precise dimensions, using the jig, in the next step.

Using the Jig to Cut the Beveled Taper

Insert one of the boards that will become one of the side pieces into the first notch of the jig, as shown, holding the plywood with the better side up. Adjust the fence of the table saw so that its blade (still adjusted to a 30° pitch) will start its cut at what will be the wide end of the side piece. Be careful to keep the long blade of the jig flush with the fence as it slides. As you push the jigged piece of wood through the saw, you will be cutting a compound miter with a 60° bevel and a 1½″ taper. Examine your cut board to be sure this is so.

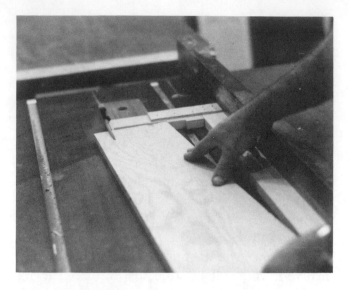

To make the second cut (on the opposite edge of the side piece), follow these steps:

1. Retain both the fence position and the pitch of the blade from the first cut. In other words, don't change any of the adjustments on the saw.

2. Reverse the jig. The short (notched) leg should now be near the saw blade; the long leg is still against the fence of the saw.

3. Rotate the plywood 180°, still keeping the better side up, and fit it into the second notch of the jig, as shown.

4. As you slide the jig along the fence, the second cut will be made.

Repeat this procedure for each of the side panels.

Assemble the cut pieces on the paper pattern in a trial setup.

Making the End Plugs

To make the top and bottom of the churn, align a bevel gauge to fit the angle formed between the joined side pieces and the flat level surface of your bench top.

Transfer this angle to the table of your band saw.

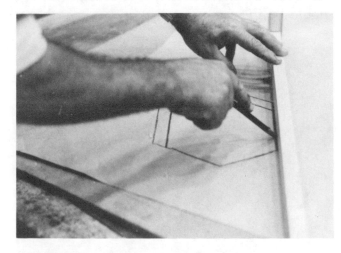

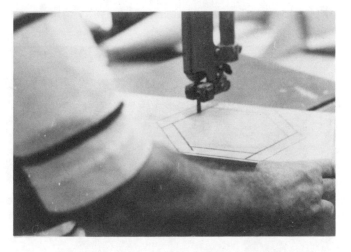

Make a pattern for the top plug on butcher paper. Reduce the size of the pattern on all sides by the thickness of your plywood (so the plug will fit inside the sides of the churn).

Attach this pattern to a piece of plywood with spray adhesive and cut it out on the prepared band saw.

Drill a hole in the center of the top plug for the dasher pole. The dasher pole can be made from a 1½″ dowel or a large broomstick.

Make a bottom for the churn following the same procedure as for the top. Draw up a pattern, making reductions to allow for the thickness of the sides; secure the pattern with spray adhesive,

Make a box-like arrangement to fit inside the churn under the hole. The dasher pole will run through this box, keeping the pole straight.

and cut along the pattern with a band saw.

Cut out the bottom plug without changing the tilt of the band saw table—the angle setting should be the same as was used to cut the top.

Assemble all of the pieces to make the churn, using white glue and 2″ staples or eight-penny nails.

This churn was textured using a torch and wire brush, as described in the section on distressing wood. It is ready to be used as a set dressing for *Green Grow the Lilacs* or its musical version, *Oklahoma!*

PVC Pipe

Polyvinyl chloride is a plastic that you encounter, in one form or another, almost every day. Furniture is upholstered in sheets of colored, patterned, or clear PVC; playing cards are protected by thin clear films of it; one formulation of polyvinyl chloride is used in the manufacture of plastic water and sewer pipe.

PVC pipe is handy in making a variety of props, wherever a round rod-like look is desired. PVC pipe comes in a variety of diameters, from ½″ to 6″, and most sizes are available with two different wall thicknesses.

PVC pipe is not as strong as metal pipe, of course, and it cannot be welded (actually it can be welded with special plastic welding equipment). But it is inexpensive; it's easy to cut, bend, drill, and bolt; and it can be cemented if you have large areas of it in contact.

PVC is easily bent into shape when it is heated to 250°F. Heating can be accomplished in a kitchen oven, by using infrared heat lamps, a hot air gun, or with the indirect heater discussed in the following section on making a shepherd's crook. Boiling water does not produce adequate heat.

Bending a Shepherd's Crook

The first step is to make a wooden jig to serve as a form for bending the softened PVC pipe. Draw the shape on plywood, and cut it out on a band saw. Bear in mind that the plywood form you are designing will define the *inside* contour of the crook.

When PVC is heated above 340°F., toxic chlorine gas is released. You can tell when this gas is being released, because the plastic will begin to blacken and ignite, and black smoke will be produced. For safety reasons, then, heat and bend PVC out of doors where plenty of fresh air is available, or use forced ventilation if you must work indoors.

The trick is to apply enough heat to soften the plastic without overheating any area to the point of producing fumes. The following instructions detail our solution to this problem.

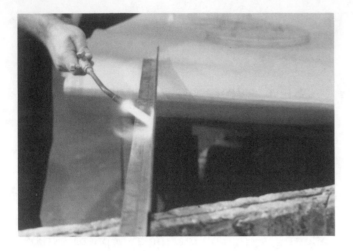

Pre-heat a piece of angle iron with a torch. It takes about three feet of PVC pipe to make the bend in the crook, so you need a little more than three feet of angle iron to serve as the heat distributor.

Lay one end of a 10′ length of PVC pipe in this bed of hot iron. Continue applying heat to the iron, but avoid allowing the torch flame to make direct contact with the plastic pipe. Rotate the PVC in the iron bed, to allow an even distribution of heat to all parts of the pipe surface. Some scorching of the white surface of the pipe may occur, but if you keep the pipe rotating this will not create any danger.

Soon the heated end of the pipe will become rubbery and ready to shape. You may need help in transporting the flexible pipe to the forming table. With the pipe heated to 250°F., gloves are recommended for handling and shaping it.

    The rubbery plastic can now be easily bent around the wooden form. It will then take about two minutes for a shape this size to cool down and become rigid.

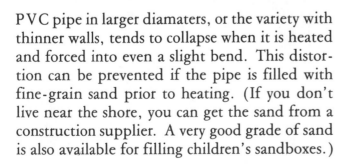

PVC pipe in larger diamaters, or the variety with thinner walls, tends to collapse when it is heated and forced into even a slight bend. This distortion can be prevented if the pipe is filled with fine-grain sand prior to heating. (If you don't live near the shore, you can get the sand from a construction supplier. A very good grade of sand is also available for filling children's sandboxes.)

Tape one end of the pipe closed with several wrappings of masking tape. Stand on a ladder and use a pitcher and a funnel to get the sand into the pipe. Tamp the sand, filling the pipe firmly and allowing no air pockets. Sand flexes very nicely, retaining the round shape of the pipe while allowing the pipe to conform to the shape of your jig.

Sculpting Urethane Foam

In my youth I stood in awe of sculptors. I was like the visitor to an artist's studio who, admiring a granite elephant, said to the artist with reverent wonder, "How ever did you do that?" And the artist's easy reply: "I just remove everything that doesn't look like an elephant, and there you are."

It doesn't have to be that hard. The intuitive removal of unwanted material is only one of several approaches to fashioning an object.

In the next few pages I will share some techniques that will, I hope, take "sculpting" out of the esoteric realm of the artist and replace it with "carving" which is within the grasp of the willing technician.

The Band Saw as a Sculpting Tool

A band saw is not commonly equated with a sculptor's chisel, but in connection with this little-known procedure and with the help of a handful of toothpicks, it will go a long way toward rough-cutting three-dimensional objects from urethane foam.

I have chosen a twin-barreled laser space pistol as a project to demonstrate this carving technique, but myriad three-dimensional objects can be fashioned this way—the only limitation is dictated by the size of your band saw's throat.

Sculpting a Space Gun

When you are carving a complex shape such as this futuristic sidearm, a scale model of the object is almost indispensible. We fashioned this one out of a small wad of Plasticine at a ⅕ scale.

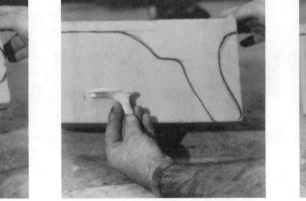

Sketch a top view, front view, and end view of the pistol onto a block of high-density urethane foam. (High-density foam is more durable than lightweight foam under the stresses of onstage use.) All three views must be represented on the block before you begin cutting.

The dust produced by cutting and sanding urethane foam is more abrasive and more dangerous to your nose, throat, and lungs than sawdust.

Always wear a face mask to filter out these particles when you are performing any operation that produces foam dust.

Select one of the outlines for your first cut and make a straightforward unbroken cut with the band saw along this line. If one of your three outlines is more complex, cut along that one first, and save the simplest shape for last.

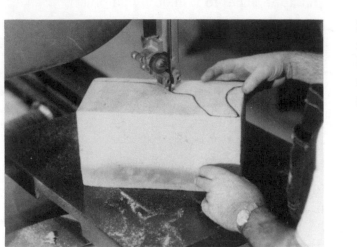

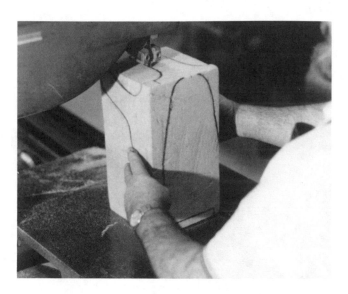

As the "scrap" foam is cut away, don't discard the pieces. Reassemble them and hold them in place as you turn the block 90° and select the second sketched outline to be cut. The reassembled block is easy to hold square on the table as the next cut is made with the band saw.

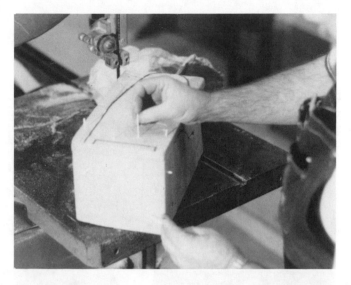

After the second outline has been cut the collection of scraps will have become too cumbersome to hold together in your hands. But the pieces are still useful and should not be discarded. Use

toothpicks this time to reassemble the foam block. Toothpicks are inexpensive, so use plenty to hold the pieces of the block firmly together while you make the final cut with the band saw.

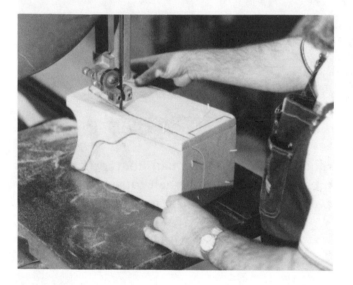

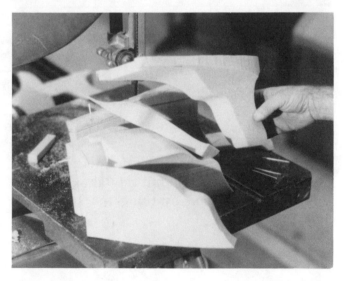

By saving the simplest outline for last you reduce the chance of error as this block of pinned fragments is cut for the third time. The band saw blade will probably pass through several of the toothpicks, but this will not hamper your project.

When the last cut is complete, pull the central part of the foam block from the pile of fragments. That will be the rough-cut enlargement of the model you began with.

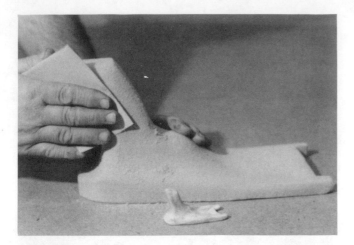

The sharp linear edges of your space gun can be easily rounded into shape with sandpaper.

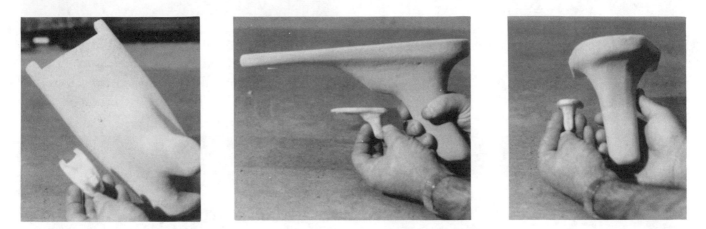

These three photos illustrate the successful results of using the band saw as a sculpting tool.

We have rough-cut architectural details (newel posts, banister rails, column capitals, etc.) from solid blocks of wood by using the same technique, but substituting nails for toothpicks. You must use extreme care when cutting, however, to avoid sawing through the nails.

Sculpting a Urethane Dog

This second project uses a related technique to carve a dog of urethane foam. However, this sculpture is a bit too complicated to be accomplished entirely with the band saw.

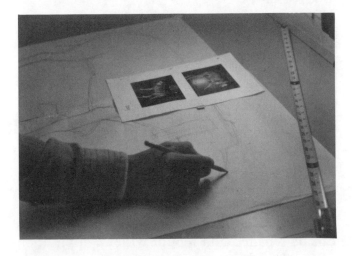

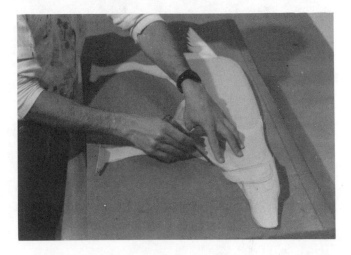

Make a full-scale sketch of a dog in an appropriate pose, working from research material. Use either a photograph or a good rendering of the correct breed of dog.

(When I feel that a sketch is beyond the limitations of my talents, I can usually find someone in the shop with the necessary skills. My ability to *carve* is not dependent on an ability to *draw*.)

Trace your sketch onto a large block of foam and cut the outline on a band saw.

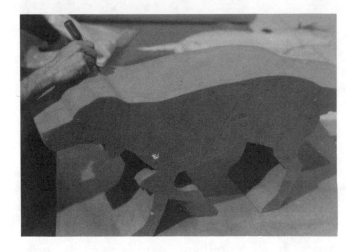

This block of foam is already beginning to look like a doggy. Now sketch onto the top of the figure more of the details — taper the head at the nose; narrow the body at the neck; bring the tail to a point. These cuts will not always go clear through the whole body, so they cannot be made with the band saw, but a hand saw will cut easily through soft urethane foam. Use a keyhole saw, a hacksaw fitted with a single handle on one end, as a carving knife.

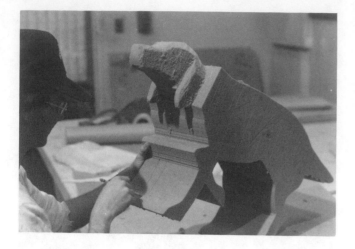 

As you carve these details, a form will begin to emerge from the block. Continue sketching in the details of the underside — the legs, belly, etc.

Sketch out additional features and carve away unwanted material. If you should make any errors and carve away too much of the foam, flaws can be repaired and rebuilt with an application of Bondo.

 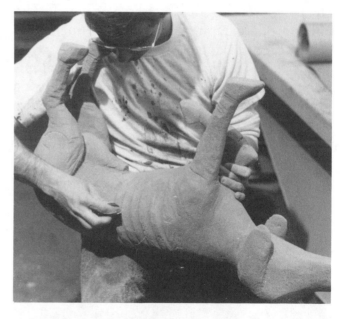

Sketch and carve. Sketch and carve. Sketch and carve.

Smooth out any remaining marks from the saw blade with sandpaper. Urethane is soft enough to be worked efficiently with medium-grit sandpaper. In fact, urethane foam is so easily workable that the final stages of carving can be done entirely with sandpaper. Our dog's ribs were worked in during the sanding process.

Machine Tooling Urethane Foam

Urethane foam can be turned on a lathe to form objects with uniformly round shapes. But better news is that the lathe is not essential to this technique. The first machine-tooled project discussed here does indeed use a lathe and demonstrates the similarities and differences of turning urethane *vs.* turning wood; the second project shows the use of a drill press as an impromptu lathe.

Turning a Large Goose Egg

Golden goose eggs were needed for a production of *Jack and the Beanstalk*. Four-inch plastic goose eggs can be purchased inexpensively from display and novelty stores, but we could not find a source for six-inch eggs and were compelled to make them.

Begin with a square block of urethane foam. You must expect a certain amount of waste as the construction progresses, so make the block a little larger in each dimension than the projected final egg.

Run a sharpened dowel through the block as near to the center as possible. When you have skewered the block down the middle, withdraw the dowel and, using its path as a pilot hole, force another larger dowel into its place.

The larger dowel should be at least 1″ in diameter. This thickness is necessary to fit the dowel safely in the tail stock of the lathe. Do not yield to the temptation of using a drill at any stage as you are installing this wooden center pin. Friction is the only force securing the foam to the rod, so a tight fit is essential.

Use a disk sander to rough-cut the square edges off the block of foam.

Mount the rod into the lathe, and run the lathe at a slow speed (1200 r.p.m.), using a sandpaper block as a cutting tool to shape the block until it takes on a cylindrical form.

Draw the outline of one-half of the egg on a sheet of galvanized iron or hardened aluminum. Cut this shape out with tin snips to make a metal template to be used as a lathing tool.

This template, even though it is not sharpened, can be fed slowly onto the rotating foam, and its silhouette will define the egg's shape.

Hold the sheet-metal template square to the foam or at a slight downward angle with the rotating foam sliding past its leading edge. Any upgrade to the cutting edge will dig into your foam and leave gouges in the work. (In fact, an upward angle can not only gouge the foam and bend the template, it might jerk the template from your grasp and endanger your fingers.) This process will generate a great deal of hazardous foam dust. The use of a respirator is essential in this dusty atmosphere.

Hold the template firmly on the tool rest and patiently work it forward until the template is touching the wooden center post and the egg shape is completely carved from the foam.

It should come as no surprise that you cannot spray gold paint onto a porous foam surface and expect the surface to look metallic. A smooth, hard "shell" is needed to cover the foam surface.

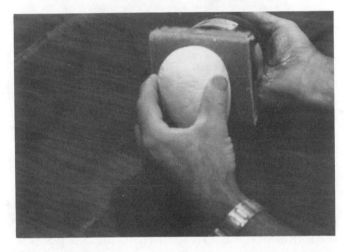

Remove the wooden dowel from the center of the foam egg and fill the void with putty. Cover the entire egg with at least two coatings of water putty to hide the foam texture.

When the putty has dried, sand it down until you have the hard smooth shell quality that you require.

A Drill Press Lathe

Sometimes the shape you want to turn will have a diameter too large to fit into the bed of a lathe. You will be pleased to learn of the next procedure, in which a drill press is converted into a makeshift lathe.

The critical feature of this conversion is the construction of a clamping center shaft which holds the foam securely while it is being turned.

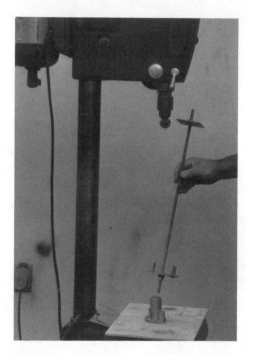

The shaft itself is a length of ⅜" threaded rod, cut about 4" longer than the foam you wish to turn. Two metal plates about 4" square are needed to make the clamp. Drill a ½" hole in the center of each plate. Center a ⅜" nut directly over each hole and weld each nut solidly to the plate.

The two metal plates thread onto the center shaft, firmly clamping the foam in place. Chucking the shaft into the jaws of the drill press will cause the foam to rotate.

Steady the lower end of the shaft by allowing it to rest in a bearing which has been bolted to the table of the drill press. The bearing in the illustration above was salvaged from an old phonograph turntable. (We have also used this procedure successfully by simply running the lower end of the shaft through a snug hole in a piece of plywood secured to the drill press table with a C-clamp. A well-lubricated bearing is secondary to the need to hold the shaft straight and steady.)

Outfit the bottom plate by welding sixteen-penny nails to it. When you force these points into the foam, you will be doubly certain that the foam cannot slip on the center shaft.

Sculpting Foam Balusters

The UCLA production of *A Feast of Youth* used a pair of sweeping handrails that required ten large balusters. We turned these balusters from urethane foam, using a drill press as a lathe and a metal template as a cutting tool.

After the foam block had been skewered on the center shaft and clamped between the two

metal plates, we tightened it in the jaws of the chuck and set it turning.

As do other procedures involving turning and cutting urethane foam, this process will generate a great quantity of foam dust. This dust is finer and more harmful than saw dust, and necessitates the use of eye protection and a respirator.

Set the speed of the drill press at about 1200 r.p.m. The rotating foam can be tooled the same as if it were fitted in the bed of a lathe. The mere touch of rough sandpaper is enough to leave a groove in the rotating foam, so the block must be worked with some care.

A wood rasp, which will shape the rotating foam quickly, can be used to define the general outline of your form. Work the file so that the rotating foam slides off the cutting edge, thereby reducing the possibility that the tool might dig into the foam.

When you use a rasp or any pointed metal tool, be careful to not allow the point to dig into the foam. Urethane foam is so soft that deep gouges

can result from carelessness, and work can be ruined in an instant.

Cut a template from sheet metal to serve as a cutting tool to refine the shape of the sculpted foam. This carefully-fashioned template will give a more specific contour to the foam. Hold the template so that the foam slides past its cutting edge, to prevent the edge from digging into the foam.

Force a slight concavity in the template as you are holding it. This bend adds rigidity to the tool and reduces vibration caused by the contact of the template with the foam.

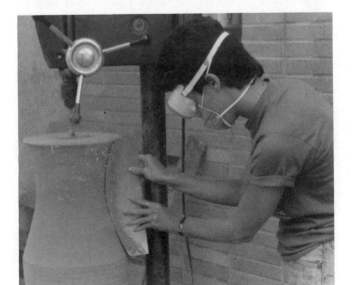

When you have cut the foam to a form that is very nearly correct, final shaping is done with a template cut to the precise final shape. A template this large requires more than one pair of hands to keep it steady and minimize vibrations. A template of this size will shape urethane foam remarkably well, allowing you to make many identical reproductions.

A drill press like this will accept a form with a radius up to about 12″. Anything larger would run into the frame of the press. Larger forms can be turned, however, if you remove the drill motor from the frame and re-mount it upside-down. Should you decide to try this, it might be necessary to tool the foam from the top of a stepladder.

The fine dust which is produced when urethane foam is turned is not only hazardous to your nose and lungs, it is also harmful to the brushes and bearings of the drill motor. When you have finished the lathing operation, it is a good idea to thoroughly clean the electric motor with compressed air.

Sculpting a Beehive

The drill press lathe makes quick work of shaping a beehive. First, though, you can save a lot of time and energy by rough-cutting a cone shape with the band saw. Just draw a circle on your foam block, tilt the table of your band saw to about 30°, and rotate the block by hand as you cut along the circle. This will yield the desired cone.

Now clamp the cone of urethane foam onto the center shaft of your converted drill press. Set the speed of the drill press at about 1200–1500 r.p.m. and you can work the rotating form with a rasp or sandpaper much the same as a potter shapes clay on a potter's wheel. Simply touching rough sandpaper to the rotating foam will very quickly groove the surface, so work the form slowly and with care.

I think you will agree that there is nothing terribly forbidding about producing a bee hive when you use this method, which puts sculpting within the reach of the average technician.

Some Tips on Sewing

This section does not purport to teach you how to make stage draperies, but rather, how to make them better.

I'll share with you a few techniques (some that I learned at a comparatively advanced stage in my career) which can make your job easier and more accurate. My first suggestion is that you construct a drapery table for your shop.

A Drapery Table

The drapery table must be large enough to accommodate curtains of a size that might be required for a stage setting—for archways, sliding glass doorways, etc. Our drapery table is 6″ wide and 10″ long. Although a drapery table is very handy when needed, it is not always in use, and a table this large can be a nuisance to store! This may be the major factor in your decision as to whether to include a drapery table in your shop. Our solution to the storage problem is to keep our drapery table on top of our vacuum form, and have it double as a work table. The fragile surface of the muslin is protected for this purpose by covering it with butcher paper or, if the work to be performed on it is more vigorous, with a couple of 4′ × 8′ sheets of Masonite.

The table top is built in the fashion of a hard wall flat—that is, the framing members are laid on edge rather than assembled flat, as is the custom with theater scenery which is to be covered with canvas or muslin.

Securely nail a covering of fiber board (Celotex) to the frame. Celotex is a soft material such as would be used for a bulletin board, and it allows easy insertion of sewing pins, so drapery fabric can be easily pinned to this surface.

Apply the muslin to the table top as you would if you were covering a 6′ × 10′ flat, with these exceptions: you stretch the muslin tighter, and you don't use any glue. Our table top is in constant use, so the muslin gets soiled and must be replaced every year or so. Gluing the muslin would make the recovering process more difficult. Stretch the muslin as tight as you can. The muslin will not be sized or painted, so the shrinking that results from wetting will not take place.

Snap a gridwork of 1′ lines on the muslin surface. Using a straight edge and a black felt marker, trace over the snapped lines to make them permanent and easy to read.

I think you will best perceive this table's advantages when you use it in the construction of a series of curtains which must all be the same size.

Pinning the curtains to the table so they stay

Grid the last 12″ in each direction with 1″ segments. This inked gridwork will provide a permanent "measuring tape" to accurately measure your draperies and curtains while they are under construction.

put during the measuring and cutting process is most helpful. You will soon begin to rely on the gridwork as a sort of jig which will make such repeated measurements precisely alike.

Sometimes you may need to make this large table even larger, in order to accommodate curtains of a larger size. You can easily add extensions by tacking plywood or Masonite to the edge of the table and supporting the overhang on sawhorses or something comparable. It would be impractical, however, to build the basic table on a larger scale.

After a few uses, you will no longer look on the drapery table as a convenient aid in the construction of draperies, but as a necessity—and you'll wonder how you ever got along without one.

Straight Cuts on Fabrics

When a curtain or drapery hangs awry on a window or doorway, you can usually assume that the fabric was not cut straight in the first place. Here are some techniques you might find useful (if you aren't already familiar with them) in making straight, square cuts across yard goods.

Some fabrics—particularly cotton—will, when new, tear along a straight line perpendicular to the selvage edge. With these fabrics, tear-ing is an effective way to reduce them to size, the results will be as accurate as could be achieved by a careful cutting with scissors.

If, however, the fabric has been hanging for a long period of time under uneven stress, or has been in a humid atmosphere where uneven shrinkage can take place, a torn line may not turn out to be square to the edge. In a case like this, the best way to make an accurate cut...

...is to spread the material out lengthwise on the drapery table, with the edge of the fabric aligned with one of the long grid lines.

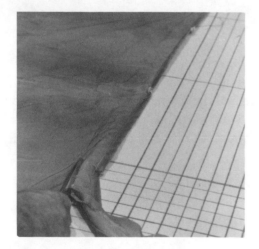

Then, using one of the grid lines as a guide, snap a line on the fabric. When this line is cut with a pair of scissors, the result will be a square end.

Some fabrics are woven on the bias, and as a result they cannot be torn effectively. These should also be snapped and cut as explained above.

Pulling a Thread

If a fabric's weave is clearly visible, it is not difficult to simply scissor a line following this weave.

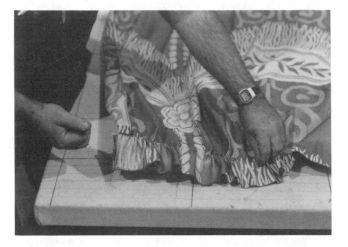

If, on the other hand, you cannot see the weave clearly, you can use the technique of "pulling a thread." Make a small cut in the fabric to begin the cut you intend to make, and pull the thread left exposed along your cut. When this thread is pulled a pucker will begin to appear across the material. With luck, this pucker may run for 6″ to 8″ before the thread breaks. It can then be extended a little farther by spreading the puckered material with your fingers.

Cut along this ''flaw line'' as far as it is visible and then grab another thread (ideally the same thread, but farther along in the fabric) and pull again. Continue this process as many times as it takes to get across the fabric. The resulting cut should be straight and square.

Sewing a Straight Hem

It is sometimes difficult to sew a straight hem if the hem is particularly wide—and draperies *do* have wide hems. Such hems are necessary to provide weight along the bottom edge. A hem can be made perfectly straight if you begin by snapping a reference line onto the material while the fabric is still pinned to the drapery table. I prefer to calculate the bottom of the drape so that it will almost touch the floor, and snap the line there. Then, as the sewing is done, the fabric is folded up following this reference line. If you follow this system, there can be no question that the bottom of the drape will be at floor level, straight, and square.

CONTAINERS

Faking a Beer Can Label

There are several plays that call for the business of popping a beer can open on stage and taking a long drink from it. The easy way to do this, of course, is to buy a six-pack and have the actor quaff the real thing. But suppose the actor doesn't like beer—or suppose the actor (by his own initiative, or at the director's behest) prefers a substitute beverage in the interest of giving a more clear-headed performance. Then the "easy way" isn't the one to be used.

What we need, then, is a method of applying a beer label to a container of some beverage the actor is comfortable with.

The following illustrations give a clear demonstration of how this label change may be easily accomplished.

Begin with a can with the desired label, and purge the can of its contents.

Remove the top of the emptied can with a mat knife. The aluminum of today's cans is very soft and easily cut.

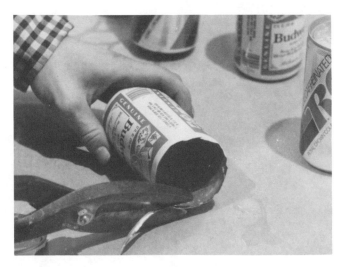

Clean up the jagged edges with a pair of tin snips or scissors.

Make a split down the middle of the can with your shears.

Then slide a full container of the acceptable beverage into the sham shell.

Making a Vile Vial

In a wicked fit of anger, Medea—a woman wronged—brews up a deadly concoction with which to seek revenge on her rival. She laces a necklace and a gown with her sorcery, and gives them to Creusa. Creusa and all in her house suffer death as a result. (There's a little more to the story, but not much.)

There are many ways of depicting this poison; the following instructions show how we did it. We obtained a small glass flask and gave it a crude, primitive-looking outer coating, taking advantage of the properties of epoxy putty.

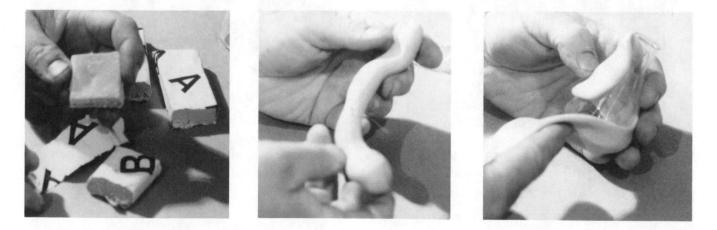

Use equal parts of the epoxy putty components. Mix the putty thoroughly and make a rope, as described in the ''Construction Techniques'' section.

Flatten the rope and wrap it around the glass. Smooth out the overlapping edges with your finger until the coating is of a uniform thickness over the whole surface. A drop of water on your finger will make this polishing easy. Do not use too much water, however, as this can ruin the properties of the putty.

In our production, Medea wore the vials on a chain around her neck (so they'd be on hand when she needed them). The chain ran through a little ring-shaped handle on each vial.

The handle can be made from a small curtain ring attached to the bottle with many wrappings of a strong nylon line. You can completely hide the nylon cord by embedding it in the soft putty.

Cover the ring with a coating of epoxy putty. Smooth and blend the coating on the ring with the coating on the bottle by rubbing the seam with your fingers or a sculpting tool.

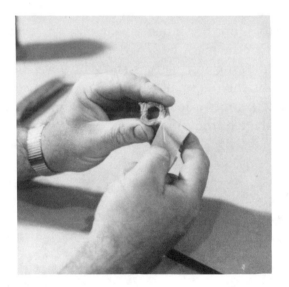

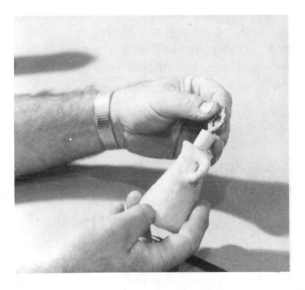

Many things could be used for a stopper. We fashioned ours from a decorative oil lamp wick trimmer. We built up the small-diameter stem by wrapping it with masking tape until it was the exact size needed to fit properly into the neck of the vial.

We sprayed the epoxy-covered glass with a coating of metallic paint. (Actually, we made two such vials. We made one "bronze" by spraying it with brass paint, using patina tones of green and aluminum. The other was made "pewter" by using the aluminum paint as the base and the green and brass paints for patina tones.)

You could make the vials fume and appear to be fearfully toxic, using nothing more than baking soda and vinegar.

Pour about a teaspoon of baking soda into the bronze vial, and about an ounce of vinegar into the pewter one. When the actress empties the contents of the pewter vial into the bronze one on stage, the "poison" will froth and drip uncontrollably — all over the necklace, the gown, and the floor.

Russian Tea Glasses

The scene is again the properties shop. The PROPERTIES MASTER *is seated in his swivel arm chair at the work table. He is studying a catalog. His expression is dour. A* STUDENT *comes striding into the prop shop with all of the exuberance of youth. He speaks.*

STUDENT   Hi there, big fella. What do you find to frown about?

PROP MASTER   I have another production in need of a set of those little tea glasses. This is the second time in six months they've been called for.

STUDENT   Seems like maybe you should break down and buy a set. What's the matter, can't you find any place that sells them?

PROP MASTER   Yes. I've located a source and a price. Specialty coffee sellers stock them, but they're a little expensive. It would cost forty dollars to buy a set of four glasses. An incidental item like this shouldn't take such a heavy chunk of the show's budget.

STUDENT   *(Looking closely at the catalog)* Why, they're nothing more than juice glasses with handles. Why don't we make a set?

PROP MASTER   Yes, but the metal work isn't really that simple. It would take some very careful soldering. I dunno—it could be done, but it's not that simple.

STUDENT   I could make one, easy. I'll bet you a dollar I can make a tea glass in half an hour.

PROP MASTER   Naw, you couldn't even get the soldering iron hot in a half hour.

STUDENT   Two dollars says I can make two glasses in 45 minutes.

PROP MASTER   You're on.

Making Two Russian Tea Glasses

The following is a re-creation of the way Jeff Brown managed to win this bet.

The first few minutes were spent assembling the raw materials. He quickly found two 4-oz. glasses, and he searched out a sheet of brass plate and—would you believe it?—a roll of gold-colored metallic tape.

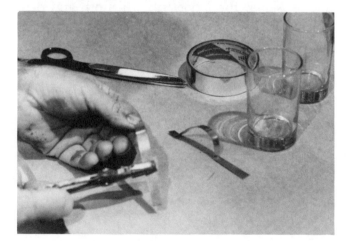

He cut two strips of brass, ½″ wide, for the handles. These strips were bent into a handle shape, leaving ½″ flat on each end. These flat tabs were meant to lie against the surface of the glasses.

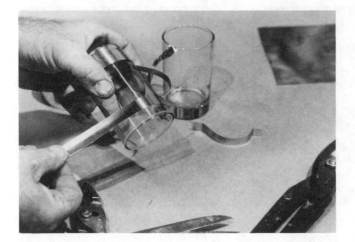

In his next step—the one I had not anticipated—Jeff taped the handle to the glass with the ¾″ metallic tape. He applied the full width at the bottom, and cut a half-width strip with scissors to fasten the upper part of the handle.

So forty minutes later, there I stood, two dollars poorer, but a wiser man.

Rustic Jugs from Wine Bottles

Period jugs and urns are rare, but wine bottles abound. Here is a method for converting a wine jug into a rustic pitcher. It might be argued that the pitcher is not precisely identifiable by period, but we have found that it is sufficiently non-descript to fit into tavern-type scenes from Euripides through Shakespeare and even to Brecht, without eliciting much criticism.

Select a large wine jug with pitcher-like qualities.

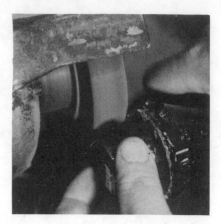

Gently begin to grind the glass bottle, working the corner of a fine grinding wheel high up on the neck of the jug where the glass is thinnest.

Score the glass around the entire circumference of the neck. Then go back and patiently repeat the process. Then gently score the circle again.

If you work with a fine wheel in good condition, one with a sharp corner, and you work the glass tenderly and with great patience, the top piece of the jug will finally fall off, doing little damage to the bottle.

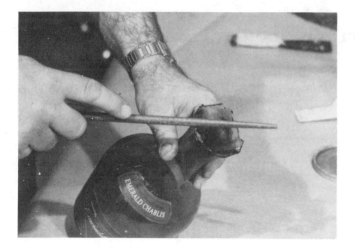

File off the sharp edges of the broken glass to minimize the danger of cutting your fingers.

Mix up some plastic filler according to manufacturer's instructions, and build up any area that was chipped away or damaged in the grinding process.

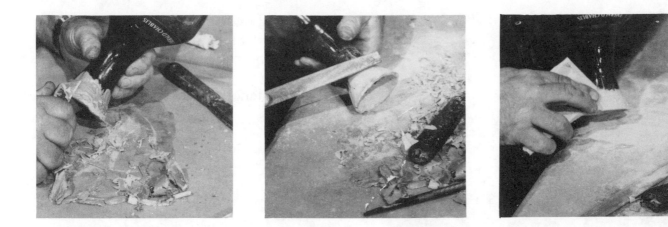

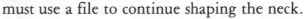

Trim away excess putty with a mat knife before the putty is fully set. Any refinement of the shape that can be accomplished now will save a lot of sanding later.

As the plastic filler cures, it will become too hard to cut with the knife. At that point you must use a file to continue shaping the neck.

Smooth the plastic filler further with sandpaper, feathering the edges to minimize the line of demarcation where the plastic filler and glass meet.

Soak off the label with water or scrape it off with a razor blade. The glass surface can now be hidden by painting it with an earth color mixed with a texturing medium, or...

...we can take a lesson from elementary-school students to give us an alternate method for treating the surface. (The children use this technique to texture their Father's Day pencil holders.)

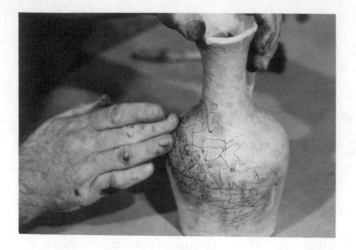

Tear off bits of masking tape and stick them onto the glass, overlapping the edges. When the entire jug has been covered, rub paint onto the tape, and the edges of the bits of tape will take on the appearance of cracks in a pottery glaze.

The table settings of the ancient Greeks included a terra cotta jar (called an *oinochoe*) for serving wine. These jars were not far removed in appearance from our doctored wine bottle.

ELECTRICITY OF LOW-VOLTAGE LAMPS

If a lighted candle should fall to the floor by accident, it would most likely go out, and the prop crew's biggest problem would be the clean-up of a hot wax spill. It's a minor problem, but one we want to avoid. But a kerosene or oil lamp fell to the floor, there is a strong possibility that an emergency call to the fire department would be in order. The conversion of candles and oil lamps to battery operation provides a safe, cold light source which can replace hazardous flames.

Sometimes it is preferable to convert electric lamps which are designed for 110-volt power to operate at a lower voltage. For example, a street lamp powered via an extension cord from backstage can be troublesome if a performer trips on the cord: not only does this pose a threat to the performer, but it can be disconcerting to the audience which has suddenly been made aware that the lamp gets its power from backstage and not from the power supply of the city where the play is set.

Rotating or slip stages also are situations where battery operation can be preferable. Turntables can be designed to accommodate 110-volt lines, but this can be cumbersome. If you rig your lamps to operate on batteries, you can simplify many of the electrical problems inherent to changing scenery on such a stage.

It is the goal of this section of the book to explain techniques for accomplishing such a conversion. A second aim is to explain some of the physics of electricity. The theory of series and parallel circuits, and their relative characteristics, will be explained in the hope that the reader's understanding will put him in a position where he can improvise with them and use them to his advantage.

Physics of Electricity

Here is the simplest electrical circuit involving a light bulb and a power source. It is so simple that even the switch has been eliminated. Touching the base of the bulb to the terminal of the battery serves as a "switch"; when the lamp is depressed to touch the battery pole, the circuit is completed and the lamp lights. Some penlight type flashlights operate in this manner.

Let us draw from this example the basics of electrical physics.

1. A battery provides a *force*. In the case of a flashlight battery, the force is 1½ volts.

2. The voltage has the power to force a movement of electrons through the wire and the lamp. This movement or flow is called *current*.

3. The filament in the lamp offers a *resistance* to an easy flow of current. The force of the battery is sufficient, however, to push the current through this resistance, and as a result, the lamp filament begins to glow.

4. Electrons (or current) will only flow when their path, which is called the *circuit,* is unbroken.

5. The function of the *switch* is to interrupt this complete path and stop the flow of electrons, thus causing the lamp to stop glowing.

There is a great deal of electrical theory contained in the foregoing five points. Basic terms and concepts have been defined. If you are unfamiliar with the fundamentals of electricity, study these points until you understand them. They are not difficult to grasp, but you should not skip over them as if they were self-evident.

Series Battery Connections

Let's complicate things just a little by soldering a second battery and a switch into our circuit. This is the basic arrangement found in a standard flashlight. In a flashlight, of course, there are no soldered connections. The circuit is completed by forcing the various components (batteries, switch, lamp) to touch under the tension of a spring.

In the photos on the following pages, all electrical connections have been made using a soldering gun and rosin-core solder.

The current flows from the batteries through the lamp, through the switch, and back to the batteries, in one path through the series of electrical elements. This electrical arrangement is called a "series circuit."

Introducing the second battery into the series adds force to the total circuit. The voltages of the two batteries are combined, and the force is now 3 volts instead of 1½ volts.

The series makes for a very compact arrangement. You can slide the unit into a sleeve and, with just a few embellishments, pass it off as a convincing candle.

Cut the sleeve from a length of PVC water pipe. Slide the components into the pipe and secure the assembly with hot glue.

An oil lamp can also be wired to be powered by flashlight batteries. This lamp makes use of

Set the unit into a candle holder and decorate it with wax drippings melted onto it from a real candle.

a series circuit exactly like the one used in the battery-powered candle.

Hide the two batteries (which will supply the lamp with the required 3 volts of force) in the base of the lamp.

In this case we were able to run the wiring through the interior of the lamp. Most lamps are not so conveniently constructed and require that the wires be hot-glued to the outside of the lamp. In such a case, conceal the wires by running them down the back side of the lamp so they won't be seen by the audience.

A four-cell flashlight has four batteries connected in a series. The voltage with this arrangement is 4 × 1½ volts, or 6 volts.

In a series circuit, it is essential that the top center post of each battery is connected to the bottom of the next battery. In other words, a series circuit is one in which the positive pole of each battery is connected to the negative pole of the next one.

Wiring the batteries in any other way will not produce the characteristics of a series circuit. If, for example, two positive posts are wired together, no current will pass between them.

Of course, a 6-volt lamp is also needed with a 6-volt circuit. The increased energy from the extra batteries forces more current to flow through the lamp; if you connect a lamp rated for 3 volts to a 6-volt circuit, the lamp would have a very bright but *very* short life.

Parallel Battery Connections

When circuits are wired in a *parallel* arrangement, current is not required to follow a single path. Electron flow is given the opportunity of choosing between two or more paths, and the rules of physics allow us to predict with absolute accuracy how these "choices" will be made.

The batteries shown here have been connected in a parallel arrangement. The center posts have been wired together, and the bases have been connected. The switch and the lamp have been connected as in a series circuit, and the current flow through these components follows the rules of a series circuit.

When batteries are wired in a parallel arrangement, the voltages are not combined to force more current to flow in the circuit. However, the current-handling capability of the batteries is increased. The total voltage of two 1½-volt batteries wired in a parallel arrangement is still 1½ volts — but the two batteries will last twice as long as a single battery would.

A practical application of this arrangement is not offered here because such applications are rare. The 1½-volt power supply is not favored by circuit designers. Sylvania's 1980 catalog of miniature lamps, for example, lists almost 800 low-voltage lamp styles, but only seven of these are rated at 2 volts or less.

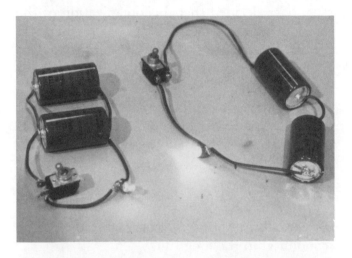

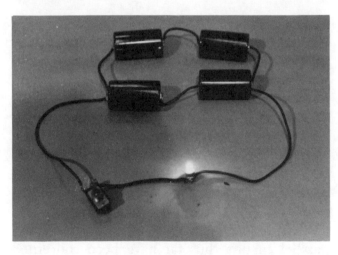

This street lamp was rigged for battery operation so that it could be used without an extension cord in a scene that was shifted on a turntable.

A 3-volt lamp was fitted into the center of the globe, and four batteries wired in a series-parallel arrangement were housed in the base of the pole (where we also concealed the switch).

Nonetheless, an understanding of parallel battery connections is important because it leads us to the concept of series–parallel connections. Such connections yield 3 volts or more, with a longer period between battery changes—and combination means greater practicality.

Parallel and Series Battery Connections Compared

This illustration graphically demonstrates the effects of parallel and series battery connections. Both lamps are rated at 3 volts. The series connection delivers a higher voltage and thus more light; the parallel arrangement has the advantage of a longer life.

Series–Parallel Battery Connections

If four batteries are wired in a series–parallel arrangement, as shown here, the voltage is twice as forceful as that from a single battery, *and* the battery life is twice as long as with two batteries connected in a single series.

The Power Supply Package

Once a wiring scheme has been decided upon, the batteries should be taped into a compact package. This package will be referred to on the following pages as the "battery pack" or "power supply." The shape of this package will depend on where it is to be hidden.

A handy and compact power supply can be found in a motorcycle storage battery, which provides 6 volts without all this soldering. This battery is more expensive, but it is rechargeable and can be economical in the long run.

Here we have revealed the anatomy of a commercially packaged battery pack. Some engineer must have decided that this organization of the components is the most compact and therefore the most efficient for a lantern flashlight. This arrangement has become standard for a 6-volt lantern battery.

It is interesting to note that a 6-volt lantern battery is made up of four 1½-volt batteries which have been internally wired in series.

Some Electronic Definitions

Perhaps it would be a good idea before we delve into other circuits and their characteristics to give formal definitions of terms that we have been using so far.

The words "volts," "current," and "resistance" have been carefully used in describing the activity within an electrical circuit. These electrical factors are absolutely predictable in terms of their effect on the flow of free electrons in a circuit.

Voltage is an electrical force which compels a movement of electrons in a completed circuit.

Current is the movement of electrons in a completed circuit.

Resistance is an opposition to the flow of electrons in a completed circuit.

A combination of voltages and resistances act to control current in a circuit. Voltages push and force electrons to move; resistances oppose and restrain the movement of electrons.

Energy in the form of heat or light (or both) is released when a voltage forces a current through a resistance.

A **switch** could be looked upon as the ultimate resistance, which will entirely stop all current flow.

The discussion and applications of series and parallel circuits thus far have been concerned with the power supply only. Frequently there is a need for multiple light sources. Light sources, or "loads," can also be wired in series or parallel and each arrangement yields very specific results.

In an electrical circuit, anything that offers resistance to the free flow of electrons — it can be a lamp, motor, heater, etc. — is called a **load.**

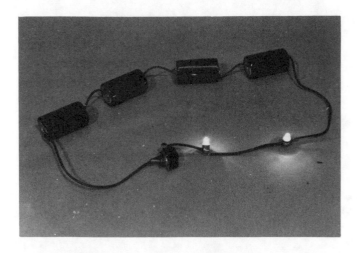

Series Load Connections

The two lamps here are wired in series with the battery pack. The batteries are also wired in series, but for now we'll concern ourselves with the load. It doesn't matter whether the power supply is a 6-volt lantern battery or some series–parallel wiring arrangement; the point is that the *load* here is wired in series with the power supply.

The following facts apply to the illustration above:

1. When two loads are connected in series, the resistance in the total circuit is increased. In a series circuit the current must flow through both loads. Therefore there is twice as much resistance in the circuit as when a single lamp was the circuit's only load.

2. The increased resistance hampers the current's ability to flow. In fact, if the lamps are precisely alike, exactly half as much current will flow as compared to the same circuit with a single lamp connected to the batteries.

3. This decreased current has the effect of reducing the voltage felt at each lamp. In the example pictured here, even though the power supply is providing 6 volts, an effective force of 3 volts is being delivered to each lamp.

Parallel Load Connections

The two lamps which make up the load in this circuit are wired in parallel with the power supply, which in this case is 3 volts. (The batteries in this case are connected in a series–parallel arrangement, but the battery arrangement is not important to the discussion at hand.)

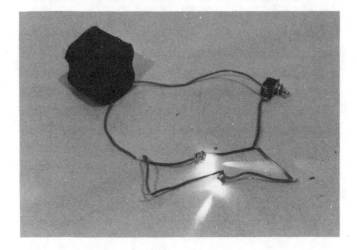

The following facts apply to the parallel load connection shown here:

1. *Both* lamps are drawing current and the total *resistance* to current flow is *decreased.*

2. As a result of this *decreased* resistance, the current flow is *increased.*

3. Battery life is actually reduced by half if the two lamps are alike.

Series – Parallel Load Connections

The four lamps making up the load of this circuit are wired in series–parallel. A force of 3 volts will be delivered to each lamp. The battery pack will provide 6 volts, with a fairly long life.

Physics of Electricity — Summary

In the interest of review and reference, here are further notes on electrical relationships that have already been defined in the discussions of series and parallel circuits:

Voltage and current flow are *directly proportional*. An increase in voltage (or force) will increase current flow.

Resistance and current flow are *inversely proportional*. An increase in resistance will decrease current flow.

Connecting a number of loads in parallel will decrease the total resistance in a circuit.

The foregoing are obvious relationships and should not be too hard for the reader to grasp.

Here are some less obvious relationships:

An increase in current will increase the apparent voltage felt across a resistance.

An increase in resistance (or loads) will *decrease* current flow in a series circuit, and *increase* current flow in a parallel circuit.

Voltage is measured in volts. Its symbol is E.

Current is measured in amperes. Its symbol is I.

Resistance is measured in ohms. Its symbol is R.

This entire list of observations can be stated mathematically according to Ohm's Law, as follows:

Voltage equals current times resistance, or
$$E = I \times R$$
Current equals voltage divided by resistance, or
$$I = E \div R$$
Resistance equals voltage divided by current, or
$$R = E \div I$$

Converting a Lamp to Battery Operation

The Top End

When a stock lamp is converted for battery operation, the conversion carries with it a compromise in the brightness of the light coming from the bulb. The lamp will not glow brilliantly, but it will glow. According to the laws that govern the universe, you may be sure that the next production to use the lamp will have a director who insists the lamp must glow brightly, so some rewiring will have to be done. And each time the poor lamp's innards are removed, altered and rewired, the technician suffers from frustration and lamp from wear and tear.

The following gimmick was devised to make this periodic conversion less of a nuisance.

Solder wires to the flashlight lamp terminals, and then secure them to the terminal posts of the male connector. Plug the connector into a screw-base adapter, and screw the assembled unit into the base, which is part of the stock lamp.

Once this unit is made up (and making it is not at all difficult), it can be removed or replaced easily, taking care of the conversion of the top part of the lamp.

This bulb unit is now intended for 3-volt operation, and the bottom end of the lamp—the power supply—must be similarly converted.

DO NOT make the mistake of plugging the 3-volt bulb unit into a household receptacle that serves 110-volt power!

Converting the Bottom End of the Lamp

I wish the solution for converting the bottom half of the lamp were as simple as converting the bulb, but unfortunately it isn't.

First you must find a place to house the batteries. Two batteries must be used to provide 3 volts to the lamp. Usually the batteries can be hidden in the base of the lamp. If there is not enough room for two "D" size batteries, perhaps you will be forced to use smaller batteries which, unfortunately, will have a shorter life than the "D" cells—but you don't have much choice. You can settle for whatever size batteries will fit, or find a lamp with a roomier base.

The original power cord for the lamp must either be wrapped into a compact wad and stored along with the batteries in the base, or snipped to a length of four or five inches and soldered to the prepared battery pack.

If the stock lamp was equipped with a working switch, it will still be usable.

A Dimmer-Controlled Flashlight

A flashlight that dims out on cue? We needed one for a production of *Family Matters*.

A battery-operated oil lamp that brightens as the wick is turned up? We needed one of those for *Pipe Dream*.

Neither of these is impossible; all that's required is a means of varying the resistance — a rheostat. The rheostat is wired into the circuit in series with the lamp.

A rheostat of what resistance?

To answer this question, we consulted a lamp catalog. Our flashlight uses a PR12 lamp. According to the catalog, a PR12 operates on 6 volts and draws 0.5 amperes.

We can calculate the lamp's resistance using Ohm's law. (Measuring the resistance directly with an ohmmeter is not accurate, as the resistance changes when the lamp gets hot.)

Remember Ohm's law? Okay,

$$R = E \div I$$

therefore, $\quad R = (6) \div (0.5)$

or $\quad R = 12$ ohms

There! The resistance of the hot lamp is 12 ohms. We know from the preceding discussion of electrical theory that two lamps in series will reduce the current flow, but both lamps will still glow dimly. Therefore 12 ohms is not enough resistance to *completely* dim the lamp. But it gives us a ballpark figure to begin experimenting with. And through experimentation, we found that a rheostat rated at 30 ohms would work.

When the actor is ready to dim the light, his thumb must execute a two-step operation. First he must rotate the rheostat knob clockwise to its extreme position, dimming the lamp to black. Then he flips the switch to its "off" position to eliminate the battery-killing trickle of current.

A rheostat rated at 30 ohms has a variable resistance from 0 ohms to 30 ohms. When the dial is at 0 ohms, there is no additional resistance in the circuit, and the lamp burns at its brightest. When the knob is rotated to the 30 ohm position, sufficient resistance is introduced to dim the lamp out.

We also discovered (the hard way) that although the lamp did not glow with the rheostat turned to 30 ohms, there was still a little current flowing through the circuit — enough to run the batteries down overnight. We introduced a switch into the circuit so that the current could be fully shut off to preserve our batteries.

A 15-ohm rheostat will dim a PR3 lamp when it is used with a 3-volt power source.

Rheostats are readily available in the larger electronics supply houses.

A slide-operated rheostat would have made the flashlight-dimming operation easier.

A Dimmer-Controlled Oil Lamp

These illustrations show an arrangement that we used to house a switch and rheostat in an oil lamp.

The component hanging out on the left side of the first photo is the switch. As mentioned in the preceding section, a switch is needed on any rheostat-controlled lamp in order to preserve the batteries.

If you use small parts, they can be compressed into a very tight space. Slipping the rheostat into one end of a short sleeve of tubing and the authentic wick control knob into the other end will allow you to connect the two and use the wick knob to control the rheostat, thus dimming the lamp in a very realistic manner.

EYEGLASSES

Binocular Replicas for the Stage

In an obscure musical called *Henry, Sweet Henry* there is a cute ensemble number called ''People Watchers.'' Our director had a great idea — each chorus member gets a pair of binoculars for some business of spying on each other as they sing and dance. If in such a situation your director is willing to substitute stylized simplification for realism, you can save money as we did by constructing replicas.

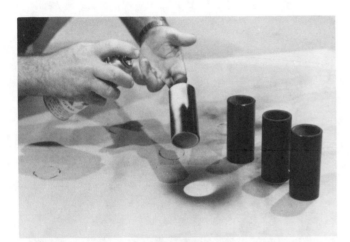

Each pair of binoculars is built from six pieces of PVC water pipe, four plastic curtain rings, and two grommets. (As we worked on this project, ideas for variations on the basic plan occurred to us and were worked into the design of some of the binoculars.) Two lengths of each of three different diameters of PVC pipe are required:

(2)   1½"dia × 4½"long
(2)   1"dia × 4"long
(2)   ¾"dia × 4½"long

The PVC pipe comes only in an off-white color, so it should be painted black inside and out before you assemble the binoculars.

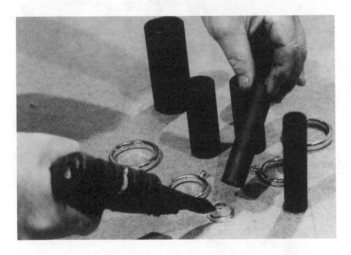

Most of the assembly can be done with hot glue. If you're not sloppy with your glue application, no repainting should be necessary.

Make the eyepieces by gluing the grommets to the ends of the smallest-diameter PVC pipe.

Make the largest-diameter pipe into the ''lens piece'' by gluing a pair of large curtain rings to them.

The smaller curtain rings will be a tight fit around the 1″ pipe, but they should be secured with a shot of hot glue anyway. Then squirt a wad of glue on the 1″ pipe to secure it inside the larger pipe.

Similarly, secure the narrowest pipe inside the other two pipe segments with a shot of hot glue.

You have now assembled the two halves of the binoculars and have only to attach these to each other. Do this by inserting a small bolt and nut through the eyes of the smaller curtain rings, and applying hot glue liberally to the larger rings.

Here is our output of binoculars, assembled for storage after the show.

Eyeglasses

Eyeglasses are rarely called for by a playwright as a necessary prop item. It is not uncommon, however, for an actor or director to request a certain style of eyeware as an aid to developing a character.

The styles and shapes of eyeglasses are quite varied: there are rimless, horn-rimmed, wire-rimmed and turtle shell; the lens shape can be round, oval, square, or cat's-eye, and there are many size variations with each shape. Then there are lorgnettes, monocles, pince-nez, aviator goggles, sunglasses, bifocals. . .and the list goes on. The list may not be infinite, but it is *very* long—there are as many styles of eyeware as there are types of characters.

If the eyeglasses are to be used as a character-building aid, it is best for the actor to be able to work with them (or a reasonable facsimile) early in the rehearsal period.

A Short History of Eyeglasses

This history on the development of eyeglasses and their use is offered to assist you in selecting the proper style of spectacles for period plays, and avoiding unintentional anachronism. A pair of glasses might make a modern character look serious or well-educated, but if you put them on Moses' nose, for instance, the effect would probably destroy the character's seriousness altogether.

Eyeglasses were invented about A.D. 1300. Some sources credit Roger Bacon with this invention; others disagree. At any rate, the first eyeglass was a "quizzer"—a single-lens magnifying glass held near the eye by means of a handle. Royalty was the first class to test the practicality of this novelty. By 1350, the two-lens version had evolved, the lenses mounted in a pivoting metal frame. These could be found balanced on the noses of select churchmen and a few of the very wealthy.

Until Gutenberg invented the printing press (around 1450), illiteracy was widespread and eye defects—especially farsightedness—caused little difficulty. In the 1500s, however, as the printed word was becoming available, the common man was becoming more acutely aware of the deterioration of close-range eyesight as a consequence of age. The need for corrective lenses was being felt, and craftsmen of the period came forth to fill it. The guild of spectacle makers received its first charter in England in 1563.

In 1665 (the Restoration period) it had become fashionable for the ladies and gentlemen of the court to wear eyeglasses even when there was no corrective need. Spectacles were used for prestige—as symbols of class, wealth and wisdom—rather than a true aid to vision.

The lorgnette, a folding spectacle equipped with a handle, was preferred by the ladies. Lorgnettes frequently hung from a chain around the wearers' necks, since they were worn more for show than ocular correction.

The fashionable gentleman used a monocle, a single lens held in front of one eye with the muscle that controls the eyelid.

All other eyeglasses of this period were either clipped to the bridge of the nose (pince-nez), or held in place either with strings running around the ears or with leather straps tied behind the wearer's head.

More than 300 years passed before anyone came up with the idea of holding glasses in place with side pieces (temples) extending to the ears. In 1728, Edward Scarlett first produced temples as an improvement to the eyeglass frames he made and sold.

Sunglasses in shades of green, blue, and gray (smoked glass) have been in use virtually from the time that glasses were first introduced.

The style of spectacles known since the 1960s as "granny glasses" were worn by Benjamin Franklin in the 1780s. The style didn't change much for 150 years, remaining popular into the late 1930s.

Building a Pair of "Granny Glasses"

The features that make this style distinctive are the thin wire used in its construction and the large round or oval shape of the lens. The temples are pretty well hidden behind the ears, and are not terribly important to the overall look of the glasses. This section, then, is chiefly concerned with the construction of convincing wire frames.

A form like the one shown must be fashioned from two disks of wood that have the same size, shape and spacing of actual spectacle lenses. Refer to authentic period glasses or to detailed photos as you design this jig for bending.

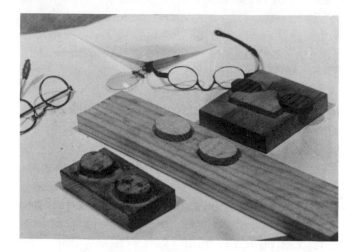

Use the band saw first, and then the sander, to shape a piece of pine until it is ¾″ thick and the size and shape of the lens in your research material. Slice this small round block directly down the center on the band saw, and you will have two identical lens forms made of wood, each ⅜″ thick.

Using your authentic spectacles again as a guide, arrange the wooden disks on a support block and glue them in place.

I have searched the city of Los Angeles for a supplier of an appropriate rod from which to fashion these wire frames, without success. I have canvassed by phone and in person the city's opticians, oculist suppliers, hobby shops, jewelers, jewelry suppliers, and craft specialty shops. No one has the raw materials, and no one has any knowledge of where flattened rod of the required size can be found. Therefore, 3/32″ brazing rod was used for the projects illustrated here. You might also want to consider 14-gauge copper wire, which is available almost anywhere. (Aluminum rod is not recommended because of the soldering required.)

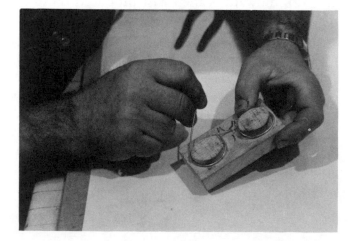

Make the nose rest and the frames for both lenses from one continuous piece of metal rod about 12″ long. Following the example of your research material, first bend a nose piece in the middle of the rod. Shape it to fit snugly between the two lens frames. Wrap the free ends of the rod around the wooden forms until the circles are completed. Then clip off any surplus metal and solder both ends where they meet the nose rest.

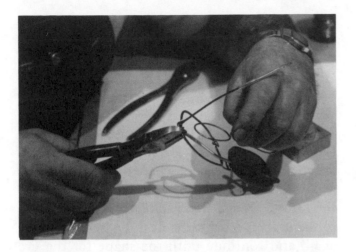

To complete the frame, appropriate some ear pieces from a discarded pair of ''modern'' wire-frame glasses. These temple pieces (complete with hinge) can be clipped off the old frames with a pair of diagonal cutters and then soldered into place.

Building a Monocle

The monocle is associated somehow with the German aristocracy, but the word itself is French, derived from the late Latin *monoculus,* meaning ''one eye.'' At any rate, the monocle gives the wearer a continental look—or at least an air of affectation.

There are several types of monocle, but the style illustrated here is authentic, easy to wear, and not difficult to build.

We constructed our monocle for a production of *The Enchanted,* and since its construction it has been used repeatedly. We were not able to locate an authentic eye piece for reference, but we did find a very good illustration in Dr. L. D. Bronson's book on the history of eyeglasses.

Select a piece of clean, strong, malleable wire from which to fashion the frame. This wire should not be springy—that is, when you bend it, it should hold its shape and not spring back. Some soldering will be necessary, so aluminum wire should not be used as it is not possible to solder aluminum. We chose a small-gauge brazing rod, but most any variety of wire (even coat hanger wire) will probably work.

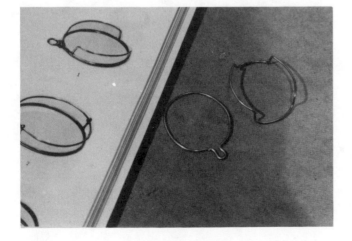

The monocle is constructed of two pieces, a lens frame and an eye clip. The frame is basically just a circle of wire to hold the lens; this circle has a lobe bent into it to receive a cord or ribbon which will prevent the monocle from falling to the floor and breaking if the wearer should unexpectedly raise his eyebrows in a moment of surprise. The eye clip is an extension of the frame which holds the monocle in place when it is pressed into the flesh at the eyebrow and cheek. The clip has a ³⁄₈″ offset built into it so that there is a clearance between the eye and the lens. This way, the wearer's eyelashes are not continually batting against the lens. This eye clip must be bent with care so that it conforms to the precise size and shape of the lens.

As you construct the clip, don't make the mistake of shaping the circle first and then attempting the bend the offsets into it. Begin instead by bending one of the angled offsets; four 90° jogs will be needed. *Then* start forming the circle. Work till you come to the spot where the next recession should be, and make the first two 90° bends for the second offset. Bend some more, continuing to shape the circle; at the next jog bend the wire again and continue until the shape for the eye clip is complete as illustrated here. Solder the two pieces of the frame together.

Lay the monocle frame on a sheet of clear acrylic and scribe the shape of the eye piece onto the plastic. Cut out this plastic disc on the band saw, smooth it with the sander, and glue it into the wire frame as a lens. This lens should have a fairly tight fit, and can be secured with epoxy cement or hot glue.

Here is the finished monocle, complete with ribbon, demonstrating the aforementioned "continental look—or at least an air of affectation."

Lorgnette

The hardware of a lorgnette is a little more complex than that of a monocle, and more difficult to build from scratch. You can, however, construct a lorgnette from parts of old eyeglasses—these glasses can be obtained from thrift shops at very reasonable prices.

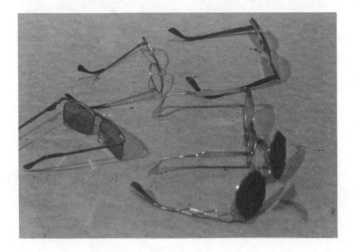

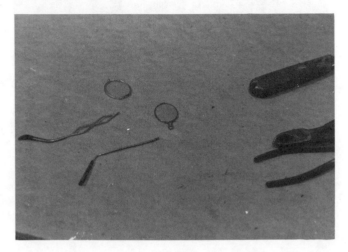

It is always a good idea to accumulate interesting eyeglasses and miscellaneous jewelry when these items turn up. You will feel less guilty about desecrating usable eyeglass frames if they were acquired expressly for this purpose.

The lorgnettes described here were made for our production of *A Man of Mode*. We began by selecting two lenses and two temples from the assortment of frames we had on hand.

Straighten the part of the temple that was meant to bend over the ear, until it begins to look like a handle. The straightened temple piece that we worked with was a little too long for a well-proportioned handle, so we took the following steps to straighten it.

The plastic tip can be removed by dipping it

in water that is almost boiling. This will soften the plastic and make it workable. (Lenses can be removed from plastic frames by heating and softening the plastic in the same fashion.)

With the plastic tip removed, we clipped the wire a little shorter, and then replaced the plastic while it was still pliable.

Fit the lens to the support, and solder the joint, taking care to make the soldered joint as strong as possible.

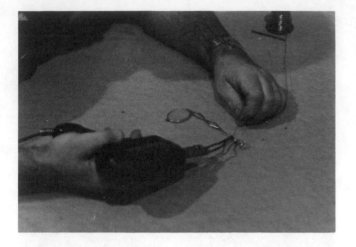

We searched through our drawer of miscellaneous jewelry and found a bauble that would look good soldered to the bottom of the handle of one of our lorgnettes. It gave the handle a finished look and provided a place to attach a chain.

Simply drilling a small hole in the end of the other lorgnette handle allowed that handle to be outfitted with a chain.

We have laid our finished lorgnettes on a page with photographs of authentic period eyeglasses. You can see that ours are not precise imitations, but they capture the period flavor.

FIRE

Blazing Fire Flames

A realistic look of dancing flames can be achieved in a manner that generates little actual heat (and is therefore very safe) by combining a sheet of clear plastic, moving air, and a light source. (This effect is used dramatically in the Pirates of the Caribbean ride at Disneyland.) The basic concept is simple: the beams from the hidden light source are reflected from the clear (and therefore invisible) sheet of plastic. The plastic sheet is rippled by moving air, and the result is an animated reflection that resembles leaping flames. What makes this effect both difficult and interesting are the experimental possibilities, and the variety of inherent problems.

To achieve a successful effect, you need to analyze the problems, experiment a little, find the right combination of components, and attune them to the specific requirements of your production.

That may sound straightforward—but bear in mind that Disneyland keeps a large and well-paid research and development staff to work out such effects. But let me share with you some of the variables you may encounter, and how we have dealt with them in our experiments.

The Plastic Sheet

The job of selecting the right sheet of plastic for this effect would be simpler if there weren't such a variety of types and thicknesses to choose from. Polyethylene has a softness that allows it to flop nicely in the gentle air currents; the trouble is, it's not quite crystal-clear, and it seems to be saying to the audience: "Hi there! I'm a sheet of not-quite-clear polyethylene up here flopping in the breeze with this light shining on me." Polystyrene and acetate are more transparent, but they have a hard surface and it takes more air current to move them. They also tend to make a rattling sound. The rattle is all right if you don't need total silence, and the sound even resembles that of crackling flames. A thin film (0.001″) ripples faster, producing a more active flame effect and more noise. Thicker plastic (0.01″) gives a less animated flame but the effect is quieter.

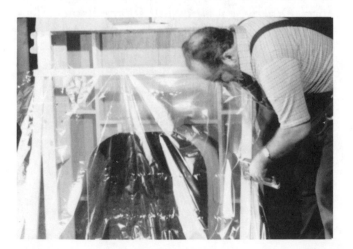

The plastic sheet must be firmly attached to a frame of some sort to keep it in place while it is under the stress of the air movement. Thinner plastics are more apt to tear away from staples; but if you put a strip of tape on the plastic and staple through it, the staples will hold better. The plastic, of course, must not be stretched tightly on the frame—and you will find that the plastic behaves a little differently when the fullness is left in the horizontal direction than when it is left in the vertical direction. Neither way is necessarily *right,* and you need to decide which gives the more desirable results for your application.

Moving the Plastic

There are two basic classes of fans. One kind, the squirrel-cage fan, moves a small volume of air under high pressure. The other, with rotating

vanes (like the oscillating fan you have at home), is used to move a large volume of air at low pressure, for a gentle breeze.

You should experiment with both kinds. Your final choice should depend on what you want the fire to look like. The air flow can be directed from the top or bottom of the plastic, or it can be blown from either side. It has been my experience, however, that the direction of the air flow is less important than its velocity.

Lighting the Plastic Sheet

The selection and placement of the light source for this effect is probably the most critical of the variables that you must control. Fortunately, light is generally easy to control. Almost any light source can be used—even a bare bulb can be used successfully if it is housed to control spill.

The light source can be spotted or flooded; it can come from one source or many. You could use PAR lamps or 500-watt fresnels. But regardless of the instrument you choose, the light source must be concealed, so it would not be practical for it to be very large physically.

In placing and focusing the light source, you need to consider both the angle of the beam on the plastic film and the sightlines of the audience. Otherwise it is possible for the flame reflections to be uselessly directed to the floor or ceiling. The old rule that the angle of incidence should equal the angle of reflection still holds. The reflection of the light source must be directed into the plane of the audience's vision.

Directing the reflection into the appropriate viewing plane can be accomplished by changing either the direction of the hidden light source or the angle of the plastic sheet.

Keep in mind that each audience member will have a unique view of the reflected flame image. If we were working for a camera's point of view, the effect could be fine tuned for the camera's one eye. But the theater audience has a wide line of sight within the viewing plane, it becomes necessary to compromise. In fact, if the theater is very wide, it is possible that those in the seats on the sides will not be able to appreciate the effect at all.

It is possible to add variety to the fire by using more than one light source. Several light sources will create the illusion of several discrete flames.

While the scene designer is the final authority when it comes to flame color, I can offer several general observations from personal experience. Red light produces corny flames. Mixing two light sources, one red and one yellow, doesn't work as well as one might expect. Orange light produces the most convincing effects, and when more than one light source is used, varying shades of amber give the most satisfying results.

Only experience can guide you in determin-what combination of light, wind, and reflective surface will yield the best effect in each situation. And no matter what creative combination you may contrive, resign yourself to the fact that there will be some in your audience who will give you no credit, saying, "Oh, look it's just like the old Pirates of the Caribbean fire effect!"

Simulating Fires

How do you fake a fire? Let me count the ways...

A fire produces light and heat. The light is orange, yellow, or sometimes blue, with occasional licks of green. It is almost never red.

A fire is the visible manifestation of burning gases. It flickers; it moves. The flames can leap violently or simmer down to glowing embers.

The fire can produce smoke.

Just as there are many faces of fire, there are many techniques to mimic them.

Let us consider a log fire first. The unit described below has been used as an open fireplace, as a campfire, and as a bed of coals under roasting meat.

A Flickering Log Fire

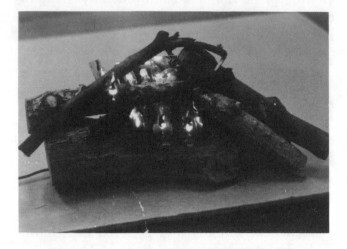

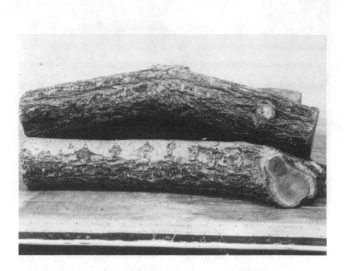

The log fire we will build consists of a series of flicker lamps mounted in a log base. When the unit is plugged in it jumps into action. This produces a non-violent fire with no flame licks —a lively, cheerily burning fire.

Begin construction by carefully selecting the logs for the effect. The most important criterion is that the logs be able to nest together. They must create a firm base, with no tencency to roll, and they should fit comfortably against one another, exposing as little air space as possible in between. The rear log must be elevated slightly to be seen above the front one.

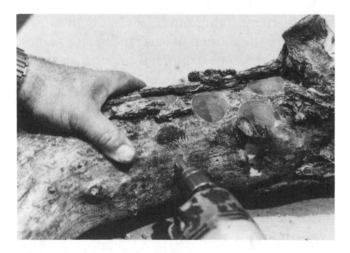

Bore holes into your logs, one hole for each flicker bulb. Each hole must accommodate a candelabra lamp base, so they should be about 1⅛″ in diameter.

Drill smaller holes (about 1¼″ in diameter) through the back of the log to the larger holes. Zip cord will be run through these holes to be wired to the candelabra sockets.

The holes that will house the lamp sockets should be located randomly, in a variety of planes, so the flicker lamps won't be lined up like a row of tin soldiers. Some lamps should be upright, some on their sides, etc.

Wire the sockets, and then slip them into the prepared holes. Hot glue will hold them in place effectively.

Collect the wires at the rear of the log assembly, and run them into a junction box. Wire the lamps in parallel. The fire effect is impressive because of the multiple lamps flickering at random—for this reason no fewer than nine or ten lamps should be used. The ''sameness'' of the lamps' color can be remedied somewhat by adding a strip of blue gel to the lower edge of some of the lights. Of course, a blue medium in front of an amber light greatly reduces brilliance, but it does add realism to the coloration.

The number of light sources can be visually doubled by backing each lamp with a reflecting strip of aluminized Mylar. The light from each lamp is then mirrored by the Mylar, creating the illusion of a greater number of flames. Disguise the top edge of the Mylar reflectors by cutting flame shapes into them.

When the power is off, this unit will not stand up to close inspection. The glass bulbs look exactly like glass bulbs, destroying the illusion. Kindling sticks added to the flame area will help conceal the glass. The problem can be remedied further by covering the lamps with black scrim or nylon netting.

Add white and gray tones to the scrim with paint, and the scrim will blend in visually and look like ash. When the power is turned on, the lamps will shine through the scrim without difficulty.

If instead of a blaze you need the effect of smoldering embers, add extra layers of scrim. This will dim the effect and produce a convincing bed of glowing coals.

Making a Camp Fire

This campfire is just the thing for campers to roast marshmallows over, for cowboys to sing songs around, and for shepherds to watch their flocks by.

Cut out a base or foundation from ¾″ plywood. Mount three standard-size sockets on this base and wire them in parallel. (The lamps in these sockets will eventually be focused upstage to illuminate a reflector of aluminized Mylar.

Assemble a group of small branches in a teepee-like arrangement around the lighting hardware. Join the branches at the top with wire or nails, and nail them to the plywood base. Leave the upstage side open for the time being so you can continue to work on the interior of this assembly.

Use scraps of colored plastic (amber shades are most convincing) to fill in the gaps and create a sort of dome or half-shell under the branches. Spray adhesive will hold the color media together. Make this plastic lining as form-fitting as possible so it will be easy to attach to the branches of the ''teepee.'' Hot glue will hold the plastic to the branches securely, if you use enough heat.

Make a second dome, this one from aluminized Mylar, to cover the upstage side of the campfire. The object is for the light from the three lamps to be reflected by the Mylar through the colored plastic to the viewing audience.

The plywood base can be hidden by laying a few more branches around the outside of the base. A few rocks glued to the base will also help disguise the plywood profile.

Some touches of paint brushed onto the firewood will make the wood look burned. A mist of black spray paint will dull the gloss of the color media. A black cloth tacked over the Mylar reflector will serve as a light seal to prevent any light spills.

A Smoldering Fireplace

If the script calls for a fire in the fireplace with no other special requirements, this smoldering log unit works well. The glowing logs tell the audience clearly that a fire has been burning and is still aglow. This unit does not, however, have flames that leap about and call attention to themselves.

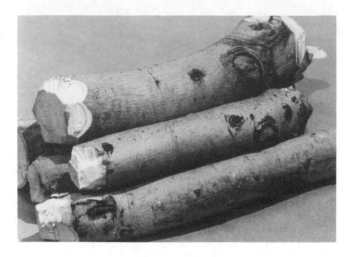

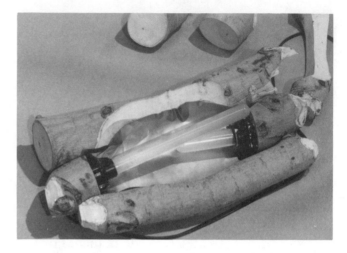

Carefully nest a group of logs. Do not fasten them together yet, but assure yourself of a good arrangement and remember it.

Remove the front log (on the bottom) and scoop a large portion out with the band saw. Cut the ends of the top and center logs complete off and retain only these ends. This leaves the interior of the unit hollow, creating a cavity that will house a pair of lamps. Reassemble the cutaway logs by nailing them to each other and a plywood base. (The plywood base used here was cut small enough that it is virtually hidden in the photos.)

Wire the two light sockets in parallel. Two long tubular lamps go into these sockets. A metal shield mounted on the plywood base will help keep the base cool.

The cut logs can be made to appear to be intact by wrapping a skin of screen wire around them and stapling it in place.

Prepare about 4 oz. of polyester resin by adding 10–12 drops of catalyzing solution to it. (Mix the resin according to the instructions that come with it.)

Brush a coating of glass fibers and catalyzed resin onto the interior of the screen. When this resin cures it will be translucent and can be colored from the inside with orange, brown, and other colored dyes suggesting smoldering coals. The lamps can be wrapped in plastic color media as well.

Work a thin coat of sawdust and flex-glue into surface of the log to restore the bark texture.

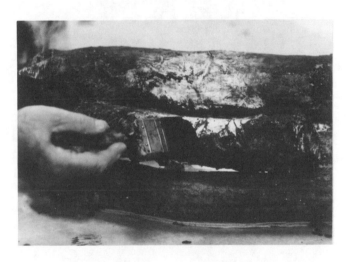

Apply black, umber, and gray paints to the surface of the fiberglass with brush and sponge. Keep the paint thin so the translucency of the fiberglass is not lost.

Finally, staple a black flameproof cloth to the back side of the unit to prevent light spill and

Much of this coloring and texturing work should be done with the internal lamps lit so you can see the final effect develop as you work.

allow easy access to the interior so as to facilitate changing lamps.

A Firebrand Torch

There are many kinds of torches, ranging from the most rustic (for medieval peasants) to the more refined (for the Statue of Liberty). The one illustrated here is utilitarian in design, intended to suggest a stick of wood with an oil- or pitch-soaked rag wrapped around one end—the sort of thing one might contrive hastily for an unplanned excursion through a forest on a moonless night. We built ours for the chase scene in *Brigadoon*.

The body of the torch is made from a 15″ length of 1″ diameter PVC pipe.

This torch can be made to operate with two ''C''-size batteries, a switch, and a flashlight bulb, all wired in series. (See the section on electricity for an explanation of series wiring.) Hot-glue the switch to the lower end of the pipe (the ''handle'' end) where it can be conveniently turned on or off by a flick of the thumb.

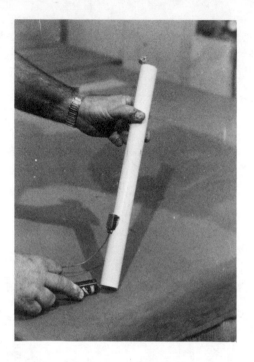

Drill a hole next to the switch so a wire can be run into the pipe and to the light bulb. It would be a boon if all the wiring could be contained in the PVC tube, but there isn't enough room for the wires and the batteries. Some of the wires must remain outside the tube—but they will be hidden in subsequent construction.

Wrap a covering of erosion cloth around the pipe for bulk. Then wrap the erosion cloth-covered tube with a coating of muslin and glue. Apply the muslin with lots of wrinkles running the length of the torch, to create the illusion of bark. (The batteries can be tucked into the tube during construction to keep them out of the way.)

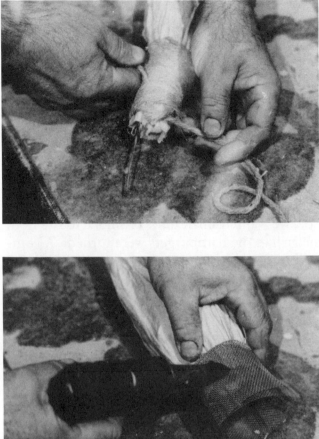

Wrap jute twine around the lower end of the torch to form a handle. Use an invisible knot (see the section on Construction Techniques) to keep the twine from unraveling.

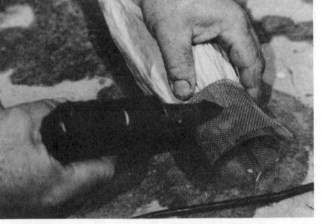

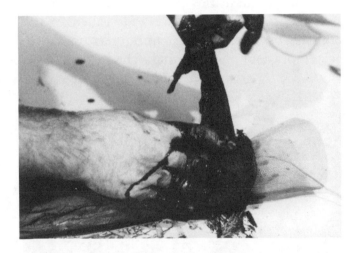

Use hot glue to attach a wrapping of 4″-wide plastic screening to the "fire" end of the torch. Wrap a strip of cheesecloth that has been dipped in black or umber paint around the lower end of

the screen. This will add texture and hold the screen in place. The cheesecloth wrapping will suggest the oil-soaked rag which is serving to fuel the torch.

Cut the screen wire with tin snips to suggest flame-like shapes. Prepare another 2 oz. of polyester resin with an appropriate number of drops of catalyst. Paint the flames with resin, filling in the screen wire "pores." This resin will catch the light of the bulb and add to the flame effect.

Daub the resin with orange ink or dye to lend the appropriate tint to the illusion.

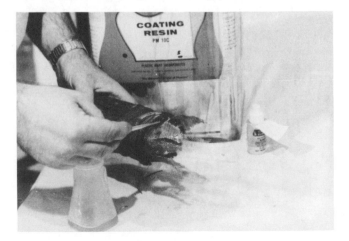

We converted our torches to 110-volt operation for a production of *Hamlet*. The small lamp was replaced with three miniature-base flicker bulbs. Three flicker lamps in concert made a lively dancing flame. The bulbs were wired in parallel and powered by an extension cord running from the switchboard. (The current drawn by flicker lamps is so small that they cannot be connected to many electronically-controlled dimmer boards. They tend to flash erratically and may remain lit when the controller is turned off. Auto-transformer dimmers work fine, though.)

Smoke Effects

Barbecue Grill

This little smoke effect can be used in situations where small quantities of smoke are needed.

Our production of *Generation* called for the business of cooking raw hamburgers on a pre-heated outdoor grill. To make the business realistic, we wanted small puffs of smoke to rise from the grill as the hamburgers were turned. A commercial fog machine was available, but we ruled it out as a smoke source because it produced only large, uncontrollable volumes of smoke.

A soldering iron was placed in the bed of the grill and was turned on to pre-heat. The surface of the grill was masked from audience view, so the movements of the actor manipulating this apparatus were not conspicuous. A small syringe was loaded with "fog juice" (the same as is used in the bog foggers); the actor squirted a small stream of this liquid on the heated tip of the iron each time he turned a burger, and each time a very safe and realistic puff of smoke rose from the grill.

Flash Pot Substitute

Dangers of fire and explosion are always present when black-powder flash pots are used. This problem has encouraged technicians to find safer methods of creating the surprise flash-and-smoke effect. One solution to this problem is achieved with a flash bulb, compressed air, and dust.

Load the dust (fuller's earth) into a small tube or funnel. Connect an air hose serving compressed air to the small end of the funnel. On cue (synchronized with the flash of a flash bulb), open the valve. The resultant burst will produce an instantaneous column of dust about 6' high.

Care must be taken, of course, that no one is standing directly over the burst as the cue is taken. Fuller's earth is not toxic (it is rated as a nuisance dust), but breathing should not be attempted in the middle of the cloud.

FOOD

One of mankind's common experiences is that of eating. It is not surprising, therefore, that so many plays depict this activity. Some scripts call for full-course dinners, others require a practical wet bar; it's hard to recall a play that doesn't keep the actors' hands busy with some kind of snack or beverage.

The following guidelines should be observed in the preparation of food to be consumed on stage.

Providing Edible Prop Food

1. The food must be clean and fresh. It's not fair to ask an actor to consume last night's whipped potatoes. The food must be served on clean platters with clean utensils.

2. The food must be palatable to the actor who will eat it. Most actors appreciate the opportunity to help select a reasonable menu, and will be eager to cooperate with you. A few will take advantage of your offer to please individual tastes and will send you on an actor fetch, a search for exotic delicacies for which they claim to have a preference. Then there are the Method types who will disdain any thought of substitution — if the script calls for a porterhouse steak with mushrooms, they want a porterhouse steak with mushrooms!

3. The food must be easy to chew and to swallow, without any danger of even momentary dryness or discomfort. The actor's voice is his most valuable tool, and his ability to use it must not be impaired.

4. The food must be consistently prepared. The actor should be secure that there will be no surprises from one performance to the next. If you have been using sliced bananas as a substitute for candy bon-bons, and you run out of bananas, it might seem reasonable to you to switch to cubed peaches — but it won't seem reasonable to the actor whose performance is thrown off by the unfamiliar taste and texture.

5. If the script calls for a specific food item, the food used should look exactly like (or, if practical, actually be) the item called for. Frequently substitutions can be made which are easier to prepare than the food specified in the script. These substitutions must be made with rule #2 in mind.

If you begin thinking in terms of substitute foods, it is possible to get into a rut. Suppose, for instance, that the script calls for an ice-cream cone. You decide to substitute mashed potatoes for the ice cream, on the grounds that the potatoes won't melt and require no refrigeration. Then suppose that in the second act the script calls for a meal that includes mashed potatoes, and you substitute ice cream, arguing that ice cream doesn't require cooking. You can understand the actors' consternation when the prop crew thinks only in terms of "substitutes"!

I knew one very skillful stage cook who could prepare virtually any menu by working creatively with scrambled eggs, banana chunks, unsliced white bread, and food color.

Yogurt, cottage cheese, and brown bread are also useful in simulating more perishable or difficult foods.

A final consideration: foods can be *too* appetizing and invite indiscriminate munching by the cast, both on and off stage. Snack foods like peanuts, pretzels, and candies can be gobbled up with such voracity that they become a budgetary burden, and the prop crew is reduced to a band of nagging policemen in the interest of keeping enough prop snacks on hand for the next performance. Filling the snack dishes with breakfast cereals (Cocoa Puffs, Kix, and Captain Crunch are convincing snack substitutes) reduces the temptation to overeat, but provides a substitute entirely in keeping with the guidelines above.

Making Beverages for the Stage

Stage drinks should not be sweet or syrupy. Most undiluted soft drinks cause phlegm to form and thus inhibit the actor's vocal performance. The guidelines given in connection with food preparation are equally applicable to the preparation of drinks.

Coffee, tea, and milk are usually used when coffee, tea, and milk are called for.

White wine can be simulated by diluting Gatorade or Mountain Dew with water. Red wine can be simulated with cranberry or grape juice (or a combination of both) diluted with water. Champagne can be suggested with ginger ale — and if you need a convincing "pop," mix in some warm 7-Up.

Water is a good substitute for vodka and gin. Whiskey, brandy, rum, etc., can be made with watered-down apple juice or brewed tea (instant tea isn't convincing because it is often cloudy).

Artificial Food

Sometimes a playwright will write dialogue in which the characters discuss an upcoming meal, and then the act ends just as the meal is brought to the table. That's considerate! The story line isn't hurt, and the prop department is spared the ongoing expense and nightly headache of meal preparation. In such a case (especially when the show will have a long run), faked food, often consisting chiefly of Styrofoam or cardboard, can be served up with the illusion that the cast is about to eat. The rest of this section will deal with the manufacture of artificial foodstuffs.

Bread

Bread is still one of the least expensive items that might turn up on a prop list. The day may come when a loaf of bread will buy a bag of gold, but right now the easiest and cheapest way to put bread on the prop table is to buy a real loaf of bread — especially if it is to be eaten.

And yet...there is a place for prop bread which is only decorative in nature. The baker selling his product on the street, or the heavily laden banquet table, require only the illusion of real bread. And once you have a few "loaves" in stock (the construction is not difficult), you'll find it easier to pull them out of storage for each new production than to run to the grocery store.

Start with a block of urethane foam about the size of a loaf of bread. Remove the edges with a band saw and a disc sander. Use a real loaf or a good picture for reference — we all know what a loaf of bread looks like until we try to sculpt one, and then the memory plays some funny tricks.

Smooth out the remaining ridges with a wood rasp. The loaf shown has a flaw which will have to be repaired with putty.

Urethane foam is a very soft material and easy to shape. My hands are rough enough that I can shape the foam with my hands alone. If yours are not as calloused as mine, try wrapping sandpaper around a finger — but be gentle. It's easy to overwork the foam.

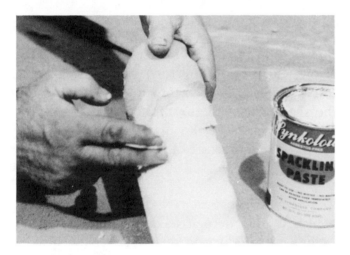

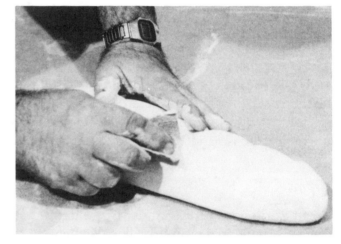

Once you are satisfied with the shape, cover the entire form with a thin coat of spackling paste. This will give you a less porous surface to finish with sandpaper. A single thick coat of paste is likely to crack as it dries; two thin coats will give better results.

Sand the loaf, smoothing the texture of the spackle to a delicate crust.

Paint your bread with shades of ochre, orange, and brown, and they will be ready for display on your banquet table.

The Greatest Compliment

Scene: The prop room. Friday morning.

The PROP MASTER is looking over the Stage Manager's Report from the previous evening. He frowns as he reads that one of the prop guns misfired.

He is interrupted as the PROP CREW HEAD enters, grinning broadly.

PROP CREW HEAD   Did you hear about last night?

PROP MASTER   I heard about the gun that misfired again, is that what you mean?

PROP CREW HEAD   No, I'm talking about that box of plaster candies.

PROP MASTER   Yeah—?

PROP CREW HEAD   Diane Henderson snuck a bite out of one, and broke her front tooth.

PROP MASTER   You're kidding.

PROP CREW HEAD   No. You'll be hearing from her. She was really mad about it last night.

PROP MASTER   Didn't anyone ever tell her that actors were not to eat the prop food except as a part of stage business?

PROP CREW HEAD   Sure, sure, she knew better, all right. Maybe that's why she was so mad, 'cause she knew she was wrong and got caught. On second thought, I bet you don't hear from her. I bet she's embarrassed.

PROP MASTER   Well, if those chocolates look real enough that the actors were fooled, I feel very flattered. I accept the broken tooth as an accolade. Now, let's go get that gun and see why it won't shoot.

Candy

Chocolates

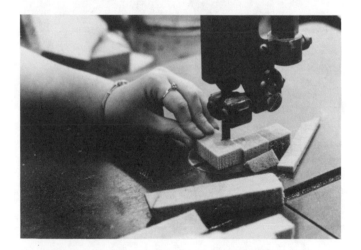

The chocolates (the ones shown were made for *A Taste of Honey*) begin their route through the candy factory at the band saw. Cut some Styrofoam or urethane foam into pieces of bonbon size. Decide what size your finished candies should be, and cut the plastic chunks to a size just a little larger.

Remove the corners and edges with a rotary disk sander. Keep the image of chocolates in your mind as you sculpt each piece to a nugget-like shape.

Each piece will be reduced in size during the sanding process, but the next step will build it up again.

Mix up a thin batch of plaster. Dip the foam nuggets into the plaster and set them out to harden on a polyester sheet. The plaster fills the pores of the foam plastic and further rounds the shape of each piece. After the plaster has hardened, you can break any surplus plaster off the bottom. You don't want to remove all of the base, though; the flat and slightly flared bottom will add to the realistic appearance of the candy.

Dip each piece in thick solution of raw umber scenic paint, for a convincing chocolate color. This process is just like that used by candy makers when the candy is hand-made—but don't get so caught up that you lick your fingers.

Raw umber makes dark chocolates. Use burnt umber instead if you want to produce milk chocolates. If you want to give the candies a shiny luster, dip them in a clear glaze after the paint has dried. Continue to set the candies out to dry on a plastic sheet, and they will be easily removable after they have dried.

Peppermint Sticks

It can be a torturous ordeal—one that will test the mettle of the most disciplined actor—if you place candy, pastries, or some other goody before the performer and warn him that he's looking at a stage prop that must not be consumed except as part of stage business. (Even the Bible says to muzzle the ox that grinds the grain.) The best way to protect the actor's conscience and your supply of props is to provide inedible replicas which will eliminate temptation. The fakes can be put into storage after the production comes

down, and will be ready when needed again.

A candy seller is one of the market vendors who appear in the *Brigadoon* production number "Down on MacConnachie Square." We provided his candy sticks by wrapping ribbon around wooden dowels. Reeds or soda straws can also be used to make these candy sticks; in fact, it's possible to find soda straws manufactured with stripes on them. The drawback is that using these soda straws exclusively gives you only one flavor of candy.

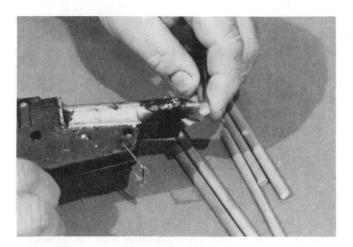

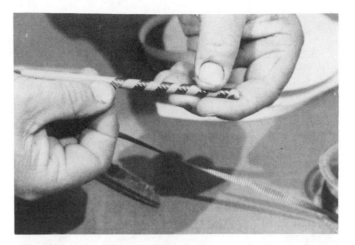

Cut the material you are using for the stick to an appropriate length and put a dab of hot glue on one end.

Attach the ribbon to the drop of hot glue and begin spiraling it around the stick to produce the characteristic stripe associated with candy sticks.

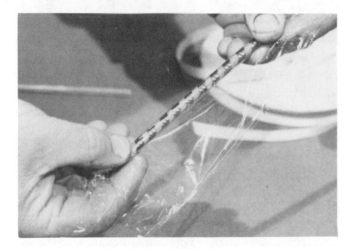

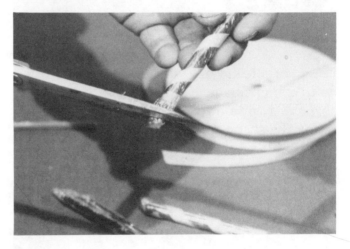

Wrap the candy stick with Saran Wrap. This plastic wrap is self-sticking, so no adhesive is needed.

Clip off the ends of the Saran Wrap with scissors, leaving enough to twist in order to seal the ends.

Arrange the candies according to flavor.

Cauliflower

We noticed that the texture of bead foam (also known by its trade name Falcon Foam) suggests the buds in a head of cauliflower, so we built some cauliflower heads and added them to a marketplace setting. (It might be argued that this is a pretty lame excuse for adding a prop to a show, but the cauliflower isn't hard to make, turned out to be interesting, and didn't detract, so...why not?)

Use a keyhole saw or a wide hacksaw blade fitted with a homemade handle to sculpt the basic shape of a cauliflower head from bead foam, and refine the shape with a wood rasp. Keep a real cauliflower nearby for ready reference.

Bead foam is very soft. You can easily form the individual buds of the cauliflower head by scraping the foam with a pointed tool — if your fingernails are sharp you might find them adequate to shape the foam.

When the produce man prepares a head of cauliflower for display in the supermarket, he cuts the leaves into a combination of short, coarse stalks and small, soft curls. You can simulate the stalks by constructing a sort of boat of heavy paper. Crush the hull so it doesn't look *too* much like a boat. This "boat" will not be evident when the cauliflower is completed; it serves as a base for the softer leaves.

Cut 12″ to 15″ crescents from white tissue paper and coat them well with flex-glue. These crescents will form the soft curled leaves.

    Press four to six glue-covered crescents around the base of the cauliflower. Twist them, curl them and trim them until they take on a leaf-like appearance.

You can add paint while the glue is still wet, if you wish. You can also add extra glue while you are painting. Flex-glue mixes well with water-base paints, and it will add gloss to paint which would otherwise dry flat.

Cheese

These cheeses have been shaped from urethane foam and have been wrapped in cheesecloth just as real cheeses are.

The waxy texture is achieved by painting the cheesecloth with flex-glue, and the color is achieved by brushing food color into the wet flex-glue. (Scenic paint will not produce a convincing texture for cheese.) Yellow and orange dyes can be used in various strengths and combinations to suggest Cheddar, Muenster, and so forth. Many cheeses, when sliced, have a dark rind and a light interior—bear that in mind when painting slices or wedges of ''cheese.'' A few careful dabs of blue will add a suggestion of mold formations.

Making a Chicken Drumstick

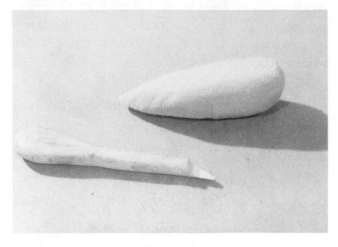

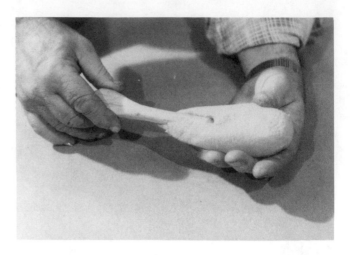

The main components of this drumstick are a shaped piece of urethane foam and a shaped stick of pine.

Push the wooden "bone" into the urethane, just a little off center. The thigh-bone of a chicken is not dead center, like the stick in a corn dog.

Build up the "flesh" on the drumstick with a heavy coating of latex rubber. If you don't keep latex in stock, several heavy coats of flex-glue will give a satisfactory texture.

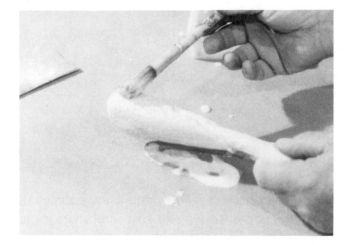

Use a light piece of flannel to make a "skin" for the drumstick. On a real chicken leg the skin is likely to not cover the entire leg, so leave one side exposed to add credibility to the form.

Flex-glue with yellow, orange, and brown inks will give convincing skin and flesh colors.

Making a Hamburger

Flex-glue plays an important role in the manufacture of many fake foods. When this glue is mixed with paints or dyes it provides a gloss and texture that enhance the credibility of a variety of food items, including both meat and produce.

In this project, as we construct a non-practical hamburger, the versatility of flex-glue will be demonstrated.

Cut a 3½″-diameter circle from a slab of ''firm'' flexible urethane foam, to make the basic shape of a hamburger bun.

The firmest of the flexible urethanes can be shaped on a disk sander. Round off the edges and sand the bun until the shape is convincing; then slice it with a serrated knife as if it were the real thing.

The urethane foam form should have all of the physical characteristics of a baked hamburger bun except for texture and color—and here's where the flex-glue is valuable.

Paint the bun with a heavy coating of flex-glue. This will seal the pores of the foam and begin to change the texture. Allow this coating to dry. It's possible to hasten drying with a hand-held hair dryer.

Coat the bun a second time with flex-glue. This coating should completely fill the pores and give the bun a smooth crust-like surface. When this coating dries it should leave the bun ready for coloring.

Shape a burger pattie in a manner similar to the way you made the bun, this time from a ½″ slab of flexible urethane foam. The texture of ground meat can be simulated with a single application of open-weave cheesecloth and flex-glue. Only the outer edge of the meat patty will be visible, so that's the only surface that needs to be decorated.

Keep the application of cheesecloth smooth around the rim, folding all the surplus over onto the top and bottom surfaces. Set the patty aside to dry. It too is ready for coloring.

Adding color to the bun and meat patty is a quick and simple operation. Mix appropriately tinted inks with flex-glue and give each element a final coat. Don't mix a sizable quantity of any color; after all, a few brush strokes will be all you need. Simply transfer a few brushfuls of flex-glue onto the plastic table covering and add a few drops of ink or dye to the glue. When you attain shades that please you, apply the glue to the bun and meat patty.

The open-hole texture of a sponge (preferably natural, but cellulose with do) suggests the interior of a tomato. Give a tomato-size slice of sponge the conditioning coat of flex-glue and set it aside.

Tomatoes are red, so use red ink to tint the flex-glue here.

A pretty convincing lettuce leaf can be fashioned from industrial-grade paper toweling. Tear out a piece of towel the shape of a lettuce leaf (be sure to tear away all the straight edges) and coat the paper with flex-glue.

Work a small quantity of green and yellow inks into the flex-glue to yield a realistic shade.

The bun requires dyes of orange, yellow, and a tiny bit of brown. The meat patty can be made to look medium-well-done with a mixture of brown, red, and a touch of orange.

Make it a cheeseburger! Cut a cheese-size slice from card stock and base-coat it with flex-glue.

Cheddar cheese is primarily yellow with a hint of orange, so mix a little of these colors into the flex-glue and apply it.

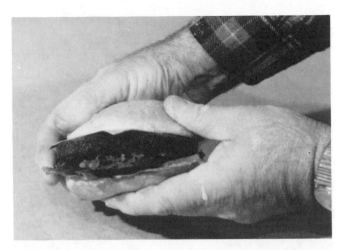

Bend the corners of the card stock down to make the cheese look melted.

If these photos could only have been printed in color, I know this sight would make your mouth water!

Making a Sandwich

A sandwich follows the same basic scheme as the hamburger, with a change in the style of the bread.

These bread slices were formed from flexible urethane foam cut on the band saw. The rough texture of white bread was achieved by coating the foam with cheesecloth. Three or four coatings of flex-glue and colored inks around the perimeter of each slice will simulate a smooth textured crust.

Fruits and Vegetables

There are times when a decision must be made whether to use a real item as a prop or to fake it. Perishables of all kinds are often subject to such a decision. My own guideline for making this choice where fruits and vegetables are concerned is simple: If they are to be eaten, or are involved in important stage business, real produce should be obtained. If, on the other hand, the fruits or vegetables are to be used only for show, time and energy can be saved in the long run by making replicas that will not rot or need replacement.

Lettuce

Prepare two pieces of heavy paper for the base coat of the head (butcher paper is a good choice). Cut each piece to a rough circle about 15″ in diameter. Cut a series of slices into the paper along the radii, stopping each cut short of the center.

Build your head of lettuce around a form with a diameter of about 6″. A rubber ball will work, or a wad of rags taped into a ball; we used a Styrofoam ball, as shown. Paint one of your circles of heavy paper with flex-glue and wrap it around the form.

Treat the second paper circle with flex-glue and wrap it around the form from the other side.

Crush the paper to form wrinkles, and your lettuce will be almost convincing. (The pair of heads in the background came from a grocer and served as an aid in recalling what real lettuce looks like.)

To make the head's outer leaves, cut several circles of white tissue paper (the kind used for gift wrapping), coat them with flex-glue, and wrap them around the head, one over the other.

Even while the head is still wet with glue, you can begin to apply color, using shades of green and yellow. We first applied a coat of light green with a brush, working it into all the wrinkles and folds. Then, using the palm of a hand as both palette and brush, we patted lighter and darker hues onto the wrinkles. Applying the paint in this fashion produces a natural effect of highlight and shadow.

Three of the five heads shown here are fake. Can you tell which are shop-made? Guess the diagonal row from lower left to upper right and you will be right.

This basketful of produce required no soil or fertilizer, and was "grown" by students with no previous experience in farming.

Making a Slice of Pie

Neatly broken bead foam gives a convincing suggestion of blueberry pie.

This impression can be made more vivid by painting the broken surface with a liberal coating of flex-glue tinted with a small amount of blue ink or dye.

White flannel or felt saturated with flex-glue makes a good imitation crust. Cut the fabric to the shape of a pie slice and fold it so that it is thicker along the "outer edge."

Trim away the excess fabric and the pie will be ready to serve with a scoop of Styrofoam ice cream.

Sausages

Anytime meat is called for in a production but is not to be consumed, a convincing fake is prob-ably the best idea. One method of making the-atrical "sausages" is shown here.

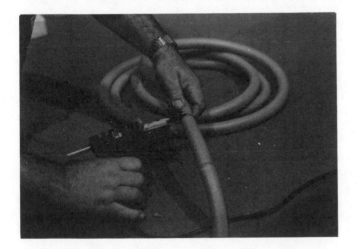

Begin with a length of ¾"-diameter Ethafoam. 1" diameter will also work—or perhaps you'd prefer to use some of each, to give a variety of sizes. Mark the Ethafoam in sausage-link lengths, and score the marks with the tip of a hot-glue gun. You do not apply any glue in this operation, the glue gun is used only to apply heat—which melts the Ethafoam and creates a realistically-shaped "link."

Cheesecloth saturated with flex-glue can be wrapped around the Ethafoam to form the char-acteristic sausage "skin."

Accentuate the links twisting each joint tight and tying it with nylon thread. Color the links to resemble raw sausages with dyes of red, brown, and a hint of purple. Work these dyes into the flex-glue while it is still wet. The blend of dyes and flex-glue will yield a convincing color and texture.

This Scottish lassie (from the chorus of *Briga-doon*) is ready to sell a basket of sausages that appear to be made from intestines and pork scraps.

Tropical Fruit Cocktails

Tropical fruit-juice cocktails—the kind that are always served with little parasols in them—can be quickly and permanently put together using paraffin wax as the main ingredient. These drinks cannot be consumed, but they can't be spilled, either.

Heat some paraffin with a hot plate. Heat the wax slowly and do not overheat—wax melts at about 160°F. and can burst into flames if it gets too hot. If there is any doubt in your mind as to whether you can apply the heat properly, play it safe by using a double boiler.

Tint the melted paraffin by tossing in a crayon (candle coloring will also work).

Place a soda straw or swizzle stick in a fancy glass and pour in the melted paraffin until the glass is about three-fourths full. (It's a good idea to warm the glass first with hot water or a hair dryer to be sure it won't crack from the hot wax.) When the wax cools it will shrink a little. Put in plastic ice cubes (see the section on Ice Cubes) or decorate the drink with an artificial flower, fake fruit, or a paper umbrella; then top the glass off with a little more melted wax.

Two of the drinks shown here were made to appear as though they had just been poured from a cocktail shaker with the addition of a fluffy topping of cotton.

Strawberries

A quantity of strawberries can be produced in a very short time. In fact, if you have the materials ready, proceed with confidence, and handle the strawberries while they're wet instead of waiting for them to dry, you can turn out several dozen in half an hour.

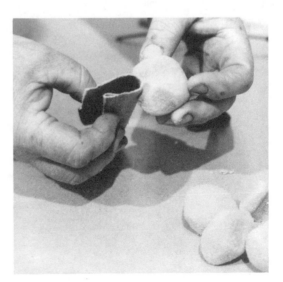

Begin by cutting 1″ cubes of urethane foam on a band saw. Use a knife to reduce these cubes to a rough strawberry shapes. Some strawberries are shaped like teardrops, others like little hearts; some are perfectly shaped, others misshapen. As always, an illustration is helpful. When we made the batch shown here, strawberries were in season, so we modeled ours after the real thing.

Refine the shape with sandpaper, removing any suggestion of corners or edges.

Dab red paint onto the forms. Using a rag for a brush can save time, if you don't mind getting your fingers into the paint. Blend a lighter red and a darker red into the basic shade to produce highlights and shadows.

Not every strawberry will have leaves still attached, but many will. We cannibalized the foliage of some artificial roses to dress our strawberries. Simply select leaves of an appropriate size and shape, and snip them into 1″ segments. You can also make stems and leaves from coat hanger wire and green crepe paper, but this will slow down production considerably.

Poke the stems of the leaf segments into the foam, and the job is done. *Voilà!* Thirty strawberries in thirty minutes.

FOOTLIGHTS

Footlights have been a symbol of the theater since performances first came indoors. Improvements in lighting equipment have rendered footlights obsolete, but decorative footlights are still used in period plays to recall earlier times.

Until the last few years of their use (when they disappeared into the stage floor before disappearing altogether), footlights did not change much over the years in their outward appearance.

The same units can be used to decorate a Renaissance stage, a frontier cabaret, or even an early vaudeville stage.

While footlights of this kind are sometimes cut from coffee cans, the design given here takes no longer to make and has a cleaner look. An extra advantage of this design is that the base, because it is made of wood, is a natural insulator and will reduce the risk of an electrical short.

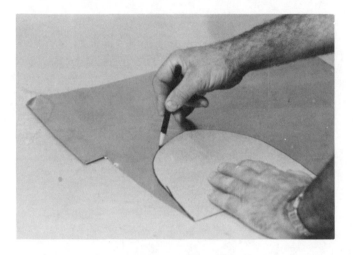

Begin construction by cutting a template from heavy paper. The old grade-school technique for cutting out Valentine hearts can be used here— fold the paper down the middle, lay out half of the pattern, and cut along the outline while the paper is folded. When you open the pattern, it will be symmetrical.

Use a grease pencil to trace the outline of the pattern onto a sheet of lightweight aluminum.

Snip the metal along the pencil outline. Use a file to remove burrs and rough spots from the edges.

Bend the aluminum into a smooth curve, as shown.

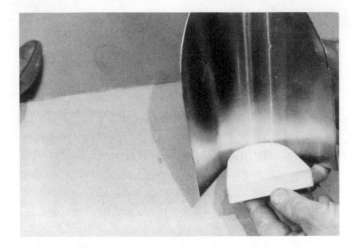

Trace the shape of the bent aluminum reflector onto a piece of ¾″ pine or plywood. Cut the base out on a band saw and attach the reflector to it with nails or screws.

Bolt a porcelain light socket to the base, and you have the first unit ready to be wired and installed.

These footlights can be painted black or sprayed with metallic paint to give the look of brass.

Various elements can be introduced to alter the design of the unit—for instance, an oil-lamp chimney can be fitted over the bulb to give the footlight a cabaret look.

GLUES AND ADHESIVES

Animal Glue and Its Successors

Gelatin glue is an animal product made, as I understand it, by boiling down hides, hoofs, bones, and animal by-products until a thick gelatinous mass is formed. When the water is removed this jelly becomes hard and brittle. This solid form is made available commercially in a block, and as flakes, granules, and powder. Only substances derived from animal protein are "glues" in the original sense; all others are adhesives and cements. In common usage, however, anything that becomes sticky and forms a bond as it dries is called "glue."

The consumer who uses animal glue must add water to bring the glue back to its liquid form, heat the mixture, and keep it warm in a double boiler so it remains ready for use.

Animal-base glue has been widely used in the theater since the glue industry began in the mid-1800s. For almost a century animal glue had no rivals, so it remained the "standard" for use as a pigment binder in scene paint, for attaching muslin to flats, and for general use as an adhesive.

Gelatin glue never becomes really permanent. It loosens in the presence of water — especially hot water. Some technicians consider this an advantage, since scenery painted with animal glue as the binder could be washed, thus eliminating heavy paint build-up. The notorious disadvantage of animal glue is its odor. As it decays, gelatin glue gives off a stench like rotting flesh.

This odor can be inhibited somewhat by the addition of formaldehyde or Lysol to the liquid glue solution.

After World War II, the burgeoning plastics industry began to produce synthetic adhesives with long names that eventually replaced animal glues for most applications. Animal glues are still on the market today; but their appeal seems to be based solely on being removable with water, so the use of animal glues is confined to specialized applications and diehard traditionalists.

In the late 1950s DuPont introduced a product called Elvanol (polyvinyl alcohol). It shares some characteristics of animal glue — it has to be cooked, for example. But it has its advantages: it only has to be cooked once, it remains flexible, it is water-resistant, and because it's not made of protein it doesn't rot. It has an odor that some people find objectionable, but this odor is a far cry from that of animal glue. Elvanol might have caught on as a replacement for animal glue, had not white glue (polyvinyl acetate, sometimes called PVA) hit the market at about the same time. White glue has important advantages over both animal glue and Elvanol which won it the approval of the theatrical world: it is convenient, strong, readily available, and odorless. The only disadvantage of white glue is that it costs a little more than the others, but given the advantages, it's worth the extra expense.

Elvanol

There are some operations for which the expense of white glue makes Elvanol the attractive choice. A pound of Elvanol powder, which produces a gallon of glue solution, costs about $1.80 at this writing. I still keep some Elvanol on hand for the times when we are doing large amounts of "cloth-mâché."

Elvanol is sold as a dry powder, with a consistency that resembles flour. A 50-pound bag costs about $90 at this writing. When the powder is mixed with water and cooked, it becomes a working glue solution. Heating is only necessary during the initial preparation. When the glue cools it remains in solution and can be used cold. Kept in an airtight container, liquid Elvanol has a shelf life of about a year.

Mix the powder in the ratio of 2 pounds of Elvanol powder to 2 gallons of cold water. Mix them before you heat the water; if you add the powder to water that's too hot, lumps will form that won't boil out. Heat the glue until it begins to boil. When the mixture cools it will have the consistency of corn syrup.

Elvanol can be prepared either with direct heat or in a double boiler. Cooking the glue in a double boiler takes several hours but requires no attention. I like to use direct heat which brings the glue to a boil much faster—you can boil 2 gallons in about 20 minutes—but the pot must be stirred constantly. If you don't continue stirring, a thick skin of burned glue will form in the bottom of your pail, and this skin will tend to trap heat at the bottom, burning the residue further and preventing the rest of the mixture from cooking properly. If there are other things you must attend to at the same time, the double-boiler method is the safe bet, but you can save a lot of time if you're willing to concentrate your attention on stirring the brew.

When the cooked Elvanol comes to a rolling boil, it should be removed from the heat. If you turn your back at this point, the glue can boil over and in very little time you can lose as much as a third of the mixture.

Elvanol is an ideal glue to use in "cloth-mâché" (or glue cloth)—the application of glue-soaked muslin to chicken-wire forms. For this application, you can extend 2 gallons of Elvanol to 4 gallons with this recipe:

> 2 gallons prepared Elvanol
> 1 gallon scrap scene paint
> 1 gallon water

If the "scrap" scene paint is truly left over, this 4-gallon quantity will probably cost about $3.50.

FEV

The FEV process is a texturing technique which produces several usable theatrical finishes. It can give a look of antique wood to shop-made furniture, or, with a minor alteration of methods or components, can make felt look like leather or wood look like metal. FEV has been a standard process in many theaters for a long time. With a little practice you can become an expert in FEV finishes.

FEV stands for French Enamel Varnish. This material is a varnish, since its primary ingredient is shellac and since the broad definition of "varnish" covers any gum or resin suspended in alcohol or oil. It is an enamel in the sense that it is a medium to which dyes are added which bring color and depth to the hard glossy finish. And it borrows the adjective "French" from an almost forgotten process known as "French polishing" which involves the patient, repeated rubbing of thinned shellac onto furniture pieces using an

egg-shaped pad of lintless cotton as an applicator.

The formula for mixing FEV varies according to the application. A basic recipe, however, goes like this:

> 1 part white shellac
> 1 part alcohol
> a small amount of dye—just enough
>   to yield a good color

I know of no hard rule as to the amount of dye that this process requires. Different dyes give different results, so trial-and-error is your ally here. Aniline dye is the traditional coloring agent. This dye is sold as a powder and is very concentrated—a little goes a long way. Other dyes that can be used with this process include leather dyes, fabric and textile dyes, and lamp dips and glass stains.

Aluminum powders, bronzing powders, and graphite can be used alone or with colored dyes to produce a metallic finish.

You can achieve different degrees of gloss and different working characteristics by varying the ratio of shellac and alcohol: using more shellac produces a thicker and glossier varnish, while an increase in alcohol yields a thinner varnish with less gloss.

My shop no longer uses FEV to imitate leather. I have found that using flex-glue in a similar process is more to my liking.

Flex-Glue

An Introduction to Flex-Glue

The scene takes place in the properties shop. A STUDENT *has arranged to make up a lab period that she missed the day before. The* PROP MASTER *has collected some materials and is just about to use them in explaining how to embed decorations onto a jewel box.*

PROP MASTER I'm going to show you how to use a product that may be new to you.

STUDENT Oh, good! I like to learn new things. You sure make these required lab sessions fun and interesting.

PROP MASTER *(Shuffling his feet and toeing an imaginary line in embarrassment)* Well now, well now, we try. You will be making a very delicately decorated jewelry box.

STUDENT A jewelry box? Imagine! I'm going to make a jewelry box. Do you know what those other people out there in the shop are doing? They're driving nails in keystones—and I'm going to make a jewelry box. Fate sure is good to me.

PROP MASTER Uh, yes. Well, this is flex-glue, and you will be using it to adhere this decoration to the box.

STUDENT Flex-glue? It looks like Elmer's white glue.

PROP MASTER Yes, it does look like white glue, it feels about the same, and it works about like white glue, but its formulation is not the same. Notice that the odor is not the same.

STUDENT Eeuu! Take it away! It stinks.

PROP MASTER It does not stink. *(Under his breath)* Everything with an odor does not *stink.* I've smelled stink before, and this does not stink.

STUDENT Gross. Is this stuff toxic or something? Is it carcinogenic?

PROP MASTER No! It's just a glue that dries to form a soft flexible coating.

STUDENT I know how to use white glue and I'm sure I can do a better job if I use a glue I've used before. Can we use white glue?

PROP MASTER No. *(With patience)* You will see as this job progresses that the glue will be laid on in very thick coats. White glue would shrink, become brittle, and crack and peel. No, this job is best done with flex-glue. Now, watch this. The box has been laid out with pencil to indicate where each ornament goes. See that?

STUDENT *(Doubtfully)* Uh, yes.

PROP MASTER Just dip the piece of filigree into a little glue, like this...and then place it onto the outline, like this...there. See?

STUDENT Is this job going to be messy?

PROP MASTER No, it doesn't have to be messy. You might get a little glue on your fingers, but it won't matter. The glue cleans up with soap and water.

STUDENT Can I wear gloves?

PROP MASTER Not for this. Gloves are too clumsy

for this work. You use gloves and you lose your sense of touch. The pieces will go on more accurately if you just use your fingers. After this initial lay-up, you can finish the job with a brush.

Applications and Aliases

I have heard flex-glue referred to as "book binder's glue," "Swift's glue," and "flex-glue" (a manufacturer in Albuquerque calls it "Phlexglu"). Bookbinders call it by its formulation number, "Swift's 43917." Swift, however, calls it a carton adhesive. I will stick with the name "flex-glue," which is the most descriptive.

Flex-glue is, as the name implies, a glue which remains flexible after it has dried. It never becomes hard or brittle. Flex-glue should be used in the construction of any costume or prop which must be bent or manipulated.

Apart from its value as an adhesive material, flex-glue has many applications as a texturing medium. Mixed with shellac and dyes, it can be

STUDENT Would it be O.K. if you do the first part, and then after it dries, I'll do the second part and paint on the glue with the brush?

PROP MASTER How are you at driving clout nails?

used to produce a convincing stage leather. It can be used as an embedding material to apply lace, fringe, or other decorative material to cloth or solid forms, and the decoration will appear to be an integral part of the form. A thick coat of flex-glue applied over a releasing agent produces a usable "skin" when it dries. Flex-glue makes a good gloss finish, similar to clear acrylic paint, but it builds up faster and produces a heavier texture more quickly than clear acrylic. This is a really versatile product; it would be more accurate to call it "flexible-texturing-material," but pretty soon that would become awkward, so "flex-glue" it is.

Making a Leather Texture

Flex-glue applied to muslin in repeated coats produces a surface that resembles thin leather. Of course, leatherette and vinyl upholstering material can also be used to approximate leather, but the hand-made flex-glue variety has a cruder and more primitive look. This "leather" can be used to decorate books, luggage, old sea chests, and so on—and even to upholster furniture. To make a thicker leather such as might be used for a blacksmith's apron, just substitute felt for muslin.

Spread a piece of muslin of the desired size on a sheet of plastic. Flex-glue soaks into and through porous material (such as muslin), but it does not adhere to polyethylene or vinyl chloride. Working on a plastic sheet of such material, therefore, allows for liberal applications of the glue without your project becoming fastened to your worktable.

Liberally apply flex-glue to the muslin. Neatness is not much of a concern here; your main objective is to get a thick coat of glue on the cloth.

Evenness of application depends on the results you want. It's possible to skip some areas of the muslin; when dyes are applied in the next step, they will "take" differently on the treated and untreated areas, adding depth and variety to the finished textures.

Thin some shellac with alcohol in about a half-and-half proportion, and mix in a small quantity of brown dye or ink. Half an ounce of prepared dye or ink should color about 4 oz. of thinned shellac. Almost any water-soluble (or alcohol-soluble) coloring agent can be used. We have

used writing inks, India ink, All-Purpose Rit dye, aniline dyes, and even food coloring with this technique. A little experimentation will tell you how much of the dye you have selected will be required to properly color your work.

Pour or brush the tinted shellac into the glue-soaked muslin. Neatness in most cases is still not

a priority. Spread the color boldly, and don't be afraid of making a mistake.

Folding the cloth onto itself and then re-opening it spreads the color in a pleasant way, making a pattern a little like a Rorschach blot. If you feel the pattern is too pronounced, fold again from a different direction, and the pattern will begin to blend out. You may like the results of this folding and blotting technique so well that you put your brush aside and use it exclusively.

If you decide at any point of the progress of your work that the color or texture is inadequate, you can add more color or glue, or whatever you feel is missing. No matter how thick you pile the ingredients on, the glue and dyes will keep their transparency and the cloth will not become brittle. If the color gets too dark, you can scrape some off with a putty knife and spread the remaining dye a little more modestly.

If you are unhappy with the results, write it off as a learning experience and start over. So far you have not invested heavily in either time or materials.

Leave the sheet to dry. Normally this will happen overnight; if you have really piled the glue on, it might take several days.

If you have applied the shellac too heavily, it may remain tacky for a long time. A thin final coat of flex-glue over the shellac usually solves the problem of shellac that refuses to dry. Even if there is no apparent stickiness, you can apply this final coat to give a smoother, shinier surface. This coat will go on milky white, but don't be alarmed, it will dry clear.

A final word of caution regarding the drying period. You may be tempted to hasten drying by leaving your sheet outside where the sun and wind can do their work. If you do, be sure to weight down the corners. We have seen a few disasters where the wind folded the cloth over and it dried with the painted surfaces touching.

The props in the photos above have been decorated with a "leather" prepared from muslin and flex-glue according to the instructions given here.

Making Skin, Membranes, and Tissue

When a thick coating of flex-glue dries, it forms a tough, flexible, and nearly transparent skin. Properly colored, this "skin" can be used to effectively simulate animal tissue. The section on Animal Forms details deveral projects which use flex-glue to construct skins for animals and birds.

The project that follows demonstrates the use of flex-glue to dress the stump of an amputated hand on a human dummy.

We made use of the skin that had formed on the surface of an open bucket of flex-glue.

This skin was laid out on a sheet of Saran Wrap (any sheet of slick plastic would have worked), and we colored the blob of glue with red, brown, and blue inks to simulate broken flesh. The glue itself dried colorless.

This sheet of tinted "flesh" was left to dry overnight.

An Embedding Material

A solid object such as a jewelry box or a metal bowl can be decorated with lace, fringe, or other cloth trim, so that the appliqué appears to be an integral part of the object. This kind of decoration can be made to appear to be integral, rather than an add-on, with the use of a medium that will make the decoration appear to be embedded into the surface of the object. Polyester resins are often recommended for this embedding process, and we have used them with some success. How-

The next morning we peeled the skin from the plastic wrap and attached strips of it to the stump of the dummy's arm. A little more dye was applied to disguise the edges where the strips overlapped.

A small piece of the glue skin was also applied to the dummy's face to simulate an open wound.

ever, experience has shown us that flex-glue is the superior material for this application. Flex-glue is convenient, fast-setting, inexpensive, easy to clean up. It is wet enough to completely saturate the cloth trim, and it is viscous enough to fill all the pores of the fabric. It remains flexible even applied in several heavy coats, and it will not become brittle with age. It also takes paint and dye well.

The surface of the object to be decorated should first be made tacky with spray adhesive. This allows for easy positioning of the trim and will hold the trim securely while the first coat of flex-glue is brushed on. This first coat of glue will probably take several hours to cure. If the object being decorated has a non-porous surface, the first coat of glue may have a tendency to run or sag. Keep an eye out for this problem, and use a brush to smooth out any uneven areas in the glue. Sags of this sort are not likely to develop in subsequent coats.

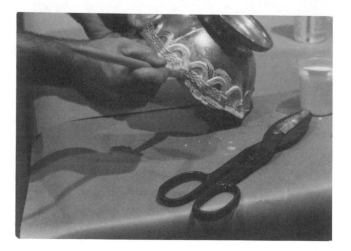

As you no doubt inferred from the last sentence, additional coats of glue — at least two — are necessary and desirable. These coats build up the surface of the glue "skin" and further achieve the embedded look. Because some of the moisture from the additional coats of glue is absorbed into the first coating, the second and subsequent coats will take less time to dry — drying time may be as little as half an hour between coats.

The final coat of flex-glue should be applied to the entire surface of the object so that the surface has a uniform texture. This time allow the glue to dry overnight, and it will be ready to paint.

The book shown was colored with tan dye to contrast with the brown leather binding. The metal bowl was given a silvery appearance with aluminum powder.

A *Paint Binder*

The fact that flex-glue dries clear and has a strong glossy finish makes it a good binder for metallic powders. Gold and aluminum are not the only colored powders that can be mixed into the binding medium; graphite mixed with flex-glue makes a dark gray gunmetal-colored metallic "paint." The graphite shown in the accompanying illustrations is sold as a dry lubricant for use in industrial machining.

As the graphite and glue mixture is brushed on, it will have a pale and un-metallic appearance. This is due to the milky color of the liquid glue. As the glue dries and becomes transparent, the painted object will take on the dark metallic look of pewter. Repeated applications of this coating will give the appearance of depth.

A little graphite or aluminum powder dusted onto the texturing medium while it is still wet will add more depth.

After the final coat has completely dried (al-low at least 24 hours), the flex-glue skin can be polished with a paste wax for a high gloss. The wax polish will also serve to seal in any loose powder remaining from the final dusting.

Shatter-Resistant Skin

Here is another kind of flex-glue "skin" that you may find useful. This skin is a coating formed on an object that is to be deliberately broken.

The glue skin is almost invisible and will help to control breakage and minimize scattering of the shattered pieces.

When you dip a ceramic object in flex-glue and allow it to dry, a tough but flexible transparent coating forms over the ceramic surface. Repeated dippings (with sufficient drying time in between) will form an even thicker skin. The pitcher shown

here was thrown violently against the proscenium, as a piece of stage business, in the Tom Stoppard play *Travesties*. Although the pitcher broke, the pieces did not splatter explosively.

Rough Textures

Many additives (but not those with an oil base) can be mixed with flex-glue to change the working properties of the glue. Thickness or viscosity can be increased by the addition of Cabosil or fuller's earth. When these powders are mixed into the flex-glue, the resulting mixture can be used like putty to make rough textures.

The skin formed by flex-glue when it dries has been discussed earlier in this section. It is worth noting that this skin can be manipulated during the drying process to form rougher textures. The surface can be disturbed by brushing or folding the skin into itself, producing a rough or corroded effect.

Hot Glue

Hot glue has been around for almost twenty years. In that time it has become indispensable to many industries, the theater among them. There are several reasons for this: hot glue is convenient, inexpensive, effective on a wide variety of materials, and fast. The glue reaches its maximum

bond in just a few minutes.

Hot glue is, however, an adhesive relatively unfamiliar to many technicians. It is indispensible only to those who observe two basic axioms:

1. Use plenty of heat.
2. Select the right glue.

Heat. A thin squirt of hot glue carries very little heat with it. When hot glue is used sparingly, the materials to be glued feel very little heat and the bond is virtually nonexistent. The bond is

further impeded if there is any delay after the glue is applied, before the materials to be bonded are brought together. There are several ways to overcome this problem.

One solution is to use a large wad of glue — more than might seem necessary. A liberal application of glue carries more heat, which is essential for a good bond. The bond still must be made quickly — no cooling should occur before the materials are brought together. If too much glue has been used, the excess can be trimmed away later.

Another solution is to transfer heat from the tip of the glue gun before squeezing the trigger. Touch the tip of the gun to materials to be glued

so that when the glue is applied, the heat from the glue is not immediately absorbed and thus lost from the joint where it is needed.

A third way to minimize heat loss is to preheat with an external heat source the materials to be glued.

A propane torch can be used to heat the materials to be glued so that the glue will melt when applied. Use the torch with discretion, however, and apply the heat slowly. Metal objects can be heated until they glow red if the hottest part of the torch flame is applied. Hot glue melts at about 300°F.; if you heat a piece of iron until it glows, you have heated it about three times too hot. Glass can be preheated with a torch if it is

The Right Glue. There are many formulations of glue sticks available, each designed to adhere to a specific type of surface. The glue guns commonly available in hardware stores have only one type of glue stick readily available. That one type is inexpensive and designed for use on porous materials — paper, cardboard, cloth, etc. It is less effective on wood, and will peel off metal, plas-

done gently, with the flame at a distance; direct application of the hottest part of the flame will shatter the glass. Thin glass is even more delicate. The basic precaution to keep in mind is that the application of heat must be gradual and general. Even wood can be preheated if it is done carefully. Wood will kindle at about 475°F., but there is no need to reach that temperature. The gradual application of heat will also allow the heat to penetrate the wood — but be careful not to allow the wood to char, as the ash produced can prevent the hot glue from bonding properly.

tic, and glass. Because this "handyman" variety of hot glue will not adhere well to all surfaces (no one variety of hot glue will), an understandable reluctance to rely on hot glue has given this adhesive something of a bad reputation.

The following chart shows the wide range of hot glues produced by only one manufacturer:

Hi-Per Product Assembly & Packaging Hot Melt—Substrate Cross Reference Chart

Formula	1X	2X	3X	5X	6X	41	232	274	342	351P	446	613	740	804	915	1942	1946	2000	2923	4046	8096
ABS	3	2	4	4	2	2	3	3	4	4	3	4	4	3	3	2	1	2	3	2	2
Acrylic	4	3	3	4	2	2	2	3	4	4	3	4	4	3	3	2	2	4	3	2	3
Aluminum	4	4	3	4	4	2	3	2*	4	4	2	4	4	2*	3	3	2	3	3	2	3
Brass	4	4	3	4	3	2	3	2*	4	4	2	4	4	2*	3	3	2	3	3	2	3
Butyrate	4	3	3	4	2	2	2	3	4	4	3	4	4	3	3	2	2	2	3	2	3
Ceramic	3	2	2	3	2	2	2	3	4	4	2	4	4	3	3	2	2	2	2	2	2
Copper	4	4	4	4	3	2	3	2*	4	4	3	4	4	2*	3	4	3	4	4	2	3
Corrugated	1	2	2	1	2	2	2	2	1	2	2	1.	1	2	2	1	1	2	2	2	2
Cotton	1	2	3	2	2	3	2	1	3	3	3	3	3	1	2	1	2	2	2	2	2
Fiberglas	3	3	3	3	3	2	3	2	4	4	3	4	4	2	2	2	3	3	3	2	3
Glass	4	3	3	4	3	3	3	3	4	4	3	4	4	3	3	3	3	3	3	3	3
Hardboard	2	2	4	4	2	3	3	1	4	4	3	4	4	1	3	2	2	3	3	3	3
Lead	4	4	4	4	4	3	4	3*	4	4	3	4	4	3*	3	3	3	3	3	3	3
Leather	3	2	3	3	2	3	3	1	3	3	3	4	3	1	3	1	2	3	2	2	2
Maple	3	3	4	4	3	3	3	1	4	4	3	4	4	1	4	2	3	3	3	3	3
Mylar	4	4	4	4	4	3	4	4	4	4	4	4	4	4	2	4	3	4	4	3	3
Neoprene (Rubber)	4	4	4	4	4	4	4	4	4	4	4	4	4	4	3	4	3	4	4	3	3
Nitrile (Rubber)	4	4	4	4	4	4	4	4	4	4	4	4	4	4	3	4	3	4	4	3	3
Nylon	3	3	4	4	4	3	4	3	4	4	4	4	4	3	3	3	3	3	4	3	3
Oak	3	3	4	4	3	3	3	1	4	4	3	4	4	1	3	2	3	3	3	3	3
Paper	1	1	1	1	1	1	1	1	1	2	1	1	1	1	2	1	1	1	1	2	2
Particle Board	1	1	2	1	2	2	1	1	3	3	3	3	3	1	3	1	1	2	2	3	2
PC Board (G7)	3	3	4	4	3	3	3	2	4	4	3	4	3	1	3	1	1	3	3	2	2
Pine	1	1	2	2	2	3	3	1	3	3	3	4	3	1	3	1	2	2	2	3	3
Polycarbonate	3	3	4	4	3	3	2	3	4	4	3	4	4	3	3	2	2	3	3	2	3
Polyester	4	4	4	4	4	3	4	3	4	4	3	4	4	3	3	3	2	3	3	2	3
Polyester (Foam)	2	1	2	2	1	2	3	2	3	3	2	4	3	2	2	1	2	2	2	2	2
Polyethylene	4	3	4	4	3	3	3	4	4	4	3	4	4	4	2	3	3	4	4	3	3
Polypropylene	4	3	4	4	3	3	3	4	4	4	3	4	4	4	2	3	3	4	4	3	3
Polystyrene (Foam)	1	1	2	2	1	1	2	3	3	4	2	4	3	3	2	2	2	3	3	3	3
Polystyrene (Rigid)	4	3	3	4	3	3	3	4	4	4	3	4	4	3	3	3	1	3	3	2	3
PVC (Flexible)	4	4	4	4	3	4	4	1	4	2	4	4	4	1	3	3	3	3	3	2	3
PVC (Rigid)	3	3	4	4	3	2	3	1	4	4	3	4	4	1	3	2	2	3	3	2	2
PVC (Semi Rigid)	4	3	3	4	3	2	3	2	4	4	3	4	4	2	3	3	3	3	3	2	3
Sand (Mold)	2	2	1	2	2	2	4	3	4	4	3	4	4	3	4	2	3	3	3	3	3
SBR (Rubber)	4	4	4	4	4	3	4	4	4	4	4	3	4	4	3	3	3	4	4	3	3
Silicone (Rubber)	4	4	4	4	4	4	4	4	4	4	4	4	4	4	4	4	4	4	4	3	3
Stainless (Steel)	4	3	4	4	3	3	4	2*	4	4	3	4	4	2*	3	3	3	4	4	3	3
Steel	4	3	4	4	3	3	4	2*	4	4	3	4	4	2*	3	3	3	4	4	3	3
Steel (Galvanized)	4	3	4	4	3	3	4	2*	4	4	3	4	4	2*	3	3	3	4	4	3	3
Teflon	4	4	4	4	4	4	4	4	4	4	4	4	4	4	4	4	4	4	4	3	4
Urethane (Foam)	2	1	2	2	1	2	2	2	3	4	2	4	3	2	3	1	2	2	2	2	2
Urethane (Rigid)	4	4	4	4	4	3	4	4	4	4	3	4	4	4	4	3	3	4	4	3	3

1 = EXCELLENT   2 = GOOD   3 = FAIR   4 = POOR   * METAL PREHEATED

Now it must be admitted, after the preceding discussion, that hot glue is not the last word in adhesives—it is not the preferred glue for all applications. Although it has been demonstrated that, with the correct glue stick and sufficient heat, hot glue will effectively bond metal, wood, and cloth, it is not likely to render bolts, nails, sewing machines, and welding equipment obsolete. But there are many jobs where, with knowledgeable use, the hot glue gun is the best choice.

Non-Adhesive Applications of Hot Glue

Hot Glue Candle Drippings. The candles shown here were made from pieces of PVC tubing sliced at an angle with a band saw. Hot glue was applied and allowed to run. Since the intent here is to use the glue for decoration rather than as an adhesive, the inexpensive "handyman" variety of glue stick is just as effective as the more expensive formulations.

Doughnuts and Danish. A very inviting glazed doughnut or Danish pastry can be produced with hot glue. Make a spiral of ½" or ¾" Ethafoam using hot glue as an adhesive. Then decorate the surface with a "glaze" of hot glue. Some patience is required with this operation. If too much hot glue is applied all at once, it will reduce the Ethafoam to a melted puddle. Apply a little hot glue and let it cool; then squirt on a little more and let that cool. Finally, when the surface is covered, apply a second heavier coating. The first layer will insulate the Ethafoam and keep it from melting.

Hot Glue Ornamentation. When the hot glue gun first became available, costumers and property builders were quick to find ways to use it as a sort of "cake decorator" for making filigree and delicate ornamentation. Very fine work can be produced by a skilled expert; but if your hands are not so skilled (and I admit mine are not), you can still use hot glue as a casting material.

Casting with Hot Glue. Since hot glue is a liquid when it is hot and a solid when it cools, it can be used effectively as a casting material.

We needed a fancy jewelry box for a production of *Little Mary Sunshine*. All we had was a plain jewelry box, so we went to work to dress it up. The first step was to produce castings to fit in the corners. We fashioned the shapes from Plasticine and glass beads, and then we made a plaster mold of the clay ornaments.

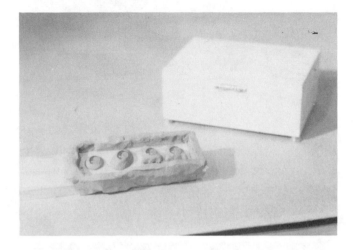

Make an enclosure of Plasticine to contain the plaster as it is poured. Coat the enclosure and the shapes to be cast with Vaseline to ensure easy removal of the plaster.

Then mix and pour the plaster.

When the plaster has set, remove the Plasticine and glass originals from the mold. Since hot glue won't stick to a moist surface, dip the plaster mold momentarily in water to assure an easy release of the hot glue castings.

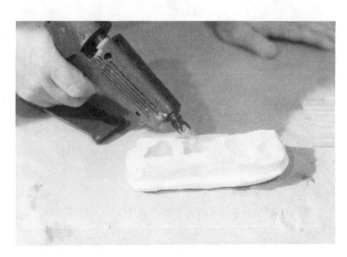

Fill the depressions in the mold with hot glue. Bubbles may form as the hot glue turns the moisture in the mold to steam. If this happens, you can burst the bubbles with a toothpick as they rise to the surface, and press the popped bubbles firmly back into the mold as the glue cools.

When the hot glue has cooled, pry it from the mold. If your casting has an uneven edge from the mold, it can be smoothed with a mat knife.

Hot-glue the castings to the box, and give the box a coat of acrylic paint. We textured our box to look like wood; you might prefer to paint it to look like marble.

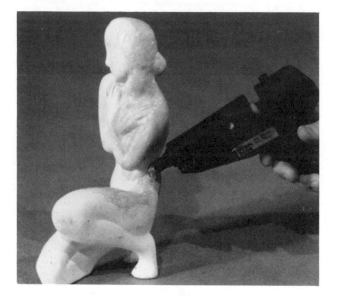

We textured a plaster statue with a coating of hot glue for a production of *Last Summer at Bluefish Cove*. The statue was finished with gold spray

paint and a gold paste rub-on paint, to give it the appearance of having been cast from bronze.

GRAMOPHONE

An authentic gramophone—crank-wound, with a horn to amplify the sound—is an expensive antique. At this writing, a gramophone in working order could easily cost you $250. With the passage of time, the rarity of these machines will increase, and so will inflation, putting the authentic object farther out of reach. For this,reason, the sensible solution is to build a stage replica when a production calls for a gramophone.

The construction of a "talking-machine" requires three forms of plastic media. If these are not already familiar materials to you, you will be using them with confidence by the time you have completed this project.

There were many different designs of gramophone horns manufactured. The straight cone that satisfied Edison's need for amplification soon was recognized by phonograph manufacturers as a potential element of design, and the shape was modified and embellished for the sake of appearance. These designs run the gamut from a utilitarian conical trumpet to lotus blossom shapes with an art nouveau flavor. More fashionable extremes included hand-painted decorations of flowers, figures, and so on. The gramophone devised here is somewhere in the middle of this austere-to-gaudy spectrum.

The sounding horn is fashioned from 20-mil or 30-mil aluminum sheets. Cut eight wedge-shaped segments, four with tabs on both sides (as shown in the photo at left) to facilitate joining the segments. Each segment is 26″ long. The width is 1″ at the narrow end, tapering to 3″ at a length of 20″. In the last 6″ the width flares from 3″ to 4½″. This flare will form the open end of the horn and should be cut with a slightly concave side. The end which will form the rim of the horn should be cut with a slightly convex curve.

Bend each of the tab strips. Ideally this should be at a 45° angle, but the precise angle is not critical. When all sides are joined together, the horn will have the shape of an octagonal pyramid. Drill ³/₁₆″ holes through the tabs and through the tabless segments at the points where they will meet the perforations in the tabs. Then, using a pop riveter, join the segments through these prepared holes. (If your shop doesn't own a pop riveter, look into purchasing one from any hardware store. It's a handy tool that you will use constantly once you have one.)

We salvaged the lamp-shade from an old high-intensity lamp to finish off the narrow end of the horn. If you don't have a scrap or salvaged part of the right shape, a metal 4-oz. glass can be used. Drill and pop-rivet this piece of hardware into place.

The gramophone cabinet is simply a plywood box. The box shown here is 12" × 15", with a height of 9". The top overhangs the sides by 1" on all sides. Make the base of two pieces of plywood. The first overhangs the box by 3/4" on all sides; the second overhangs the first by an additional 3/4" all the way around. We added a little extra decoration to the front of the cabinet in the form of plastic Corinthian columns salvaged from a wedding cake. When these columns were cut down the middle on the band saw, they formed excellent ornaments for the gramophone case.

A word of explanation is in order concerning the large square hole in the face of the cabinet. This gramophone was built for a production of Tom Stoppard's *Travesties*. The sound designer insisted that the gramophone "sound" was to come from the gramophone—not from behind the unit, but from the unit itself. Our solution was to put a speaker grille in the face of the cab-inet to accommodate a loudspeaker which would simulate phonograph music. Gramophones with exposed reproducing horns do not have speaker-grilles in the cabinet, but theatrical license prevailed. And apparently we got away with it—no one in the audience ever mentioned the duplicity of sound sources built into our machine.

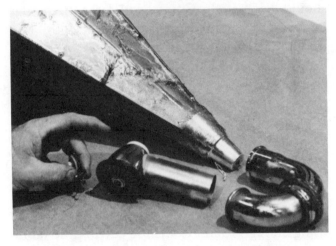

Duplicating the hardware unique to old-fashioned talking machines is a challenge which inevitably must be confronted.

We assembled a collection of "junk" that seemed to have possibilities, and some photos of gramophones to use for reference. The found objects included lamp and projector parts, plumbing elements, drawer pulls, and a trumpet.

A little thought and a lot of trial and error led to the selection of parts shown in the second photo. The trap from a bathroom sink was chosen for the sound chamber (in a real gramophone this curve channels sound waves from the needle into the horn). We were able to modify the trap later so that it served also as a swiveling mounting bracket. The "pickup head" is a composite of four items: the backing plate from a drawer pull, a bottom-mounting fixture from an electric light socket, part of a shower head, and a porcelain drawer knob. We even found an earring to suggest the needle clamp and its attachment to the diaphragm in the pickup head.

"A–B" epoxy putty was used to attach the sink trap to the shower head, and to join the trap and the assembled horn. (See the section on Construction Techniques for instructions on using epoxy putty as a bonding material.) The "pickup head" was bolted together with a 6–32 machine screw which, fortunately, matched the threads on the porcelain drawer knob. The earring—which had seemed like such a fine idea—was finally discarded when we realized that the audience would not be able to see such a detail from 20 feet away.

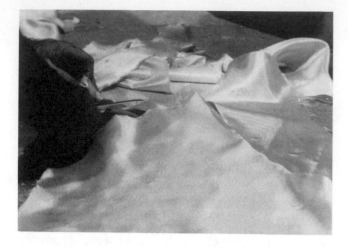

Now that the basic parts have been assembled, the next step is to make them attractive. Let's work on the horn first.

You can fill in gaps and rivet holes, smooth imperfect bends, and add strength by applying a fiberglass coating to the entire surface of the aluminum. Both the inside and outside surfaces should be coated. Cut several large triangular patches of medium-weight fiberglass cloth. Mix up about 4 oz. of polyester resin with about 20 drops of catalyst—or according to the proportions specified in the instructions provided with the product you are using.

Brush the catalyzed resin into the fabric. Saturating the fibers of the cloth will make the fabric transparent. Make sure no areas remain white. Any remaining white indicates that you are not using enough resin. Continue cutting the fabric and mixing and applying the resin until all of the aluminum is covered. There will be areas where the fiberglass cloth is overlapped—this adds further to the strength of the fiberglass coating.

The surface of the horn will now be very rough. A quick sanding with coarse sandpaper will even out some of the roughness and prepare the horn to be filled and smoothed with a plastic putty such as Bondo. (Bondo is a trade name for a plastic filler putty. Refer to the section on making a turtle, under Animal Forms, for instructions on the use of this material.)

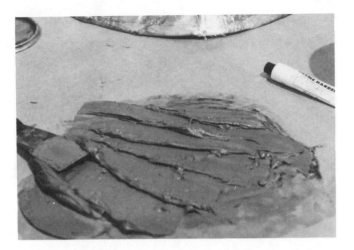

Mix the putty with a cream hardener according to the instructions on the can. Spread a thin coating over the entire area of the horn. Since the putty cures so rapidly, it is necessary to work in small quantities. You may have to mix and spread several batches before the horn is completely covered. Spread the putty as evenly as you can with a putty knife.

The next step is the final sanding. You can use a power sander or do the work by hand. Plastic filler is designed to be sanded, so it can be worked easily. This material hardens progressively as it cures, and as it hardens it becomes more difficult to sand. It is advisable, then, to begin sanding with coarse sandpaper within an hour or so of applying the filler putty. As you continue to smooth the surface, it is likely that you will sand completely through the Bondo in some places. A second and even a third application of Bondo may be necessary to smooth over-worked areas and fill holes. These subsequent applications should be made sparingly. The first coat can be troweled on like plaster; later applications should be applied like spackling paste.

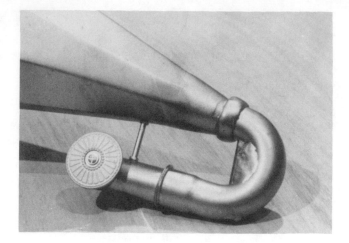

The joint between the horn and the sink trap can be strengthened with a support near the pickup head. Drill the trap and insert a ½" tube to act both as a support and a swiveling mount to the cabinet. The tube can be securely attached to the unit with two-part epoxy putty. Solidly mount a ½" wooden dowel to the rear of the cabinet, and slide the tube onto it.

Now the cabinet needs attention. Use wood putty or spackling paste to fill any imperfections in the wood, and to coat the routed edges of the plywood. Sand the wood and the putty, and give the cabinet a paint job to simulate close-grain wood. Dress the top with ornamental brass gew-

gaws. We used the pulls from a chest of drawers. Inkwells would have made good needle holders (the needle on a gramophone had to be changed every third or fourth record, so the machines often had little cups to hold a supply of needles), but we couldn't find any of these.

We salvaged a turntable from a discarded phonograph and fashioned a crank from an old patch-cord jack and a piece of scrap iron. Then we fitted a piece of open-weave fabric over the inside of that ridiculous speaker grille. And we had a finished talking machine ready for an audience.

ICE CUBES

When your stage bartender is ready to make an old-fashioned or an amaretto-on-the-rocks, what could be simpler than making a trayful of ice cubes in the refrigerator? Answer: Going to the bar supplies drawer and pulling out the ice-cube box.

Of course, the ice cubes must be made first. Here are the steps.

Cut ice-cube-size squares from a sheet of ⅝″ or ¾″ Plexiglas on the bandsaw.

Using a sander, smooth off the marks left by the saw blade, and round the sharp corners and edges slightly.

Use a propane torch to heat-polish the surfaces marred by the sander. Do this with patience— a little overheating can discolor the plastic, and extreme overheating can cause the plastic to ignite.

The finished ice cube has a realistic appearance, a realistic tinkle when shaken, and an unrealistic tendency to sink to the bottom of the glass. A glass filled with artificial ice cubes looks real; a glass with only one or two does not.

If you don't have a thick enough sheet of Plexiglas on hand, there is an alternative method— you can cast a convincing set of ice cubes using polyester resin.

Use a new, unscratched, clean, flexible plastic ice cube tray as a mold. (Metal trays won't work; the resin welds to the tray.) Plastic trays are designed with tapering sides for easy removal of the ice cubes. Spray the tray with mold release. You might want to make a test with a little resin to be sure the acrylic will separate from the tray— the fact that we've never had trouble with poor release only validates the tray and mold release we have used.

Catalyze 2 oz. of clear casting resin with 10 drops of MEK peroxide for a normal mix. You might be tempted to make a "hotter" mix for a faster set, but you're apt to be troubled by discoloration and air-bubble entrapment, so exercise patience.

Thoroughly stir the catalyst into the resin.

Small air bubbles in the mixture should give you no trouble—they will settle out in the mold, leaving the casting clear and bubble-free.

Pour the resin into the tray. It may take two or three mixes to completely fill the tray.

Wait 12 hours, and give the tray a twist. The plastic cubes should pop right out, just like real ice cubes would do.

JUNK ART—FOUND OBJECTS

Support Your Local Scavenger

As the scene opens, the designer and technical director look up from their sketches to see the properties master enter the shop, his arms filled with assorted brown paper bags. The bags are overflowing with assorted paraphernalia.

DESIGNER Uh-oh. It's Monday. And he's got his shopping bags. And I know that smile on his face. If you'll excuse me, I'm gonna skip this.

TECHNICAL DIRECTOR Aw, come on. He likes to show his stuff off. Don't go. It'll only take a minute or two.

DESIGNER I've heard his song and dance, and I don't want to hear it again. I get tired of humoring him. *(He exits hurriedly)*

TECHNICAL DIRECTOR *(To fleeing* DESIGNER*)* Chicken. *(To* PROP MASTER*)* Can I help you there?

PROP MASTER *(Handing over two of the bags)* Thanks. Take these bags till I get the prop room door open.

TECHNICAL DIRECTOR *(Entering the room and peeking into his bags)* Whatcha got here? Been shopping?

PROP MASTER *(Unpacking some paper bags)* Yes, "garage sale-ing." You can pick up some very special things if you get out early enough.

TECHNICAL DIRECTOR Special? I guess! What's this?

PROP MASTER *That* is a rotisserie motor.

TECHNICAL DIRECTOR I know. Are we doing a show that needs a rotisserie barbecue?!

PROP MASTER No. But that's a good one. I tried it out. It's quiet, and it has an r.p.m. of only 15.

TECHNICAL DIRECTOR What're you going to do with it?

PROP MASTER I'll put it in a box up there with those other motors.

TECHNICAL DIRECTOR No, I mean where'll you ever use the motor?

PROP MASTER I'm not sure yet.

TECHNICAL DIRECTOR *(Digging through the sack)* What's this? Isn't this a hydraulic door closer?

PROP MASTER Yeah, I got that for fifty cents. A real buy.

TECHNICAL DIRECTOR You gonna put it in the box with the hydraulic closers?

PROP MASTER Yeah, I'll store it there for a little while.

TECHNICAL DIRECTOR Till when?

PROP MASTER Till I need it. *(Smiling)* Someday when we need a cuckoo clock, and I use that door closer as a cuckoo-bird mechanism, you're going to think I'm pretty clever.

TECHNICAL DIRECTOR *(Digging some more)* This is a good-looking cameo brooch. *(Fooling with it)* But it's broken. Are you going to be able to fix it?

PROP MASTER Probably not, but I got it and this matching earring for only a quarter.

TECHNICAL DIRECTOR There's only one earring. That's not worth anything by itself. It's junk! Boy, are you clever. You bought twenty-five cents' worth of junk.

PROP MASTER Oh, no, I doubt if I'll use those pieces as jewelry, but I'll use them.

TECHNICAL DIRECTOR You'll store them with the jewelry, though?

PROP MASTER Probably. Those cameos will work

real good as decorations for something — sometime.

TECHNICAL DIRECTOR Why don't you just wait till you need the decoration and then buy it as it's needed?

PROP MASTER Well, I probably couldn't find it when I need it — and if I did find it, it surely wouldn't be at this price.

TECHNICAL DIRECTOR You know what I think? I think you're a pack rat. A pack rat, bringing a lot of junk in here. And when you get canned, someone will have to go through all of this junk and throw it away.

PROP MASTER *(With complete confidence and assurance)* These are found objects. You won't have found objects when you need them if you don't start finding them.

TECHNICAL DIRECTOR *(Walking away, shaking his head)* A pack rat. But, he's a jolly old fool, and he's harmless.

The Use of Found Objects

If you have a little imagination and a flair for envisioning the unusual, you can become expert in the esoteric art of "found objects." Specialized hardware can be used to construct many prop items in ways that the manufacturer never intended. Plumbing and electrical hardware is particularly applicable to this art, and I recommend that you accumulate such hardware for the express purpose of misusing it in this way. Success with found objects depends not on chance, but on advance preparation: these objects must be gathered and organized even though their eventual use will probably not be known at the time they are collected.

This section gives brief suggestions of sources for such objects and ways they can be used.

This assortment of relays, solenoids, and connectors was saved when we threw out a junked pinball machine. Where will these parts be used? It's hard to say...yet.

The only thing we can claim as ingenious in the construction of this undersized piano is that we had the foresight to salvage and store the keyboard a couple years ago when we discarded a piano that was no longer usable.

The body of this coffee grinder was made of plywood, with a routed base and top—pretty straightforward stuff. The crank, however, is a fanciful assembly of found objects.

The crank consists of the following parts, listed from the bottom upward: a lamp base, a curtain rod bracket, half of a drawer pull, a small lamp flange, and a porcelain drawer knob.

For a production of *When You Comin' Back, Red Ryder?* we needed decorative bases for nine café stools. Each stool consisted of a padded seat mounted on a 2″ pipe, threaded at each end and screwed into a mounting flange. The flanges were bolted and screwed onto the seat at one end of the pipe, and to the floor at the other end. There is nothing out of the ordinary here; the manufacturers of the parts intended such usage.

The designer was asked to make a selection for a base for the stools from this assemblage, which included industrial and decorator lamp shades, a highway construction marker, and a ceiling canopy for a chandelier. He felt most of these found objects were too large and chose the small object in the foreground—the ceiling plate.

Using the ceiling canopy as a model, we cast nine copies from fiberglass and polyester resin.

This oversized hourglass was built for *The Wizard of Oz* and reused in *Once upon a Mattress*. It consists of a pair of liter-size plastic soda bottles, filled with fine sand and hot-glued together at their mouths. The bases were chromed ashtrays.

This covered bowl, which was used in *Faust,* was made up of a variety of miscellaneous articles. The "antique" was made from a plastic bowl set on a lamp base. This was decorated with a piece of gimp and two filigree ornaments; the lid was made from an upturned ceiling plate from a light fixture topped off with a plastic cap from a wine bottle and a drawer pull. The entire bowl and its lid were painted with a coating of flex-glue and graphite to simulate pewter.

This repair of one of a pair of vases was done using a wood block and two lamp parts.

The repaired vase is strong, but not really a perfect match. The vases, however, were used on opposite sides of the stage, so the mismatch was hardly noticeable. It might be argued that the best solution would have been to go out and buy a replacement. But this repair took only half an hour and was done inexpensively; no one had to leave the prop shop, and the prop man had a chance to be clever.

LAMP PARTS

We have found lamp parts to be extremely adaptable, lending themselves to the construction of many hard-to-find property items. Lamp parts are not dirt cheap — but when you compare their cost to the purchase price of the item you are mocking up, the economy is readily apparent.

The lamp parts shown here were assembled to make non-lamp objects. In the descriptions that follow, names for the various parts have been taken from a catalog published by Crystal Lamp Parts, a firm located in Los Angeles.

Using lamp parts to construct a candelabrum is not too far removed from their intended use...

So let's go farther afield, and make something unlikely. This rapier has been put together using a real épée blade and five lamp parts. The handle and guard consist of a cast metal lamp base, an embossed steel shade holder, a 4½" turned brass spindle, a turned brass candle cup, and a check ring. Finally, the threaded tip that was part of the fencing foil from which we appropriated the blade was screwed onto the handle end of the blade to hold all the pieces securely.

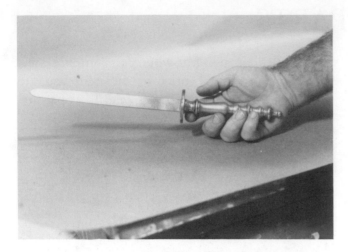

The blade of this knife was shaped on the grinding wheel from a piece of 3/4" sill iron. The handle is the same turned brass spindle used in the rapier, with a pyramid knob and a drawer-pull backing plate. The blade was brazed to the handle assembly. (I have tried to minimize the projects in this book which require welding, but here there is no other way of effectively securing the blade to the handle.)

This hookah (water pipe) was built for *La Quinta de Pancho Diablo*. The pieces used in its construction were as follows: a cast metal lamp base, a four-way fixture body, a brass spinning (an old chandelier body), a 3" canopy collar, and a large candle cup. This assembly was held together with a section of 1/8 IPS threaded pipe and two lock nuts. Look at the four-way fixture body in the photo and you will see a sawed-off fixture arm bolted to it. The end of this arm supports a 3/8" rubber tube which has been fitted over it.

We happened to have an old Irish bagpipe in stock from which we appropriated a mouthpiece for the mouthpiece of the hookah. If you're not fortunate enough to have such an exotic part lying around, you could make a very serviceable brass mouthpiece from lamp parts: a cast metal bobesche, a 4" brass spindle, and a pyramid knob.

This goblet was made from the two halves of a two-piece brass fount, with the top of the fount inverted to serve as a base for the goblet. (Our goblet was not practical, and one would not want to attempt to drink from it without sealing the holes. Filled with liquid, this goblet would function as the world's fastest dribble glass.)

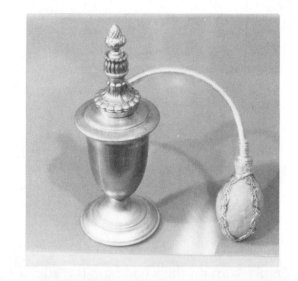

The goblet can be converted to an oversize perfume atomizer by the addition of a brass vase cap, a cast finial (cannibalized from an old lamp; not in the Crystal Lamp Parts catalog), and an acorn finial. All of these parts are held together with standard ⅛ IPS threaded pipe.

The cast finial was drilled and fitted with a ¼″ bolt. A length of rubber tubing was secured to the body by sliding it over the bolt. The squeeze bulb is a partially inflated balloon decorated with latex and lace.

A scroll suitable for a Hebrew scholar or synagogue setting can be made of four fixture body covers, four 2⅞″ urn finials, and two 14″ threaded rods. Make the body of the scroll from 1¼″ PVC plastic water pipe.

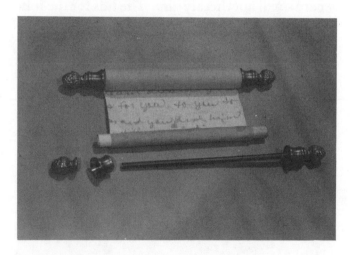

A scroll with a royal or heraldic look can be built from four acorn finials, four turned brass candle cups, and two 10″ threaded rods. The body is made of ¾″ PVC plastic water pipe.

This ear trumpet was made of a brass fount, a piece of a fixture arm, and an ear tip from an ear syringe.

The inkwells in this elegant pen holder and desk set are small apothecary jars. The lids for the inkwells are made from cast metal bobesches. The

decorative trim on the wood base is made of ¾" banding. The brass banding is a standard lamp item and can be ordered from a lamp catalog.

Planning a production of *The Front Page*? Here is a plan for producing the 1920s "candlestick" telephones you'll need.

The photo shows two telephones in two stages of construction. One is nearly finished; the other has been left loosely assembled to show how the parts fit together.

The parts of the telephone in the foreground, from left to right, are: a flashlight reflector, a faucet wall flange, a 2¼" ball shade holder, a "Ward Locktight" swivel, a turned brass candle cup, and a length of brass tubing (PVC water pipe or EMT conduit would have worked equally well). The base is made of a check ring and a 5" collar canopy. The telephone is held together with threaded ⅛ IPS steel pipe and two lock nuts.

We couldn't find stock lamp parts that suggested the shape of a receiver, but we discovered that the plastic container made for "L'Oreal" brand hair set is about the right size and shape.

The receiver cradle was forged out of ½" sill iron.

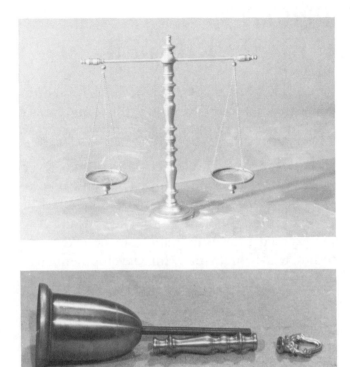

This balance, bell, goblet, and censer were all constructed from lamp parts. In the light of the instructions on the preceding pages, you should have little difficulty discerning the scheme.

This brass bed headboard was commercially made, but you can duplicate it in your shop — from *lamp parts!* The frame consists of brass tubing in four sizes, all available as standard lamp hardware. You will have to bend the two uppermost sections of tubing yourself. The bedpost knobs are spun brass founts; the knobs on the insides of the curlicues are stamped brass caps. The center finial is made up of three brass coupling necks, a turned spindle, and a four-way armback, topped off with a pressure-cast bud knob.

The bent brass tubes are held in place with brass coupling necks, ⅛ IPS threaded nipples and decorative brass nuts. The vertical tubing forming the rungs is secured with long threaded lamp piping and small threaded ball knobs. Each rung is ornamented at the top with a brass stamping and at the bottom with a brass check ring.

OLD-TIME PHOTOS
PROCESSED ON A BLUEPRINTER

Large framed portraits of Great-Grandma and Great-Grandpa, *circa* 1900, make interesting set dressings. A large portrait of this kind could be made using standard photographic darkroom techniques, with soft focus, sepia toner, etc. But an associate who has some experience using a blueprinter for printing photos assured me that very authentic turn-of-the-century photo quality could be achieved with this process. I was eager to give it a try. The process is explained in detail here.

Some specialized equipment is needed, none of it terribly exotic. You will need a 35mm camera with a close-up lens, a 35mm projector (a slide projector), brownline paper, and access to a blueprint machine.

The camera could be borrowed, and if you can't borrow a close-up lens, you can purchase one at a photo supply store for about $15. The projector should not be a problem to find. And the exposed brownline paper can be taken to a commercial blueprinter for development at a modest cost.

Select a photo to be reproduced. Our designer found these in a book. You might want to use an authentic photo of your ancestors, or pose some actors in period costume and photograph them.

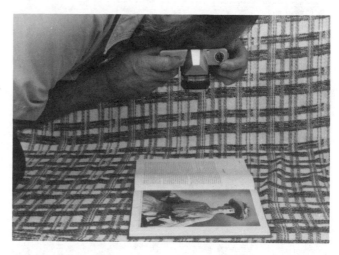

Make a black and white slide of the photo you have selected. The preparation of this slide is probably the most critical step in the whole process, so a detailed explanation of its preparation is in order. Use a 35mm camera with through-the-lens focusing to assure that the whole frame is accurately filled with your subject and that the focus is sharp. When you come to the printing step later on, you will want to print from the full frame, so you don't want any white border on the slide film.

Best results are obtained from a high-contrast black and white positive slide. The easiest way to obtain this is to use color slide film and photograph a black and white subject. Experience has taught us to shoot the slides outdoors in bright open shade, using daylight Ektachrome film.

If you have a copy stand with incandescent you may be tempted to use it—if so, use it outdoors and don't use the lights. Artificial lighting will almost certainly result in the slide having a yellow cast. This yellow tint will act as an ultraviolet filter, foiling your attempts at exposing the UV light-sensitive paper.

Now, about the close-up lens...I am suggesting that you obtain a copy lens (sometimes called a portrait lens), which is really an inexpensive set of three lenses. You do not replace the existing camera lens, but augment it by attaching the copy lens over it. This is analogous to outfitting the camera with reading glasses—the copy lens permits a close focus on the subject. With this lens attachment you could focus on a postage stamp, or even a cockroach.

Use the whole roll of film. Take shots with a variety of exposure times and lens openings. You are after the highest contrast you can achieve, so give yourself plenty of slides to choose from.

If you decide to pose actors to make the slide, you'll eliminate some problems and generate a few new ones. Dress your actors in black and white, and have them apply makeup using cool tones and accentuating contrast. Eliminate warm tones from the composition. You still only need one slide to print from, but it's better to take many and choose the one that will work best.

Take the roll of film to a photofinisher or your neighborhood drug store. When you get the slides back, select the one with the best contrast and complete absence of yellow tones. This is the slide you will print from. The paper you want to work with is Ozalid brand #408 ZT. This is a brownline paper that will give your picture its sepia tone.

Everything You Never Wanted to Know About Brownline (But Were Afraid to Ask)

If you are at all familiar with ordinary darkroom techniques, some parts of this project may puzzle you. You will be making a positive image on brownline paper using a positive slide—that may seem like a reversal of the usual rules of order, but that's the way this paper works. The thinner parts of the slide allow light rays to strike the paper and burn off the emulsion; when the paper is processed, these areas will stay white. The dark areas of the slide hold back the light, preserving the paper emulsion; when the paper is processed these areas turn brown.

Another surprise—the paper is only sensitive to ultraviolet light and is not affected by short-term exposure to normal incandescent lighting. It may seem strange to be doing work which ordinarily requires a safe-light and a darkroom out in the open in the prop shop, with so much ambient light. The photo below shows a safe level of working light; this photo has not been retouched.

Tape the brownline paper to a wall or easel and use the projector to focus the projected slide onto

It is possible to monitor the progress of the exposure by making periodic comparisons between the brightest portions of the exposure and a sheet of white paper. Make the check by standing in the path of the projected image and holding the white paper alongside of the brownline. When the lightest areas of the brownline match the white paper, the exposed brownline paper is ready for processing. (The unexposed brownline paper has a solid yellowish color on its light-sensitive side. As the exposure progresses, the bright areas of the projected image cause this yellow tint to gradually fade to white. When these areas are completely white, the exposure is complete. The properly exposed sheet will have the appearance of an extremely pale version of the finished portrait, with the darkest areas a very light yellow. The exposure shown in the photo above took 2½ hours.

it. Here is something else that those with dark-room experience will find odd: Using the brightest setting on a Kodak Carousel projector, it will take from 2½ to 3 hours to make the exposure. (If you have access to an HMI projector, which produces much more ultraviolet light, you can reduce the exposure time to 15 or 20 minutes; but since it's not very likely that you have one of these on hand, we won't discuss this possibility further.) Just think—you can set the projector up in a nice, quiet place where it won't be disturbed, and take a friend to dinner and a movie, and when you return, the exposure will be complete! Of course, you can stick around and watch the exposure take place if you're patient and have a lot of time on your hands.

I must confess that my limited experience with this process has not been sufficient for me to have become comfortable with the notion of doing photographic processing with the lights on —in fact, I kept the work lights off during most of the exposure time when making the prints shown here. I only turned them on to make periodic checks of the progress of the exposure; the accompanying photo was taken during one of these checks.

The exposed sheet can be processed immediately, or it can be packed away in a light-tight envelope and taken to a blueprinter for development tomorrow. If you must take the picture to a blueprinter elsewhere, be aware that you must guard against any sunlight touching the exposed sheet. Sunlight includes ultraviolet rays, and even a little sunlight will instantly ruin the picture.

Developing the print is the easy part. Just run the exposed sheet through the ammonia developer bath of the blueprint machine. *Do not run the paper through the first phase of the blueprinter which will expose the paper to ultraviolet light.* The "light bath" is useful when the machine is used for blueprints, but it's not helpful here. All you need from the printer is the ammonia vapor. If you are using the services of a commercial blueprinter, you should explain your intentions carefully so he doesn't spoil your project by running the brownline paper through the ultraviolet light and erase the image that you spent so long exposing.

Mat and frame the finished portrait, and your set dressing is ready to hang.

The first time you attempt this process you will find that it isn't difficult; the length of the instructions here reflect only the fact that it is such an unusual technique.

Postscript: When the finished portraits shown here were hung on the set of *The 5th of July,* the director hated them. Feeling that they were too prominent and demanded too much attention, he insisted that we take them down. But we have kept them in stock, and they are available for use the next time "antique" photos are needed.

PLANT FORMS

A Landscape Hedge

Sometimes a set will include a sliding glass door or a picture window that opens upstage to reveal a patio garden. We built two units of the design shown here to dress just such a patio garden in a production of *The Big Knife*.

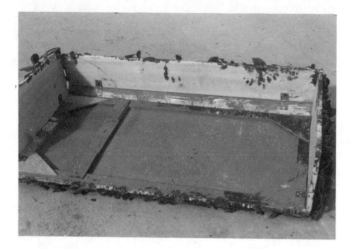

Begin to reproduce this unit by making a 3 ′ × 5 ′ scenic plug with standard flat construction. The sides can be made of 1 ″ × 12 ″ pine lumber or two more 1 ′ plugs, hinged to fold tightly against the main body.

After the frame has been hinged together, paint it with a ground coat of scumbled green tones.

Staple chicken wire over the painted frame. Allow enough play in the chicken wire so that the frame can be folded easily.

Now comes the long process that can be made much easier with many hands helping. Tear strips of muslin into 1 ″ × 6 ″ pieces. Dip each each strip into green paint and tie it onto the chicken wire. Each opening in the chicken wire should have a green strip tied to it. These strips are to simulate leaves, so they should be carefully

The top is constructed like the sides, and is equipped with a 3 ″ toggle so it can fold over the two side pieces. The folded hedge will consume about 5 ″ of storage space.

smoothed to leaf-like flatness after they are tied on. There are many holes in the chicken wire, so many strips of muslin will be required. A more convincing look can be achieved if three or four tones of green are used. Work from several paint pails, with a different shade of green in each, some lighter and some darker.

In spite of the most painstaking efforts at creating natural color and texture, the hedge will still appear flat and unrealistic except when viewed from a very great distance.

Adding a few commercially made artificial plastic leaves will help the appearance greatly. Real magnolia leaves dipped in green neoprene flame-proofing will work well for this purpose. Leaves of higher quality should be placed strategically where they will add the most to the hedge's appearance. Placing them at the corners of the hedge break is an especially good idea.

If the hedge were made up exclusively of artificial leaves of a high quality, it would appear exceedingly realistic, even on close examination. It would also be exceedingly expensive.

The hedge was such a popular item, and it took up so little storage space, that we decided to build another pair. We now have four of these hedges in stock ready to dress patio gardens.

Topiary Bushes

If you were gratified building the hedge, this project will take you near to ecstasy. It incorporates refinements in the leaf-making technique that make the foliage even more realistic.

Fashion a framework of plywood and chicken

wire to serve as a three-dimensional representation of the desired shape. Our trees were to look as if they were pruned to spherical shapes; your design might use another of many possible forms, including animal shapes.

To make a spherical framework like ours, make two disks from plywood, and cut one into quarters along the diameter. Drill a 2″ hole in the center of the uncut disk. The uncut disk will be the horizontal support, and the center hole will allow for insertion of a pole (the "trunk") in a later stage of construction. Nail the sections of the quartered disk perpendicularly to the radius lines drawn from the center hole of the uncut disk (the quarters should not obstruct the hole). Heavy-gauge chicken wire will help the tree or bush hold its shape with a minimum of internal support.

You can't leave the framework the color of raw wood. No matter how densely you "foliate" the tree, some tiny holes will be left that allow the interior to be seen—so it needs to be dark in there. Dark green is a good choice. The wise thing would be to paint the interior before the chicken wire is applied. But if you are less cunning and apply the chicken wire first (as we did), the only sensible way to get paint onto the plywood is by using a spray gun.

Dip a large piece of erosion cloth in green paint and lay it onto the wire frame. Tear 1″ × 6″ strips of muslin and begin the tedious task of tying them onto the chicken wire. Try to tie each strip of muslin around both a strand of the chicken wire and a string of the erosion cloth. Spread the ends of the muslin strips open to suggest leaves. Spreading the strips will cut down the number of rag strips that will be needed, and the use of the erosion cloth will further reduce the quantity — but you'll still need a staggering number of them. Many hands make light work. (Compare instructions for the Landscape Hedge in the section immediately preceding.)

When one side of the form has been covered with little rag ties, rotate the form and begin covering the other side. Continue until the whole surface has been covered.

Dip real leaves in green neoprene (see the following section on Foliage Flameproofing) and insert the stems into the chicken-wire openings. This will add a touch of realism to the tree.

Our leaves were clipped from an India hawthorne bush. These leaves were chosen for their substantial thickness which lends itself to being preserved with a neoprene coating. The wet neoprene flameproofing will act as an adhesive when it dries, holding the leaves in place.

You'll need a large supply of flameproofed leaves to make the tree look full — ideally, a leaf should be stuck into every opening in the chicken wire.

Here is our little grove of topiary bushes used to dress a garden setting for a production of *Man of Mode*. Actually, a total of four trees were made, two that were double-tiered and two consisting of a single round form each. (I'm still looking forward to the day when a production requires a fantasy garden of topiary unicorns, dragons, and trolls.)

Foliage Flameproofing and Preserving

The most convincing way to dress a scene with foliage is to use real leaves. The problem is that real foliage, once cut, begins to wilt and then dry out. Wilted, dry foliage soon looks convincingly *dead*—and creates a fire hazard besides.

California Flameproofing of Pasadena manufactures a green flameproofing solution for cut natural foliage. This solution also serves to preserve the foliage.

The compound, called #57 Green, is a thick dark olive-green liquid. When a branch is dipped in this preparation, it is coated with a layer of flame-retardant rubber. The flexible skin molds around the surfaces of the foliage, preserving perfectly the leaf shapes, sealing in the plant's moisture to retard the natural drying process. When the foliage finally does dry out, this tough green rubberized coating prevents the leaves from falling off.

#57 Green can also be brushed or sprayed onto the foliage—with large bushes and trees this is the only practical approach.

The formula has a neoprene base, and the manufacturer's label warns that it is "dangerous if taken internally." It would appear from the label that the chemical is otherwise safe to use, with the user taking such standard precautions as washing hands after using the solution and being careful to not let the solution enter the mouth. A respirator should be worn when the chemical is to be sprayed.

The solution must be thinned for spraying, and one coating will not be sufficient then. Repeated applications are required in order for the solution to perform effectively as either a flame retardant or a preservative.

When you want to preserve a leaf, and you need it to last for a long period of time, select a leaf with some thickness and body. Magnolia leaves, lemon leaves, holly, and evergreens such as fir, pine, and spruce have enough thickness to be good prospects. Oak, aspen, and maple are thin in cross section and will soon go limp, even with a neoprene coating.

Here are magnolia leaves being preserved and flameproofed. A thin wire has been twisted onto the stem of each leaf. When the leaf is dipped, the flameproofing solution will coat this joint and make it secure.

The leaves need to be hung up while the flameproofing dries. The leaves should not touch, for the rubber coating will seal leaves together if they are in contact while they dry.

The leaves can be applied after they have dried for a few hours. They can be tied to the branches with the little wires that were applied before dipping. (This method is recommended only for smaller bushes—the time required to dress a large tree would be prohibitive.)

We made two palm trees to contribute to the tropical atmosphere of *The Night of the Iguana*. We made sure they would survive the run of the show with brushed applications of #57 Green.

A Bale of Alfalfa

Bales of alfalfa or straw play a part in several frequently produced plays, including *Green Grow the Lilacs* and *The Matchmaker*, and their musical incarnations, *Oklahoma!* and *Hello, Dolly!*

Real hay bales are inexpensive, but they are also messy, heavy, and hard to flameproof. Fakes are so easy to make that it's sensible to construct them and keep them in stock if you have storage space.

First construct a crate-like form. If you can control the position of the bale on stage, you can leave the bottom open. Note that the edges of the form in the photo are oblique—square edges would produce an unrealistic bale. If the bale is to be more than ornamental, the top surface should be stout enough for an actor to stand on

it. (Building this sturdiness into the frame will also ensure that the finished bale will be suitable for re-use in a later production.)

Cover the frame with any spongy padding material—cotton batting, foam rubber, or rug padding. The ends should be thickly padded to avoid a "flat" appearance.

Use grass mats to cover the form and to give it the appearance of straw. Grass mats are too vibrantly green to pass for cured alfalfa. Mix a gallon of bleach solution consisting of 1 part laundry bleach (such as Clorox) and 3 parts water. A heavy spray with this bleach will change the green to tones of yellow and brown.

These mats can be stapled down in most places; use three-penny nails where the padding is thick.

Tie the bale with jute or sisal hemp. Then give the bale a final spray of bleach, paying special attention to the places where mat edges overlap.

Dressing a Hay Cart

Loading a cart with real hay or straw brings with it the same problems encountered with a real bale of alfalfa: straw is messy, hard to store, and a fire hazard. The following technique, that of constructing straw mats which can be draped or piled, is offered to overcome these objections.

Flameproof about a tenth of a bale of straw. The only way to do this effectively is to immerse the straw in a strong flameproofing solution to thoroughly saturate it.

Allow the straw to dry.

Spread a thin layer of straw on the ground covering an area a little larger than the mat you intend to make. Straw is being spread in the photo to construct a 5' × 7' mat.

Cut a piece of erosion cloth to the desired size (the one in the photo is 5' × 7') and dip it in glue to thoroughly saturate it. Elvanol is a good choice for this because it is inexpensive and dries flexible. At any rate, select a glue that is not stiff or brittle when it dries.

Wring out the surplus glue, but keep the erosion cloth soaked. (This is an operation that calls for old clothes.)

Spread the wet erosion cloth evenly over the bed of straw. An extra pair of hands will be helpful.

The straw will adhere to the underside of the mat and add some thickness to the erosion cloth —and, most important, keep the saturated fabric from sticking to the floor.

Now distribute more of the flameproofed straw (which has been allowed to dry) to completely cover the erosion cloth. Walking on the straw as you perform this operation will help work the glue into the straw fibers. Use your hand as a dipper and sprinkle more glue over this new layer of straw. Imagine yourself doing a sort of war dance (not a shuffle) and stomp the straw, glue, and erosion cloth together. Be organized about this to be sure that the entire area is "stomped." Allow the mat to dry.

After 4 or 5 hours, lift the mat and move it to another location to prevent its sticking to the floor.

Two identical mats were made for this hay cart. One was cut down the middle and used to cover the sides; the other covered the top. The upper mat was draped over a lightweight framework to keep it elevated. A handful of flameproofed straw should be stuffed into any spot that appears too sparse.

Our cart was built and dressed for a production of Shaw's *Saint Joan*.

A piece of business called for an actor to crawl into the straw and go to sleep. The framework with an open interior made this business possible.

This set is from our production of *Brigadoon*. The bed of hay in the shed was made up of a pile of small mattresses covered with a straw mat. The edges of the mat were hidden with a few handfuls of loose straw.

Making Stylized Plant Foliage

Usually your best source for obtaining artificial leaves is a retailer. Artificial florists (well, the *florist* is probably the genuine article) can be found in metropolitan areas in the Yellow Pages under the heading "Artificial." However, you may discover that large-leafed plants will quickly exhaust your prop budget.

The technique detailed here is not very good if you need a highly realistic plant; on the other hand, it's not bad if you need a large stylized or fantasy plant. We found that this need crops up from time to time when designers loosen up their creativity. The foliage shown in progress in these photos was made for *Man of Mode*, but similar gardens have come from our shop for productions of *Little Mary Sunshine* and *The Enchanted*.

You will need a couple of yards of lightweight fabric for this project—something like satin, silk, or a lightweight rayon. This is not to say that you should go out and buy several yards of China silk—that could be more outrageously expensive than the artificial leaves. Perhaps your costume shop has some useful scraps or even used fabric. We were able to recycle a large pillow covering from an earlier production.

Try to find a fabric of an appropriate color. It's better to start with a color that approximates foliage from the beginning; a touch of spray may be useful for adding highlight or shadow to the final leaf, but if you start with an odd-colored fabric and try to change the hue with paint, it is likely that the paint will spoil the texture of the foliage.

Coat the fabric with a liberal application of flex-glue. (The fabric in the photo is so wide that only half its width was coated in the first step.)

The flex-glue will soak into and through the fabric, so be sure to work on a sheet of poly-ethylene or vinyl. The dried glue will not stick to the plastic, thus providing easy separation of the leaves from the work surface when the glue has dried.

The flex-glue will deepen the color of the fabric. If you have the time it is a good idea to test a bit of fabric to be sure that there will be no surprises in store when the glue dries.

Proceed efficiently through the rest of the steps outlined below. You need to finish this job while the glue is still wet, so don't tarry.

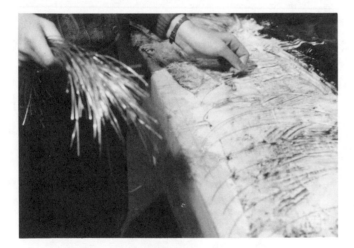

While the glue is still wet, lay wires cut to the intended length of your leaves onto the coated fabric. Each wire will serve as the central vein of a leaf. Almost any soft, inexpensive wire will do. Stove-pipe wire will work well; coat-hanger wire is too stiff. We used an aluminum welding wire cut to 14″ lengths — 12″ to form the vein and 2″ left exposed to make a stem. A curve remained in our wire from having been wound on the spool. We took advantage of this bend, allowing it to define the center of a long, narrow curved leaf.

Lay a second piece of fabric over the first one, creating a sandwich with the wires in the middle. (We were able to fold over the previously un-treated section of our wide piece of fabric to form our sandwich.)

Paint on another coat of flex-glue to saturate the fabric. Leave the project to dry overnight.

The final step in producing the leaves is to cut out the leaf shapes with scissors. The narrow leaf shape that we chose proved to be very economical in that many leaves could be produced from the fabric with a minimum of waste. This is not, however, the only leaf shape possible with this technique.

Oak, philodendron, or rubber plant leaves are a few other possibilities.

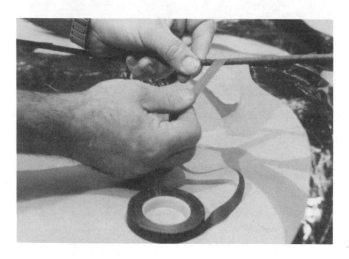

Fashion a stalk from heavy clothesline wire or from a piece of small-diameter metal tubing. Bend the stalk into a slight curve for a realistic look. If the tubing or wire is shiny, cover it with florist's tape or paint it brown, green, or olive.

Attach the leaves to the central stalk by wrapping the stem wire with florist's tape. You may wish to alternate sides of the stalk as you attach the leaves—in some plants more than one leaf grows from the same place on the stalk, in others only one.

If you want a flowering plant, attach one or more blossoms to the top of the stalk. The blossoms may be made of tissue paper, or they may be stolen from a bouquet or from another artificial plant.

A Sapling Tree

Joyce Kilmer admitted to a talent for making poems, but ascribed the making of trees only to a higher authority. Kilmer was no stage techni-cian, for even he, had he only known of the procedure described here, could have produced a passable tree.

The "sapling" pictured here is made from eucalyptus branches. The tree will stand up if you bolt the truncated end to a short but heavy base, such as is used on a lighting standard.

Strip most of the leaves from the branches if you want to simulate a winter tree.

The problem created by using a tree *branch* to simulate a complete tree is that the secondary branches grow from the limb with a natural up-ward curl (botanists call this tendency to seek the sun "heliotropism"). When you stand the branch on end, this curl gives it a windswept appearance.

If, however, you bolt two such branches together, one curving to the east and one to the west, the effect is of a young tree with natural symmetry.

The joint where the two branches come together should be bolted for a firm attachment. Dress the branches with a cosmetic wrapping of muslin where they come together, to disguise the bolted joint. If the muslin is wrinkled as it is applied, it will take on the appearance of bark.

REHEARSAL FURNITURE

The Problem of Rehearsal Furniture

The scene takes place in the DESIGNER*'s office. A meeting has been called to discuss maintenance of the furniture pieces used in the rehearsal rooms. The* PROPERTIES MASTER *is the last to arrive, and is taking a chair.*

TECHNICAL DIRECTOR We're getting complaints about the rehearsal furniture again. It needs to be repaired—again.

FACULTY DESIGNER Why don't we buy some stronger furniture? Maybe something made of metal.

PROPERTIES MASTER *(With a knowing smile)* Yeah? Something like they put in mental and correctional facilities?

TECHNICAL DIRECTOR Sure! Someone must make durable chairs, tables, and sofas.

PROPERTIES MASTER Well, maybe someone should. Last year I talked with the juvenile hall buyer, who put me in touch with the supplier of all the furniture for California state institutions. I brought the catalog with me.

TECHNICAL DIRECTOR Let's take a look at that. *(Business of flipping pages, etc.)* Why, this isn't new, it's made of square metal tubing, but this is the same furniture that our students routinely tear up in the student lounge.

FACULTY DESIGNER This? This is the stuff they use in mental institutions?

PROPERTIES MASTER Yep, it wouldn't stand a chance in a rehearsal room.

TECHNICAL DIRECTOR Rehearsal furniture really takes a beating. I wish I knew how they could be so rough on those pieces.

FACULTY DESIGNER I recently saw a broken chair lying against a broken door frame. I naturally assumed that an actor tried to express rage by throwing the chair through the door.

PROPERTIES MASTER All we have to do then is make the chair heavy enough that it can't be thrown.

FACULTY DESIGNER Naw. If an inspired actor gets an urge to throw a chair, he'll get a friend to help him throw it.

PROPERTIES MASTER Why don't we talk to the acting instructors and see if they can give us any guidelines for what kind of punishment a piece of rehearsal furniture should take.

FACULTY DESIGNER Well, we know it's got to be able to bounce off a door frame. Have you thought about casting it out of rubber?

TECHNICAL DIRECTOR There are a few pieces that have been around a long time. You know the pieces I mean? Those oriental-styled, block-like things. They've been using them for rehearsal cubes.

PROPERTIES MASTER Yes, they were built about 15 years ago for a touring show, and they've survived pretty well. Maybe we should use their basic concept and design a set of rehearsal furniture that will have some longevity.

FACULTY DESIGNER Make a chair that won't self-destruct when it's thrown into a door, and you'll be on the right track.

Rehearsal Furniture

The rehearsal furniture described in this section has been constructed following a design concept used some fifteen years ago for tables and cubes built in our shop for a touring show. In the light of the fact that so many other pieces of rehearsal furniture, some made of wood and some of metal, have been broken, repaired, broken again, and finally discarded—I marvel at the longevity of these pieces which have withstood abusive treatment for so many years and yet are still in service.

This furniture is made of 1 × 3 frames, laminated together in such a manner that they have the strength of 2 × 4s. The frames were assembled so that their members overlapped at the joints, and as these pieces were glued together, the half-lapped splices took on the strength of mortise-and-tenon joints.

Using this construction concept, I've worked out plans for some rugged pieces of rehearsal furniture: a arm chair, a sofa, a rehearsal cube, and a bench.

The instructions given in this section include precise details for measurement and construction. For each piece of furniture there is a cutting list and step-by-step assembly instructions. The value of this section is not in its lengthy explanations, however, but in the overall design concept presented. If you would like to test the soundness of this design concept without being bound by the precise measurements given here, I encourage it as a viable option.

These instructions make repeated reference to the use of glue and staples. The glue can be any good polyvinyl white glue—Elmer's, Weldwood, Willhold, Suregrip, etc. Staples can be replaced by either 1½″ wood screws, 1¼″ drywall screws, or cement-coated nails. If you use nails, fourpenny cement-coated can replace the 1½″ staples, and eightpenny cement-coated can replace the 2″ staples. Do not attempt this construction without glue.

All of the white pine referred to in this section will have an actual thickness of ¾″ rather than 1″ as the lumberyard idiom would lead you to believe (see "lumber" in the glossary for an explanation of this convention). All widths and lengths specified, however, refer to precise measurements and are not to be confused with this jargon notation. This means that these widths cannot be ordered from a lumberyard as a stock size, but must be ripped on a table saw to the exact width specified in the cutting list.

The Rehearsal Chair

Cutting List of All Parts:

1 × 4 white pine:
    one 19½" length

1 × 3 white pine:
    two 21" lengths
    four 19½" lengths

1 × 2¼" white pine:
    two 36" lengths
    two 27" lengths
    one 24" lengths
    two 19¾" lengths
    two 19½" lengths
    two 18" lengths

1 × 2 white pine:
    two 36" lengths
    two 27" lengths
    seven 21" lengths
    five 19½" lengths
    two 17" lengths
    four 14" lengths
    four 12" lengths
    six 7" lengths

1 × 1¼" white pine:
    two 9" lengths

¾" plywood:
    19½" × 19½" for the seat
    21" × 19" for the back

Begin assembly by building the chair seat. Using glue and 2" staples, assemble the two 1 × 3 × 21" pieces alternately with two of the 1 × 3 × 19½" pieces into a square frame with outside dimensions of 21".

Make this frame sturdier by laminating 1″ × 2¼″ pieces inside the 1 × 3s. Again using glue and 1½″ staples, attach the two 1 × 2¼″ × 19½″ pieces to the insides of the 21″ lengths. The 1 × 2¼″ × 18″ pieces should then fit snugly between the 19½″ lengths and should be secured there.

The butt joints will be self-reinforcing, as you can see from this photo. You can also see the ¾″ inset in the frame which will accommodate the plywood seat. The frame is not very strong yet, but it will be after the seat is inserted in the next step.

Use glue and 1½″ wood screws to secure the 19½″ × 19½″ seat into the frame. Set the screws into both the edges and the surface of the seat to

attach each piece of the frame solidly to the plywood and to form the structure into a solid square unit.

Gather up the eight pieces which will form the legs. Four of these will be 27″ long, two 2¼″ wide and two 2″ wide. These will be joined to make the front legs and arm rests. The rear legs and back support are made with four 36″ lengths, two 2¼″ wide and two 2″ wide.

Lay each 2¼″ piece on edge on top of a 2″ piece of the same length, making a rail with a T-shaped cross section. Use glue and 2″ staples to make each rail a secure unit.

It is important that each 2¼″ length be centered with precision, because you will need an offset of exactly ¾″ on each side to execute the next step.

Glue and staple the four 14″ blocks to the bottoms of the legs. Attach these to the two front legs so that either leg is a mirror image of the other. Likewise, attach the two remaining blocks to the back legs so that each is a mirror image of the other. The photo above should clarify this idea.

Now go back to the seat unit. Make a block to serve as a spacer exactly the width of the seat edge. Theoretically this width is 3″, but any variation that may exist must be reflected in the width of the spacer. This spacer will be used to insure a tight fit when the seat and legs are assembled.

A 1 × 2 × 7″ piece is now added to each front leg. As shown in the photo, the spacer is held in place with the right hand until the 7″ piece is glued and stapled in place; then the spacer is removed. The spacer has thus reserved a space of just the right size to accommodate the seat with a tight fit. If all the parts have been fitted together according to plan, there should be a 2″ inset remaining at the top of each front leg, where the arm rest will later be fitted.

The front legs are completed with the addition of two more 7″ blocks on the outside edges of the "T"-rail and two 12″ blocks on the inside of the "T"-rail. The rear legs are assembled in the same fashion, with one variation: there is no 7″ block on the inside of the rear legs.

Now attach the legs to the seat. Apply glue first and fasten the legs with 1½″ screws.

The back (the 21″ × 19″ section of plywood) can now be fitted into place and secured, first with an application of glue and then with 1½″ screws. Now the unit is beginning to look like a chair.

Three pieces make up the top edge of the chair. Two of these are 1 × 2s, measuring 21″ and 19½″ in length, which will have the plywood back sandwiched between them. The third board measures 1 × 2¼″ × 24″; this board is screwed in place on top to cover the upper edge of the plywood back, thus protecting unsuspecting fingers from plywood splinters.

Fasten the 1 × 4 × 19½″ board to the rear of the chair seat. This board will provide a surface to which the lower edge of the plywood back can be attached to keep the plywood from flopping.

The next step calls for eight pre-cut sections of 1 × 2 lumber. The front and rear stretchers are 21″ long, the side stretchers are 19½″ long, and the reinforcement pieces are 17″ and 19½″ long.

Secure the front and rear stretchers to the bottoms of the legs, and then add the side stretchers. Strengthen all the stretchers, making them twice as thick, by attaching the reinforcement pieces with glue and staples.

The legs can be clamped to assure that they remain parallel as the screws are inserted. You may have noticed that there have been no instructions cautioning you to keep the parts of this unit square. This is not an oversight; if the cuts have been made accurately and the joints have been kept tight, a unit this small will turn out very square. The shape of the plywood seat and back will contribute significantly toward keeping the unit square. There is also an absence of cross-bracing in this design. I am certainly aware of the strengths gained with triangle bracing; if you would feel more comfortable adding diagonal braces, by all means add them. The chair on which these instructions are modeled, however, is not showing signs of suffering from the lack of cross-bracing, even after fifteen years of rugged use.

Next secure one of the 1 × 3 × 19½″ pieces to each side of the leg frames, alongside of the seat.

In this closeup view of the underside of the chair, you can see how the pieces nest together. The arrangement of the framing members is such that each piece adds strength to each adjacent piece.

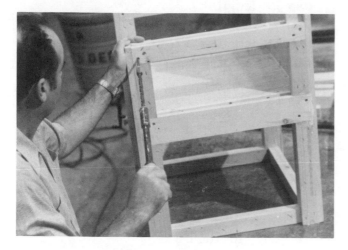

Assemble the remaining pieces to make arms for the chair. Attach two 1 × 2 × 21″ pieces to each side of the chair, to make a frame for the armrest.

Now you can staple a 1 × 2¼″ × 19¾″ board in in place on each side to cap the top of each armrest. Now fill the open spaces in the upper portion of the rear legs with the last two small pieces of wood from the cutting list.

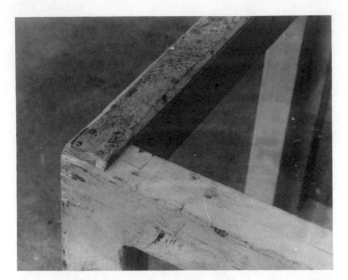

Add a strap of ¼" plywood to the bottom of each side stretcher. This further ties the pieces together and provides a secure foundation with fewer points in contact with the floor. It also raises the unit ¼" so the seat will be 18" above the floor.

A lot of spackling and sanding, and a coat of paint, will make the chair ready for use.

The Rehearsal Sofa

The rehearsal sofa is a longer version of the chair design that has just been detailed. The two are so similar that the cutting list is almost the same. You will notice that the seat, back, and spreaders which run the full width are necessarily longer, and that seven pieces have been added to form the support frame in the center of the seat. Apart from these alterations, however, the lumber and construction method are the same.

Cutting List of All Parts:

1 × 4 white pine:
  one 55½" length

1 × 3½" white pine:
  two 22" lengths
  two 19½" lengths
  two 57" lengths

1 × 2¾" white pine:
  two 55½" lengths
  two 18" lengths

1 × 2¼" white pine:
  one 60" length
  one 57" length
  one 55½" length
  two 36" lengths
  two 27" lengths
  two 19¾" lengths
  two 17" lengths
  two 14¼" lengths
  two 18" lengths

1 × 2 white pine:
  two 57" lengths
  two 34" lengths
  two 36" lengths
  four 27" lengths
  two 25" lengths
  four 21" lengths
  two 19½" lengths
  two 18" lengths
  two 17" lengths
  four 14" lengths
  four 9" lengths
  six 7" lengths

¾" plywood:
  19½" × 55½" for the seat
  18" × 57" for the back

The sofa is so much like the chair that detailed assembly instructions would be redundant. The photos show how the center frame support fits under the seat, and how the longer pieces expand the basic plan of the chair into a 5' sofa that will seat two people comfortably.

Consideration has been given to the problem of stacking rehearsal furniture for storage when not in use. A rehearsal cube and bench will fit neatly between the arms of the sofa for storage (as shown in the lower photo on page 209).

The Rehearsal Cube

Cutting List of All Parts:

1 × 2¼" white pine:
    four 18" lengths
    four 17" lengths
    four 15" lengths
    four 13½" lengths
    four 12½" lengths
    four 12" lengths

1 × 1½" white pine:
    four 17" lengths
    four 12½" lengths

¾" plywood:
    18" × 18" for the seat

A rehearsal cube is made up of four strong frames and a plywood top. As with the chair and sofa, we will assemble the frames in such a way that each piece is helping to support the adjacent pieces at the joints.

The front and rear frames are identical, and each is made of eight pieces.

Horizontal members:
two 1 × 2¼″ × 18″
two 1 × 2¼″ × 13½″

Vertical members:
two 1 × 1½″ × 17″
two 1 × 2¼″ × 12½

The pieces are assembled with glue and 1½″ staples into a frame as shown. Keep all joints tight and retain a ¾″ setback on the outside of each vertical edge.

The two end frames are also identical to each other. Each is made up of eight pieces:

Horizontal members:
two 1 × 2¼″ × 15″
two 1 × 2¼″ × 12″

Vertical members:
two 1 × 2¼″ × 17″
two 1 × 1½″ × 12½″

These frames are assembled in the same fashion as the front and back frames, using glue and staples. Again, a ¾″ setback must be retained on the vertical parts of the frames to allow for the proper fit when the end frames are secured to the front and back frames.

Glue and clamp the frames together, and then measure the cube before stapling. The photo shows the cube lying on one of its sides. The bottom is facing you, showing how the small end frame fits between the front and back frames. You should now have a cube which measures 18″ in all dimensions except height; the height should be 17″ at this stage of construction.

The notched frames offer many surfaces to be stapled; make the cube as secure as possible by driving staples through all of them.

Add the lid to the framework before the glue has dried. The plywood lid will serve to square the cube if any of its members are slightly askew. If the lid is not flush all the way around, but you know it was cut square, force the frame to accommodate it. Be sure to use glue to secure the lid before stapling it in place.

The exposed end grain of the plywood should be filled with wood putty, sanded, and painted to eliminate the danger of splinters.

Here is a photo of the three finished pieces of rehearsal furniture, showing relative proportions.

The Rehearsal Bench

The bench is very much like the cube in design and construction, but it is twice as long.

Cutting List of All Parts:

1 × 2¼″ white pine:
   four 36″ lengths
   six 17″ lengths
   two 16½″ lengths
   four 15″ lengths
   six 12½″ lengths
   two 12¼″ lengths
   four 12″ lengths

1 × 1½″ white pine:
   six 17″ lengths
   four 12½″ lengths

¾″ plywood:
   18″ × 36″ for the seat

Assemble the long frames first. Each consists of seven pieces of lumber:
   two rails, each 1 × 2¼″ × 36″
   three stiles, each 1 × 2¼″ × 12½″
   two vertical slats, each 1½″ × 17″

Lay out and square up the rails and stiles the same as you would in any scenic construction. Fit the slats into place, and secure all members except the center stile with glue and staples. The center stile should not be fastened into place yet. Make sure there is a full ¾″ setback when each slat is attached.

The two end frames each consist of the following eight components:

Horizontal members:
   two 1 × 2¼″ × 12″
   two 1 × 2¼″ × 15″

Vertical members:
   two 1 × 2¼″ × 17″
   two 1 × 1½″ × 12½″

Assemble the end frames by overlapping the horizontal and vertical pieces. Use glue and 1½″ staples to secure each joint. Again, each edge should have a ¾″ setback; if the pieces of lumber have been cut accurately, the setback will automatically assume the correct depth.

The center frame is made up of eight pieces:

Horizontal members:
  two 1 × 2¼″ × 12″
  two 1 × 2¼″ × 16½″

Vertical members:
  two 1 × 2¼″ × 17″
  two 1 × 2¼″ × 12¼″

The center frame is assembled with no setback.

The end frames should be glued and placed between the longer front and back frames. Clamp the unit tight and secure it with 2″ staples. Drive the staples into the joints from both directions.

Secure the center stile, which was left unfastened earlier, by gluing and stapling it to the center frame.

Fit the plywood lid in place squared with the sides, and fasten it with glue and 2″ staples.

Finish the bench by applying wood putty to the exposed ends of the plywood, and then sanding and painting the unit.

If you have followed the measurements given here, the cube, bench, and sofa will nest as shown for compact storage.

RUNNING WATER

The need for running water on stage is not unusual. A practical sink may be called for in any production that includes kitchen fixtures in its setting. The climactic scene in *The Miracle Worker* requires a working water pump. A director or designer may want to have rain falling outside the doors and windows of the settings of any of a number of plays. There are at least four ways of making water flow on stage to fill these various needs.

The easiest way is to connect a hose to an off-stage faucet to bring water from the city water supply, run the hose on stage, and adapt the hose connection to serve your on-stage plumbing. When an actor turns on the faucet, water flows. The disadvantage to this system is that a hose is susceptible to breaking or leaking. And if you do spring a leak, an awful lot of the city's water supply can end up on stage before anyone detects the leak and runs to the tap to shut it off.

Gravity-Fed Water Supply

A safer way to provide a water supply is to rig a 5-gallon bucket with a gravity feed.

The pipe threads of a water faucet can be adapted with standard plumbing parts (available at any hardware store) to be fed from a small-diameter copper tube. Solder a similar piece of tubing to the bottom of the bucket, and connect the two copper tubes with a length of rubber hose that fits tightly over them.

Rig the bucket behind the set, well above the level of the sink faucet. Pour a gallon of water into the bucket and gravity will cause the water to flow when the sink faucet is opened. The water flow will be steady and quite acceptable. If a leak develops in this system, no more than a gallon of water can spill onto the stage — messy, but not a disaster.

Running Water — Under Pressure

Here is a variation on the same theme. Rig a garden insecticide sprayer to the faucet and you can pump up a little pressure to force the water to flow when the sink faucet valve is opened. The sprayer can be stored either behind the "kitchen" wall or under the sink. This device will give you running water under pressure, and you still need not work with more than a gallon.

A Recirculating Electric Pump

A recirculating electric pump can keep a fountain operating smoothly for a long time. These pumps are used in the "real world" for this purpose; they work just as well on stage.

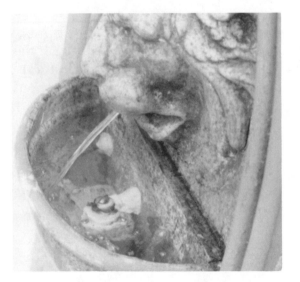

This photo shows the electric pump lying in the catch basin. The water level must be high enough to cover the pump, but since the water recirculates, it cannot overflow.

Here is a side view of the scenery on which the fountain is mounted. A hose must connect the pump to the gargoyle spout. The pump's electrical cord must also pass through the scenery. The holes accommodating the hose and the cord must then be sealed to make them watertight. There are many caulking compounds that can be used to make this seal, since the joint is not under pressure.

The disadvantage of fountains on stage such as this one is the sound of falling water. There are ways of softening the sound—with netting, rags, or sponges in the catch basin—but the sound almost always remains audible and distracting. This is a problem that should be discussed in an early production meeting to determine how nec-

essary the effect really is. I can testify to the frustration incurred by the crew in a production where such a fountain was rigged at the behest of the designer, where various exercises in softening the sound of falling water were attempted, and where the effect was ultimately cut by the director who found the noise too distracting.

This pump, used in *The Miracle Worker*, represents an adaptation of the recirculating pump. The original pumping mechanism has been removed, leaving only the cast iron shell. The handle no longer operates a valve; instead, each time the handle is operated, it makes temporary contact with a microswitch which has been wired in series with an electric water pump. At each stroke of the pump handle, the switch is closed momentarily and a stream of water spurts through the tubing and out the mouth of the pump.

The electric pump is housed in the catch basin, where it must be completely submerged in water. It only takes about half a gallon of water to keep

this pump operating and recirculating. It was not difficult to keep the tubing and electrical connection hidden inside the hollow pump housing.

Rain Effects

The traditional method of making rain fall outside of a window is to use a pair of water troughs and rig them so the water falls from the upper one to the lower one.

Make the upper trough from a horizontal rain gutter. Seal up both ends and drill lots of ⅛" holes in the bottom. The lower trough can be made of wood lined with polyethylene if it is only expected to last the run of one production; if you want to build a stock prop to be kept in storage, line the wood with sheet metal. Make the lower trough about 14" wide so it will catch not only the falling "raindrops," but also their resultant splash. The trough should be about 7" deep so a water pump can be submerged beneath the water line.

The pump lifts the water up and into the upper gutter. The water then falls through the perforations, in the form of small droplets, back into the lower trough, and the pump recirculates the water back to the top.

This effect is only effective when the audience can see it! Frequently the area behind the window is too dark or is shielded by drapes or curtains. In these instances it is helpful to open the curtains wide and rig a special spotlight, from a side position, focused on the plane of the falling raindrops. If it is not possible to open the curtains, then it is probably advisable to not attempt the effect as it will not be seen.

This device also makes a convincing pitter-patter sound which adds to the visual effect and is sometimes even more impressive than the raindrops that can be seen.

A very simple but also very effective method of depicting rainfall is to outfit a window with acetate panes, and to spray water onto them, using a spray bottle or insecticide sprayer (the pump-up variety) from a position out of sight lines. The water gathers and runs in highly visible little rivulets. This suggestion of rain can be more visually effective than the effect of falling raindrops which the audience cannot see.

STAGE MONEY

Real money is so familiar to us that it is difficult to fake it on stage. We are all so intimate with its color, sound, texture, and weight that we know when we've encountered the real McCoy. You can "see" the weight of coins in a coin purse; they have a distinctive shine and glitter; they jingle in pockets; they have a distinctive size that must be approximated, especially in intimate theaters. Paper money has a color, size, and texture that we recognize from a distance. We can almost tell from its smell when we are being duped with a stage counterfeit. Of course, aesthetic distance is inversely proportional to the degree of realism required of stage money in a larger auditorium.

Coins

Toy stores sell plastic coins which will stand fairly close visual inspection, but they have a plastic sound. If you need a stuffed money bag with a convincing weight and jingle, and the actual coins won't be seen, metal washers may be the simple and reliable answer. But if the coins will be removed from the purse, washers do have holes through them that, even from a distance, make them look like washers.

Metal slugs the size of nickels can be harvested from a site where homes or offices are under construction. Wherever electrical outlet boxes are being installed, these slugs, called "knock-outs," litter the floors. If you visit an apartment complex at just the right time, you can pick up a ten-year supply in ten minutes.

Molière's *The Miser* calls for a treasure chest filled with gold coins. The chest can be filled with poker chips (of the familiar red, white, and blue variety) that have been spray-painted gold. The coins are not handled much, so the unconvincing plastic sound is not objectionable. Besides, gold does not have the kind of "ring" that silver does.

Our production of *A Comedy of Errors* included a piece of business in which a handful of coins was thrown at a merchant. The show was played on a raked stage, and, predictably, the coins rolled down the rake and into the auditorium. Did it every time; it couldn't be helped. Then we filed flat spots on the edges of the coins, and that pretty much solved the problem. The audience was far enough away that they couldn't detect the flattened edges. But then, as the scene would play, the audience was distracted by the question: "Why don't those coins roll down the ramp?" There are times you just can't win.

In an arena theater the best thing to use for real coins is real coins. We once supplied a 50-cent roll of pennies for use in an on-stage poker game. At that show's strike, after a two-week run, 37 pennies were returned. Where can you buy or rent acceptable prop coins for thirteen cents? Dimes and quarters sometimes walk away, but the lowly penny seems not to be afflicted with wanderlust.

We needed stacks of gold coins for a production of *Molière and the Cabal*. The prop crew head came up with the useful idea of purchasing foreign copper coins from a currency exchange.

Here is the bag of unsorted copper coins that we obtained from the International Currency Exchange in Los Angeles. We bought 3 pounds of foreign coins for $6 — probably not a good exchange rate monetarily, but we were happy with the deal because the bag contained so many British and Mexican copper coins which were about the same size as American quarters.

We gave the coins a bath in Tarn-X to remove tarnish and make the coins literally "bright as a penny."

It must be admitted, though, that copper coins, whether polished or bright, look like copper coins. No amount of cleaning makes copper look like gold.

If you want coins to pass for gold, their color must be altered. This can be accomplished with a light misting of gold spray paint. A heavy coat is not necessary; a quick dusting is all you need.

If you need an even larger quantity of gold coins, hot-glue stacks of ¼" (or larger) washers together, and cap each stack with a real coin. Spray each stack with a light mist of gold paint.

Paper Money

A vast quantity of bills in large denominations plays a featured role in *Everything in the Garden*. Stacks of bills are found all over the set as the play progresses, and each discovery is significant to the development of the plot.

We needed especially good fakes, because the show was to be played in the round in a very small theater. Playgoers in the front row would probably be able to read the face values of the bills. Using real currency was out of the question because of the quantity needed. Play money from a toy store was no good; the quality and color gave it away as phony. It occurred to us that magicians use high-quality fakes in money-producing tricks — but magic dealers informed us that the Treasury Department had cracked down and confiscated these bills.   There's no sense in having your inventory liable to confiscation, so the magic suppliers no longer kept fake money on their shelves. It had been removed — at least temporarily, until the political climate shifted.

Our search led us next to a property-rental house that deals with motion-picture studios, where we found that we could *rent* counterfeit currency of a very high quality. (We never did find out why we could hire fake bills but not purchase them.) Further research brought to our attention a printing company, Earl Hayes Press, that prints extensively for the motion picture in-dustry. This company prints bottle labels, Wells Fargo signs, vintage newspapers (in several lan-guages), and...high-quality stage currency.

Good printing is not cheap, but it beats the cost of using real money. So we acquired our prop cash and the show went well.

(We were cautioned by Earl Hayes Press that we could incur the wrath of the Treasury Depart-ment by trying to pass these notes off as the real thing off stage. We respect the intent of the law. But if the Feds really think this currency would pass for genuine, they must think this is a nation of near-sighted fools. Hayes prints convincing stage money — but not *that* convincing!)

Do-It-Yourself Stage Money

The illustrations here and on the next page are intended to serve as "originals" that you can reproduce on a copy machine. They capture the flavor of legal tender without any of the actual wording and without specifying a denomination. They were made by cutting and pasting scraps of certificates and awards, with a little pen-and-ink work. If you encounter the obstacles we did in trying to acquire stage money, you will appreciate these mock-ups. It is against federal law to copy real money in this fashion.

These "plates" were designed for reproduction on a machine that will copy on both sides of a sheet of paper. You will need to be careful in aligning front and back—but even the Bureau of Printing and Engraving isn't always perfect!

U.S. Currency is printed in green on the reverse, of course, so you will have to treat the copies with a wash of paint until you attain the right shade of green.

Foreign Currency

Most people are aware that foreign money is different from ours in that it is larger and sometimes a different color. These originals offer a different size; you can supply the color with colored pencils or Highlighter felt-tip markers. We used this design for rubles in two different shows. Russian currency is often needed for incidental business in Chekhov's plays, and it is an important prop in *The Inspector General*.

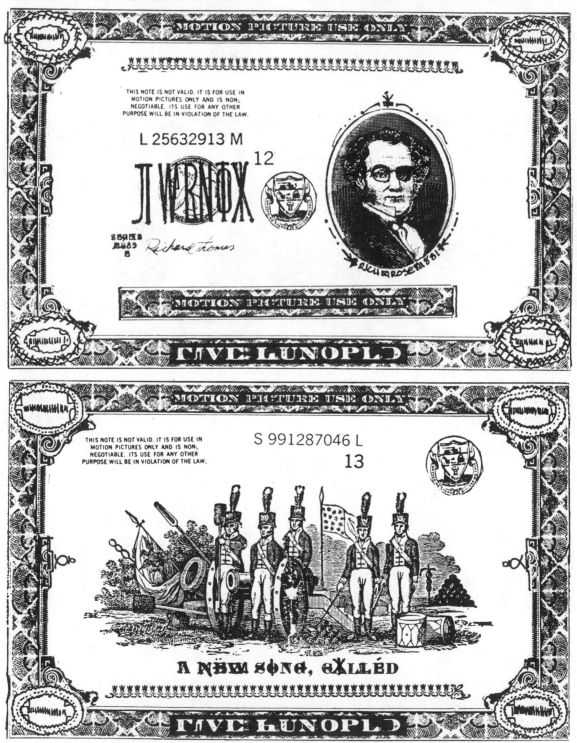

SIMULATING STAINED GLASS

For a good many years, I knew that anytime I was called upon to produce stained glass, I was in trouble. I was never satisfied with either the staining medium or the lead lines. A dye that would adhere to glass was not readily available. (Well, lamp dip was available, but in a limited number of colors, and it was hard to work with.)

I could find no putty that would stick to glass, so I made the lead lines with string, cord, or tape — or painted them on. All the results were very unsatisfactory.

In recent years, this dilemma has been resolved by (of all things) the hobby market. Such a popularity for simulated leaded windows has sprung up among hobby enthusiasts that hobby shops and crafts suppliers have been motivated to devise several products to meet the need. The products are inexpensive and convenient, and the results are highly presentable.

This section will take you through the steps of producing a leaded window, and propose some materials for this purpose.

Laying Out the Window

First you must make a full scale drawing of your window design on paper.

The drawing must be done full-size. Butcher paper is available in large sizes and is a good choice for this drawing.

Don't be content with a beautifully rendered pencil sketch of your window; it probably won't be adequate. You can draw delicate lines with a pencil, but you may not be able to reproduce all the detail in the leading. Small grapes, facial features, or veins in leaves are easily sketched in pencil, but achieving this detail in the thicker lines of the leading is a different matter.

The leading lines must be laid out in full width so you don't fool yourself as to what can be achieved.

You will lay a sheet of "glass" over this paper plan. Because of the danger of breakage, real glass is almost never used on stage; Plexiglas or acrylic should be substituted. Thin plastic sheets are marginally cheaper than glass, anyway.

The plastic sheet must be cleaned thoroughly to remove any oils, fingerprints, or anything else that might interfere with the application of dyes.

Make Your Own Leading Paste

It was a red-letter day in 1978 when I discovered a "secret formula" for concocting a water-base lead-line mixture. A scenic artist from one of the Hollywood studios put this recipe together, but was guarded with his secret. The formula is so simple that, once you know it, you wonder why you didn't think of it yourself.

These are the ingredients needed to mix your own leading paste: clear vinyl acrylic paint, white glue, metallic pigment, and powdered graphite.

Mix equal parts of white glue and clear vinyl acrylic paint. Some manufacturers call the latter vinyl glaze. It's the same stuff you apply to painted scenery to give it a gloss. The white glue can be Elmer's, Wilhold, or any polyvinyl glue.

Add aluminum powder and graphite to the glue–paint mixture until the solution becomes a thin paste. The aluminum powder should be pigment quality—such as you might mix with bronzing liquid to make aluminum paint. The graphite recommended is available in several grades for use as a lubricant in industrial machining. Actually, the graphite is an optional ingredient whose function is to make the paste a little darker.

Add black acrylic paint to taste. Without a touch of black, the leading paste will probably be too light — more like aluminum than lead. You can add a little black until you feel that the mixture has more of a leaden look.

Strain the mixture through a sheet of screen wire.

Hobby shops stock a commercially-prepared product called "Window Leading." I don't know its formula, but I bet it's not far off from that outlined above.

Leading the Lines

Squirt the leading paste onto the plastic pane (laid out on top of the paper plan), following the lines of the plan.

You can do this using any plastic squirt bottle — a ketchup squeeze bottle or an empty bottle of white glue can be used. The operation is like decorating a cake with a tube full of chocolate icing.

A few years ago, the best material you could get commercially for simulating leading lines came ready to use in a squirt tube. It was an aluminum-colored silicone caulking. This material is still available from hardware stores and building suppliers. Silicone caulking does adhere well to plastic panes, but...clean-up is next to impossible, and there is no margin for error. If you squeeze out a line too wide or too narrow, because you have moved your hand too slow or too fast, or because you're nervous or you took a step or you bumped your hand or sneezed, you can't just remove the part of the line that's wrong and then move on. No, silicone caulking is too messy for that; the whole line must be removed — completely removed — very carefully cleaned right up to where it touches any adjacent line. And if you aren't careful when you reach the adjacent line, and you smear a little bit of *that,* you'll have to remove it, too. But why deal with this kind of frustration, when the water-base paste is so easy to mix?

Mistakes do occur from time to time. This rose got lumpy when the artist got sloppy.

It takes a lot of rags to remove a bad line. Clean-up is messy, but...

...since the paste is water-soluble, clean-up is possible.

Here's the improved "leading."

We needed a pair of stained-glass windows which were to be mirror images of each other. In order to produce the reversed image, we turned the paper pattern over and re-traced the design. Another window pane could then be laid over the new pattern and taped in place, and the lead lines could be applied.

Allow 5 to 6 hours of drying time before you handle the "leaded glass," lay a straight-edge

over the leading, or touch the finished lines for any reason.

If your pattern contains a row of small square panes, lay a straight-edge directly on the dried work and use it as a guide to apply the leading perpendicular to the first set of lines. Squirt the paste alongside of the straight-edge, but *not actually touching it*. Any contact of the paste with the straight-edge will result in a serious flaw when the straight-edge is removed.

Staining the Plastic Panel

Clean the plastic pane again, to remove any trace of oil, before you begin to apply the dye.

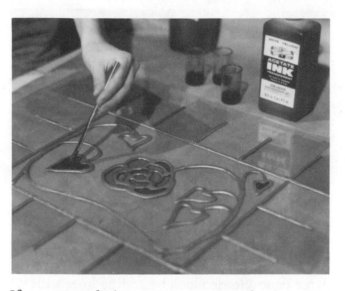

There are many stains and dyes on the market that can be used to color the leaded panes. Acetate inks are available in many colors; these are water-soluble and can be applied with a paint brush or, if you prefer, with an airbrush.

If you want darker or more saturated colors, use the glass lines as "levees" to contain pools of color until the ink dries.

A lacquer-base stain called "Crystal Craze" is available from hobby shops. It works best when applied with an airbrush, and it dries quickly. The name refers to its tendency to crystallize as it dries, giving texture to your pane as well as color-

ing it.

Another option you may wish to consider is fogging the pane with "Glass Frosting." This preparation has the effect of giving the pane a pearly translucency (and thus less transparency) which may be desirable for some applications. Spraying the frosting through a stencil gives the look of patterned milk glass.

Making a Polyester Window Pane

When a translucent pane is desirable, the following technique is recommended. The result is a good substitute for the pebbled acetate panes sometimes used in shower doors and office windows. A window up to 12' wide can be made of this material quickly and inexpensively; the finished window will be fragile, but no more fragile than real glass.

The material is nonwoven polyester cloth — a very thin fabric, about the weight of butcher paper. It is sold under various names, including "Pellon" and "Vantex," and can be purchased in rolls 12' wide for less than $1 per running yard. You can stretch it on a window frame and staple it in place. The synthetic cloth must be stretched tight, because it will not shrink at all during the following steps.

Coat the stretched polyester fabric with catalyzed laminating resin. As you work the fluid into the fabric, the white fibers in the fabric will become translucent.

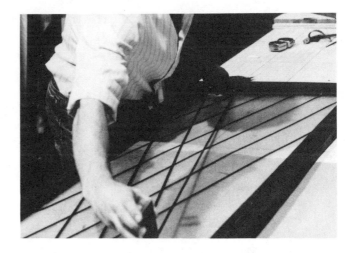

When the material has dried, you can give the large pane a leaded look by adding lines with ¼" artist's matting tape.

The polyester pane can also be colored with acetate inks or dyes. We found that water-base inks can be troublesome because of a tendency to form droplets and puddles rather than spreading evenly. It was as if we were spreading water on an oily surface. We got the ink to behave by adding a few drops of liquid detergent to the ink. The soap reduced the surface tension and allowed for better spreading action.

Be careful about adding too much soap. A drop or two will "condition" an ounce of ink. Four to six drops will be enough for a juice-glass full of dye.

TEXTURES

Distressing Wood

patina (pat′ə·nə) [It., from Lat., ''plate''] *n.* **1.** A green or brown corrosion that develops on the surfaces of copper and copper alloys (such as bronze) as a result of oxydation. **2.** Any surface of ancient or antique appearance produced by age and use.

Our goal in this section is to give wood the appearance that its surface has weathered the storms of time.

The British term for removing the ''newness'' of any property item is ''breaking down.'' In the American theater, the traditional term for the same process is ''distressing.'' So much for the linguistics lesson; let's distress some wood.

If the audience will be separated from the wood by some distance, the job of aging the wood can be made simple. The square edges of the wood can be modified with a band saw so the wood doesn't appear to be fresh from the lumber mill. Then a painting technique to suggest a coarse wood grain can be used. A fine spatter of dark paint can produce worm holes almost as effectively as taking the time to drill them all.

A rustic effect can be given to smooth milled wood by treating the edges with a draw knife. Even more dimensional detail is possible if a hatchet is used instead of a knife — but if you use a hatchet, exercise controlled caution rather than hacking with uncontrolled abandon.

Another effective way of removing the ''new'' look is to beat the wooden surface with a chain. A tire chain is an especially good tool on soft wood; the same metal spikes that grab the ice on a frozen road will grab at the wood and loosen chunks of the grain as you belabor the wood.

Torch and Brush Weathering Technique

Soft wood can be given a convincing weathered look with a torch and wire brush. The results are very realistic; the method is very easy, very fast, and very messy.

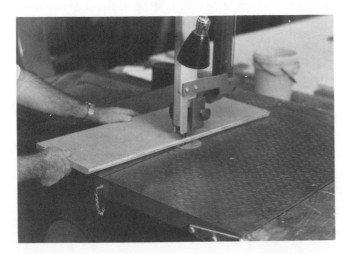

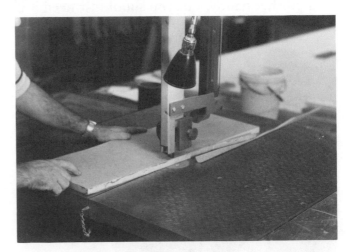

Use a band saw to remove the square edges of a piece of lumber. Make the first irregular cut with the wood held flat on the saw table; then tilt the board at a slight angle for subsequent cuts. The tilt gives a bevel to the edge of the wood and removes any remaining suggestion of squareness.

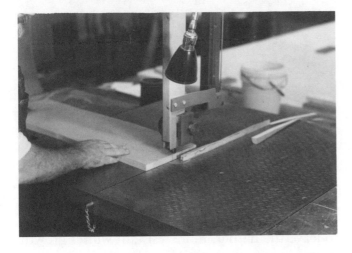

Don't neglect the ends of the board. Ends of boards get weathered, too.

Once the square edges are gone, it's time to burn the board. Use an acetylene welding torch or a propane hand torch to sear the surface of the wood. Apply the torch aggressively; the idea is to reduce about ⅛″ of the wood surface to ash. Keep the torch moving to prevent the danger of the wood bursting into flames.

Some common sense is in order with operations requiring a torch. Work outside in a clear space away from any combustible materials or flammable fumes. It's a good idea to keep a fire extinguisher handy, but you shouldn't need it if you have followed the instructions given here.

The photos show this work being done with the board supported on a wooden sawhorse; the sawhorse was never even scorched. If the wood sustains a blaze, it will be because the torch was held too long in one spot. You should be able to blow the flame out and continue.

Keep working the wood until a heavy crust of ash covers the entire surface. Pay particular attention to the end grain. Aside from the fire hazard, you will see that the amount of smoke and soot produced by this process is another good reason to do the work in the open air—generating that much smoke indoors would pose a respiratory threat and make the shop smell pretty nasty as well.

Now resign yourself to getting dirty. Attack the wood with a wire brush, running the brush along the grain of the board. The goal here is to scrape away the softer summer growth of the wood, which was more easily charred by the torch, and to leave the harder, more resistant winter growth standing out in relief. When you have finished, the board should have a color, texture, and finish in keeping with the second definition of "patina."

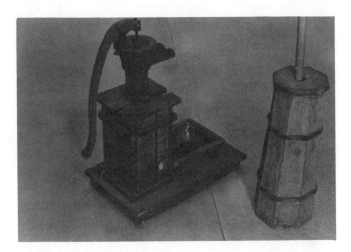

The pump and churn shown here were distressed with the torch and wire brush technique. The wood surface can be sealed, so that the ash no longer rubs off, by rubbing the wood with paste wax or linseed oil.

Marbleizing

Perhaps when you were five years old and in kindergarten, you made gift book markers with a technique like the one that follows. Or perhaps this technique is entirely new to you.

Begin with a container you don't mind getting stained, and fill it almost full with tap water.

Dribble a small amount of oil-base enamel paint (*not* latex-base) into the water. The paint won't mix with the water, but floats and swirls on the surface.

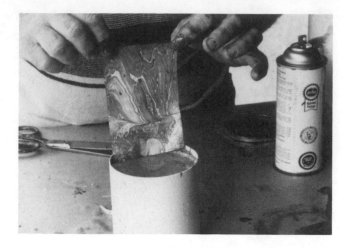

Dip a strip of dry paper into the center of the paint slick. The paint will adhere to the paper as the paper is immersed. Immediately withdraw the paper strip, and you can almost hear those little voices: ''See how pretty!'' ''Won't Grandma like this?'' And the teacher, wearily: ''Oh dear, let's get that paint off those precious little fingers...''

That's the way the kids do it, and it works well for them. If the teacher is adventurous, they might also be allowed to dip pencils into the marbleizing bath. This method is on too small a scale, however, to decorate anything larger than bookmarks and pencils.

For larger work, you need to build a vessel

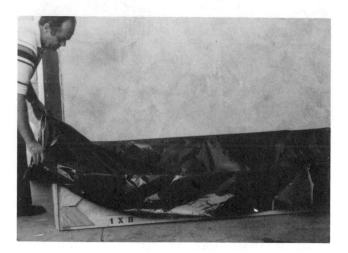

resembling a wading pool. For large-scale marbleizing, a shallow reservoir is acceptable. Unless you're willing to sacrifice your swimming pool for the project (I wouldn't sacrifice mine), you can slide the object you're decorating sideways into the water, or maybe just lay the object on the surface of the water.

To construct the ''tank,'' just nail some 1' flats around a base. We built the one shown around a 4' × 8' sheet of ¾" plywood. We intended ours to be a temporary structure; double-headed nails were used, and all the parts were reusable afterwards. This frame does not have to be terribly strong. The water will be only a few inches deep, so the pressure on the sides will not be great.

A polyethylene drop cloth can serve as a liner to keep the frame watertight. (The day we built the tank in the photo, the wind was blowing and it was necessary to staple the edges of the plastic down. On a calm day just laying the plastic sheet over the frame should suffice.) Fill the tank with water to a depth of 3" to 4".

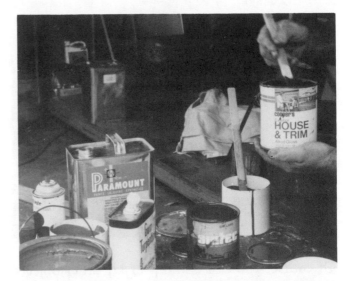

Pour a small quantity of oil-base paint onto the surface of the water. The paint should behave as it did in the kindergarteners' pail: the paint will not mix with the water but will be buoyed up to the surface where it will spread in varying thicknesses and in patterns. You should have no trouble creating a large random pattern suitable for marbleizing.

Some experimentation on your part may be required. Oil-base paints are not all formulated the same, and so they can't all be expected to react the same way when they come in contact with water. Sometimes thinning the paint will help in obtaining the desired results. It would be nice to be able to report that every brand will yield the same results, but it just isn't so. One preschool art director insists that only Testors brand model enamel will work with this technique. We have tried Testors, and the results were excellent—but other brands work just as well. You can even spray aerosol enamels onto the water's surface.

Once you have found workable paints, you can drizzle two colors in the water around each other. The blending of the two colors will be minimal, and you can get an attractive two-tone pattern.

Lay or scoop the dry paper into the wet paint slick. As the paper comes in contact with the paint, the color will adhere in a wonderfully marble-like pattern.

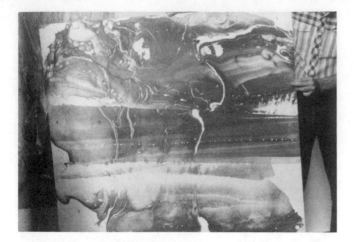

Though you have some control over the colors in your pattern, there is no way to effectively control the patterns themselves. But this marbleizing system is so simple, and paper so inexpensive, that the best solution is to repeat the operation, adding paint as needed, until you achieve a pattern that pleases you.

Of course, you can also dip or lay other objects into the water, as the kids did with their pencils. Wood that has been base-painted takes this marbleizing technique well. If you're not happy with the results, just re-paint the object (water-base scene paint will work fine), let it dry, and dip it again. The quality of the finished work depends chiefly on the limits of your patience.

Glare Reduction

Reynolds Wrap?

DIRECTOR (*Giving notes after a technical rehearsal*) What are you using for glass in that upstage mirror? It looks like a piece of tin. I mean, don't you know what a mirror looks like? Really! The whole thrust of this production has been for realism, and now we have a piece of Reynolds Wrap hanging in that frame.

PROPERTY MASTER It's aluminized Mylar.

(Lights fade; when they restore, it is the next day)

DIRECTOR (*Giving notes after first dress*) —And that mirror. . .I know it's a real mirror now, but why is it so fogged down?

PROPERTY MASTER It's been soaped down to reduce reflection.

DIRECTOR Well, it doesn't look right. Soap should make it look clean—and it looks dirty. Like it should be hanging in a haunted house. All it lacks is the cobweb machine. Can't you afford some glass wax? I can bring some from home.

PROPERTY MASTER We have glass cleaner.

(Lights fade; when they restore, it is the next day)

DIRECTOR (*Giving notes after second dress*) Oh yes, that mirror. You know, the one hanging up center—well, you sure spiffied that up, didn't you? I've never seen anything so distracting. I spent the whole evening watching myself. I mean, it looked like a three-act play about a director taking notes. Really! Isn't there something you can do?

PROPERTY MASTER I can spray it down again.

(Lights fade; when they restore, it is the next day)

DIRECTOR (*Giving notes after final dress*) —And here's that mirror again. . .I don't know what to do about that mirror. It's making more trouble than it's worth, I'll tell you that. Now it looks like a smoggy day in beautiful downtown Burbank. Well, it doesn't look like a mirror at all, that's what. You've done everything else so well, it seems a shame to spoil the whole effect by allowing this one shabby piece.

PROPERTY MASTER I thought the aluminized Mylar looked best.

DIRECTOR I guess so. *(Heavy sigh)* Goodness.

The control of audience attention is, without question, one of the big concerns in a production. The director's purpose is to focus this attention on the telling of a story. The designers must all cooperate in this endeavor, emphasizing physical elements that the director deems important and de-emphasizing elements that he sees as less important.

The viewer's focus, as he looks at the stage picture, largely depends on the contrasts that the picture presents. The eye will be attracted to and will follow whatever is easiest to see. Usually this should be an actor who is moving the plot along toward its conclusion. However, if the brightest and most eye-catching thing on the stage is one of the elements that the designers should have de-emphasized, then the design becomes counterproductive.

This section will deal briefly with ways in which a properties man can assist the director by removing visual distractions.

The Use of White on Stage

I once worked with a director who was so sensitive to the distractions of white that he made it a policy that white was *never* to be seen on stage in one of his productions. A flower could be yellow or pink, but not white. A tablecloth would have to be dyed beige or light blue or some other pastel shade; bedsheets were treated the same way. Dinnerware had to have a touch of color — the designers could pick the color, but white would not do. Even a bottle of milk had to look like it was mostly cream.

One problem with removing all white from a stage picture is that anything that *has* to be white takes on undue importance — a cold-cream jar or a stick of chalk practically glows. But I include this mention of the director's obsession because he had a real point. There was truth in what he said, even if he carried his zeal to an extreme. When an actor's shirt is changed from white to blue, for example, the effect is as if the lighting designer had increased the light level on the actor's face.

The Problem of Light-Colored Furniture

A light-colored sofa can create so much glare that no actor sitting on it can be clearly seen. For this reason, fabrics with a sheen, though they may be beautiful in themselves, should not be used for on-stage upholstery. If you bring a piece of furniture of this kind into the stage picture, you'll immediately be faced with the problem of how to tone it down.

Let's consider the problem of how to tone down a light-colored or shiny fabric.

If your organization owns the piece of furniture, your first thought might be to change the color by spraying it with fabric dye. Well, think again. Unless you are extremely well-versed in the subtleties of this technique, you will probably ruin the piece of furniture for future use. It's a curious phenomenon that when a designer sprays down an expensive item until it is perfect for the current production, it will never be used again. The next designer (or even the same designer) will dismiss the piece as too dull, too dingy, too dirty, too water-marked, or just too run down.

To maintain the quality of your stock, unless you are equipped to re-upholster furniture for each use, it is best to tone a prop down in a way in which it can be restored to its original appearance after the production.

Black nylon netting is one answer to this problem.

Softening Glare with Nylon Net

Nylon net (or Nylonet) is an inexpensive fabric with an extremely open weave. It can be pinned or whip-stitched to the existing upholstery on a piece of furniture. If one thickness of the netting is not sufficient to dull the furniture's brilliance, doubling or tripling the fabric should do the job.

Nylon netting is also effective on pictures that are too prominent. Such a picture should be removed from its frame, covered with the netting, and re-mounted in the frame.

The weave of this netting is so loose that it can be pulled and stretched to form-fit over many shapes. Covering this lamp shade, however, put the plasticity of the fabric to an extreme test. The net can be held in place with a very scant application of hot glue. A light coat of hot glue on glass can be removed later to restore the lamp to its original appearance.

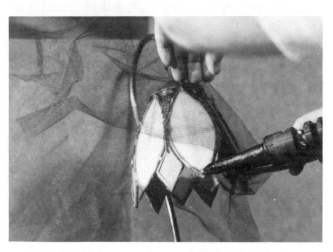

Spray adhesive is an alternative to hot glue for holding the netting on glass. If you plan to remove the net later to restore the article to its original condition, be sure to use a very light coat. When the netting is removed, a solvent such as paint thinner can be used to remove the adhesive.

Other Methods of Glare Reduction

A washable prop, such as this leaded-glass lamp shade, can be toned down with a *thin* wash of diluted acrylic paint with liquid detergent mixed in. The soap removes the permanence of the paint, allowing it to be washed off later to restore the prop.

This soapy dulling coat does, however, tend to come off when the prop is handled.

Krylon makes a dulling spray which is widely used by photographers to remove the gloss from shiny objects. It can be used successfully on expensive items such as silver and jewelry. The spray has a wax base that makes it easily removable by wiping with a soft rag.

A common mistake in the use of dulling spray is overuse, piling it on too heavily. A light coat should be sprayed on and allowed to dry. It will not appear dull while it is wet. Let it dry for 5 minutes or so, and if the object is not dull enough, *then* give it another light coat. Applying too much of the spray is wasteful and messy.

An inherent drawback to using this spray is that the dulled prop cannot be handled without becoming fingerprinted.

Expendable items can be similarly toned down with a light misting of spray paint. Dark brown gives much more pleasing results than black. Hold the can of paint about 18″ from the object and keep the can moving. Spray paint is not recommended for this use on any prop of value. The can could suddenly emit a blob of paint that renders an expensive prop—well, expendable.

WEAPONS

Toy-Store Plastic Replica Pistols

You might not be aware that the manufacturers of plastic toy guns are turning out such a good line of replica pistols for children to play with. (In fact, watchdog consumer groups that guard the juvenile market are alarmed that the realism has been carried too far.) Four of the six guns in the photo are plastic toys. The largest gun, left of center, is a full-scale replica of a .45 magnum; our starter's pistol is at the upper right; all the rest are toys. The toys are scaled down just a bit to fit a child's hand, but they are not substantially smaller than the guns they mimic.

Stage Firearms

Just having a practical gun on stage presents some safety problems that many producers would rather not have to deal with. Close security must be maintained to prevent theft; then there's the obvious problem of accidental firing that is inherent to any firearm. If your production calls for a gun to be fired, you're stuck with using a practical firearm and blanks, and with the attendant problem of providing responsible security. If, however, you need firearms that do not have to be fired, it is not difficult to produce mock-ups according to the plans that follow.

As we were building these shotguns for a production of Brecht's *Arturo Ui*, I was struck by the realization that this project calls for skills no more exotic than those required in my junior high school shop classes so many years ago. Cutting and sanding the wood stock here is no more taxing than cutting and sanding the wood for the clothes fork I made for my mother 38 years ago. And cutting, drilling, and riveting the pipe for the barrels is awfully similar to working on the set of wind chimes I made about the same time. My point is that while the thought of making a shotgun may seem intimidating—the actual process is not.

Building a Shotgun

The stock of the shotgun is 1½" thick, so take two pine 1 × 6s and laminate them together to make a board of the correct thickness. (If you have a piece of 2 × 6 fir in good shape, you can skip the lamination step.)

Laminate the boards by painting both surfaces with white glue and clamping them together. Clamp them tightly—some glue should ooze out at the seam if you have applied enough pressure with the clamps.

This lumber looks like it is almost clear (free of blemishes). Actually, we took a piece of scrap 1 × 6 pine that had knots, and made a few judicious cuts to "liberate" the portion between the knots. By doing this you can have a clear piece of wood to work with without paying the clear price.

While the boards are setting up under the pressure of the clamps, you can go ahead with the construction of the barrels for the shotgun. Refer to a gun catalogue or gun book to select an illustration of the desired style. We selected a picture of a double-barreled shotgun, the type that presumably would break open to be loaded by hand. We could have constructed the gun with a hinge so it actually could be opened, or we could have built a pump gun; but we decided to keep the construction simple.

Cut two pieces of ¾" water pipe to identical lengths, to be used for the barrels. The length can vary from 20" to 26", depending on the model you choose. If you make the barrels shorter than 18", you will have a "sawed-off" shotgun —which would not be in the hands of a law-abiding character.

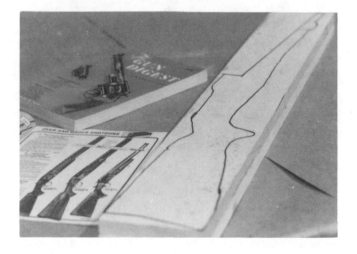

Paying close attention to your reference material, sketch the outline of the stock for the gun on your wood. If you can get an authentic shotgun to use for reference, you can make this sketch the easy way by tracing around the real stock. (The outline in the photo is severely foreshortened by the angle from which it was photographed.) Cut along the outline with a band saw.

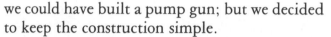

Stack the water pipes alongside of the rough-cut stock, take encouragement from how well the pieces fit, and continue.

Use a router with a half-round cutting bit to round off all of the edges except the face where the barrels will be fitted.

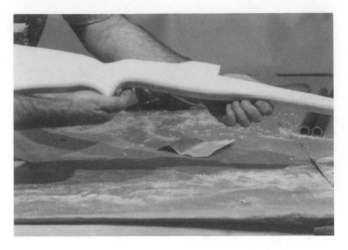

Smooth up the scars left by the band saw and the router with grit #80 sandpaper.

Connect the barrels by drilling and riveting them. Drill two holes through each piece of pipe about an inch from each end. Use an eightpenny common nail for the rivet. Cut the point off the nail if necessary, and batter the tip with a hammer until it cannot be removed. (If you have a welder available and prefer to weld the pipes instead of riveting, drop two spot welds between the pipes on the bottom side where the welds won't show.)

Attach the barrels to the stock by drilling holes and riveting according to the method outlined at left. Select an appropriate place for the drilling —someplace where there is sufficient thickness to the wood.

To complete this weapon you need to add the detail features that will help the stock and barrel "read" as a shotgun from the audience.

A trigger and trigger housing are essential; you might decide also to add the sights, a fancy stock butt, or other decoration. These are op-tional features—we decided to finish just the trigger area of our gun and to add a thumb lever used for unlocking the barrel and allowing the stock to break open for loading. (Actually, our stock didn't open, but we put the lever there anyway.)

This series of photos demonstrates how to make the trigger housing. You might devise a simpler way to make the trigger shield; this one can be built with a hammer, a vise, a pair of tin snips, an anvil, and a disk sander.

Clamp a 6″ piece of 18-gauge sheet metal in a vise. Tighten the vise leaving ⅜″ exposed above the jaws. Use a ball-peen hammer to bend this ⅜″ strip over at a right angle.

Remove the sheet metal from the vise and com-plete the fold, flattening the metal by tapping gently and repeatedly with the hammer. Cut off the surplus metal with a pair of metal shears. You should now have a metal strip folded in half, 6″ long and ⅜″ wide. You can drill two small holes through the metal now, one about ¼″ from each end, or you can wait till after the trigger guard has been shaped.

Use a disk sander to grind away the fold along the first inch of each end. Don't use a grinder for this operation; it is too coarse and might tear or mutilate the metal strip.

Where the fold has been removed, you will be able to separate the ends of the strip with a mat knife. (You won't actually be cutting the metal with the knife, just using the blade to force the two pieces apart.) Form the curved portions

of the trigger guard by bending them around the tip of an anvil. The ends that you have split open should be bent in opposite directions to form the mounting brackets.

Now the brackets will have to be drilled, if you didn't do this earlier. It is possible to get the drill into this tight spot, but you may wish at this point that you had done the drilling before the grinding.

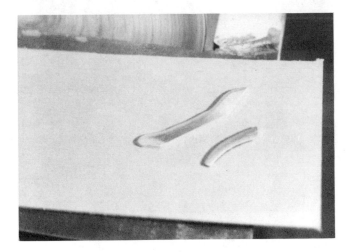

Make the thumb lever and the trigger from ⅛″ aluminum. Aluminum is a soft metal (even at this thickness), and it can be cut on a band saw to make these parts. Long, repeated cutting would eventually dull the band saw blade, but a few cuts will do no damage. Smooth the rough edges left by the saw blade with a disk sander. The photo shows a finished trigger and thumb lever.

Be cautious any time you perform an operation that generates metallic sawdust. Wear goggles to protect your eyes; and when you have finished

with the machines, use compressed air to blow the filings out of all bearings, belts, and motor parts.

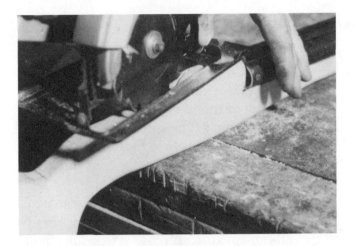

Lower a running skill saw into the breech of the gun at a jaunty angle. Drive the thumb lever into

this slot with a hammer. It should be a tight fit.

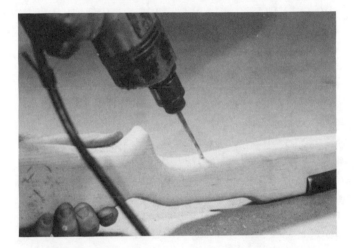

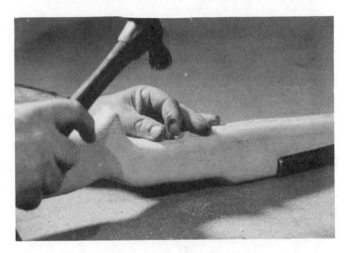

Determine where the trigger should be installed and drill a 1/4″ hole there at a slight angle. When

you drive the trigger into this hole, the fit should be so tight that no other fastening is necessary.

Finally, install the trigger guard. At this point we gave our gun a coat of watered-down raw umber as a stain before considering the shotgun finished.

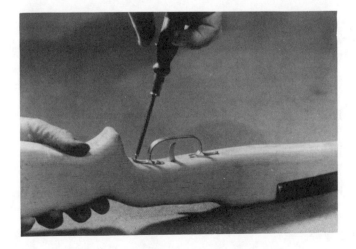

Thompson Sub-Machine Gun

The Resistable Rise of Arturo Ui, by Bertolt Brecht, is a play of 1930s violence involving gangsters of two widely separated countries. Our director felt that the noise and flashes of three blazing Thompson sub-machine guns would best convey the brutal savagery of the time and places.

He knew that this realism could be expensive, so he called an early budget meeting so we could research and plan for the costs that this effect would incur. We called the rental houses in Los Angeles where film studios rent guns, and we put together the following information:

1. A working machine gun rents for $150 per week.

2. A man who is state and federally licensed to handle automatic weapons must secure the guns from the rental house and must be responsible for them during the run (we were looking at a two-week run).

3. The blank ammunition would cost $.50 per round.

That information was the basis for the following budget:

      3 guns @ $150 = $450
              times two weeks = $900
    Licensed operator @ $25 per hour,
          minimum 4 hrs = $100
              times 10 nights = $1000
    40 rounds of ammunition = $20
              times 10 nights = $200
                  TOTAL: $2100

Obviously this one effect could not be allowed to consume so much of the total show budget. Even if we just used one gun, we would only save $600 of the total expenditure—a good savings, but leaving a total still beyond our range. The director was shown these figures; he was impressed with the expense, but insistent nonetheless on the need for the violence of the effect.

Another plan was proposed and researched. We called some of the special effects departments of the motion picture studios. At the Burbank Studios we were put in touch with Doug Pettybone, who was most cooperative. He described a gas machine gun that operates on acetylene gas and compressed air. We made an appointment, and soon we learned all about a system of tanks, tubes, valves, and glow plugs that will produce repeated flashes and explosions. It was apparent that we would be bringing a flame-thrower onto a stage where candles and oil-lamps were not allowed. And we would have to trade off a stand-by munitions expert for a stand-by fireman. All in all, this was no solution.

We had time to think about it, and we finally decided we would make our own Thompson sub-machine guns. We had no construction plans, and it was difficult to gauge dimensions from a small encyclopedia illustration—so we rented a replica machine gun and copied it.

This replica gun was rented from Stembridge Gun Rentals, Glendale, California. It is a very detailed mock-up that will pass for a real gun on stage in every way, with one exception: it will not fire ammunition, either live rounds or blanks.

This mock-up could be broken down, just like a real gun, by removing a few nuts and bolts. We had the gun in our possession for three days and it served as our "set of plans."

We examined the metal work of the gun and found that it could be broken down into five parts:

1. A barrel (with cooling fins).
2. The body of the gun, which is basically a piece of 1½" square tubing.
3. A trigger housing.
4. A rear sight.
5. The barrel tip and sight.

The biggest problem in constructing this weapon was solved simply by selecting appropriate pieces of raw stock. We were fortunate in having a large assortment of scrap water pipe, strap iron, and square metal tubing which had been salvaged and saved from other projects. If you do not have similar resources, a trip to the metal yard and a few dollars will net you the small amount of metal that you will need to make a machine gun mock-up.

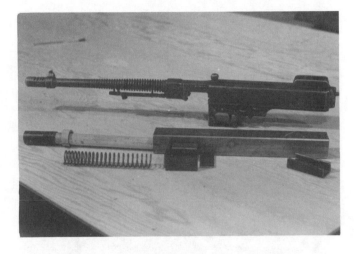

You can cut the barrel from a piece of ½" water pipe. A tight-fitting spring will serve for the cooling fins. We chose to ignore the taper in the barrel, and you probably should do the same.

Cut the body from a 15" piece of 1½" square tubing. This piece will need further refinement; we'll get back to it in a later step.

The trigger housing is a 2" piece of ¾" square tubing and three pieces of ¾" strap iron.

Cut the rear sight from a piece of channel iron.

The barrel tip is 2" of ¾" conduit and a ½" piece of ¾" water pipe.

We debated at length over the necessity of the strip under the cooling fins — it is hidden almost completely when the hand grip is in place. Finally on the second day we decided to include it.

The metal work can be made with nothing more than a vise, a hacksaw, and an acetylene welder. (Actually, we *have* more sophisticated tools, but the particular weekend that we undertook this project, our costume department had taken over the scene shop to provide a guest lecturer with a large space to conduct a workshop on fabric dyeing. We could not use the power tools because of the noise we would generate, so, rather than wait until Monday, we fitted a sharp blade in the hacksaw and made all the cuts by hand in the welding room. Certainly if you have a fully-equipped scene shop you know there are short-cuts to the procedures that follow; the point is that this work *can* be done with just a hacksaw, a welder, and a grinder — for smoothing the welds.)

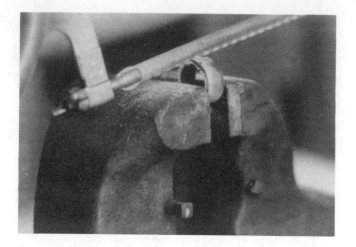

The piece of ¾" pipe that goes on the barrel tip needs a slot in it so that the front sight can be fitted in place.

Most of the cuts are made straight and square, simply cutting the pieces to the correct lengths. This is not too taxing for a hacksaw.

The only piece that is a little complicated and requires extra attention is the 1½" square tube that forms the taper where the barrel joins the main gun body. This taper is too prominent in a real machine gun to be ignored in the mock-up.

The taper is made by cutting away some of the metal on both the top and bottom of the tube and then beating the sides into the desired taper with a hammer. The method may be a little crude, but it works.

With the pieces refined a little more, we have assembled them in their approximate positions in order to compare them with the rented replica (at top). The barrel of the mock-up has been slipped together but not yet welded. The main body has the taper bent into it. The trigger housing has been welded and deburred and buffed up on the grinder. The rear sight has also been deburred and shaped a little more with the grinder.

Making the Gun Stock

While these metal pieces were being cut and welded, one member of our crew was fashioning the wooden stock and hand grips.

He traced a pattern of the stock onto a 1 x 6 and then glued it to two similar pieces of pine. This lamination makes the lumber 2¼" thick — thick enough to cut the gun stock from it. He used white glue and furniture clamps to bond these pieces into a single unit.

As soon as the glue had set, he cut out the pattern with a band saw.

The stock also has a profile in its thinner dimension. This shape can be achieved easily on a band saw.

A good deal of rounding still must be done to shape the stock. A router will not finish the job, but it is a good way to start. Further shaping must be done by sanding the stock, both by machine and by hand.

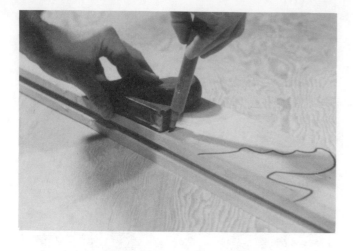

Sketch or trace the hand grips onto a piece of 2 × 6 lumber (or two 1 × 6's laminated together). Then cut out the tracing on a band saw, and you have all the wooden parts roughed out.

    The tongue-in-groove lumber in the photo is not necessary—or even desirable. But it was the best and cleanest 2 × 6 we had on hand.

A 2 × 6 is a little thicker than is needed, so its width can be reduced with a disk sander. Then it can be routed with a router.

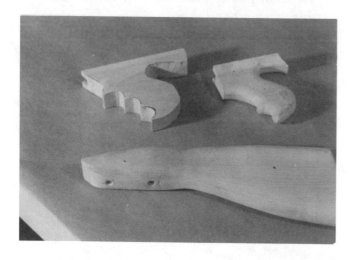

Here are the stock and hand grips that we made, shown as they appeared in three progressive stages of their development.

At the end of the first day of work, the pieces looked like this. Nothing had been fully assembled, but all of the pieces had been roughed out.

Finally it is time to assemble the metal parts into a single unit with a welder. We also welded ³/₁₆″ bolts to the body of the body of the gun, to which the hand grips and stock would be attached.

Painting a Gun-Metal Finish

We had planned to provide a blued finish on the metal parts of the gun with a bluing process just like that used by real gunsmiths. This process is available from gun shops, but unfortunately, we had used too many types of iron and steel in the construction. The steel used in the barrel and rear sight were second-hand and had been painted before; the main body was cut from stainless steel. These parts would not take the

bluing process. So, on to "Plan B"...

We decided to use the venerated theater technique of making an object appear to be metallic with FEV (French enamel varnish). (For details on FEV and its use, see the section on Glues and Adhesives.)

The body and barrel of the gun required very little paint, so a very small quantity of FEV was all we mixed.

We used a brown textile paint to color the shellac. The transparent coloring of this dye works well with the FEV process. The addition of graphite gave the shellac the desired metallic sheen. Since we needed such a small quantity of the varnish, we mixed the ingredients together on a piece of brown butcher paper on the table top.

After the FEV has dried, its luster can be improved by burnishing it with very fine steel wool.

The cartridge cannister was made from plywood. We spackled the entire surface to conceal the wood grain, and then we used the same FEV technique to give it a metallic appearance.

A Property Master's Dreams

The time is 2:30 a.m.

The **PROP MASTER** *is home in his bed, asleep. He stirs slightly as his slumber is disturbed by the distant sounds and visions of sub-machine gun fire.*

The gun is heard again. This time the bursts of flame are answered by a second series of pulses from another nearby Thompson.

He rolls over in an effort to find a more comfortable position for his large frame. A sawed-off shotgun belches twin blasts of light.

In his dream, the **PROP MASTER** *sees himself enter the picture. He strolls with a series of quick steps reminiscent of Gene Kelly toward the source of the flashes. His body has now taken on the form of Kelly or Astaire, clothed in tailored white overalls, silhouetted in the brilliant twinkling flashes.*

He glides with confidence into the stroboscopic effect of the pulsing lights. The noisy staccato of machine gun fire is somehow transformed into a repetitious rhythmic sound pattern.

The white blazes now change to tones of red and violet. The overalls change to skin-tight leather, and the figure now resembles John Travolta performing a disco number through a rainbow of flashing colors.

A host of applauding fans and followers converge from the wings and the dancer is surrounded by admirers who ad-lib:

"He's so wonderful."
"Isn't he grand?"
"Terrific! Just terrific!"
"What form. What grace!"
"God-like."
"When I grow up, I want to be just like him."
(Sigh.)
...etc.

His dance is short and spectacular, and it ends in a frozen pose.

The figure has once again become the **PROP MASTER**, *in overalls, holding a Thompson sub-machine gun. All of the multicolored flashes now have merged and are issuing from the gun's pulsing barrel.*

There is a crescenco of applause; the acclaim increases:

"It's beautiful in its simplicity."
"He's a hero—a champion!"
"So modest—so humble—so great!"
"He's so clever."
"Yes, Yes, he's clever."

"Such a clever old fellow!"
The PROPERTIES MASTER *awakens.*

PROPERTIES MASTER That's it. That's it! I'll put a strobe light into the tip of the barrel.

PROP MASTER'S WIFE Wha—? Honey, it's the middle of the night. Go to sleep!

PROPERTIES MASTER The trigger will be a double acting switch. It can activate both the loudspeaker and the strobe flashes at the same time.

PROP MASTER'S WIFE Hush! I've got to get up early in the morning.

PROPERTIES MASTER It will be perfectly safe!

PROP MASTER'S WIFE Oh, please. Give me a break.

Simulating Machine Gun Fire with a Strobe Light

Fitting a strobe light into the tip of a gun barrel is possible—but not easy. The project seemed to be plagued with trouble from the start, but the effect was successful in the end.

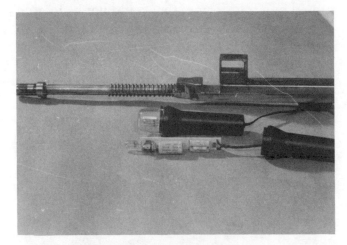

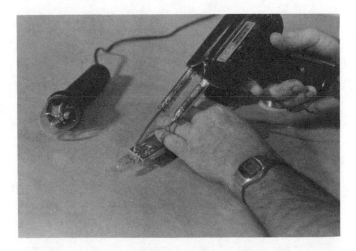

We purchased a small strobe light (called a Star Strobe) made by The Great American Market, which is based in Los Angeles. The first problem we encountered was that the strobe flashed too slowly. The Star Strobe is set to flash about once each second; we needed a rate of about eight flashes per second. We called the manufacturer, who assured us that a simple resistor change should solve the problem. A 10 meg resistor making up a r–c circuit controls the pulse rate. Replacing this with a resistor of smaller value, about 2 megohm, will increase the pulse rate.

We obtained the recommended resistor, and made the circuit-board conversion. (A radio or television repairman should be helpful in making this alteration if you do not speak of megohms and r–c circuits with ease.)

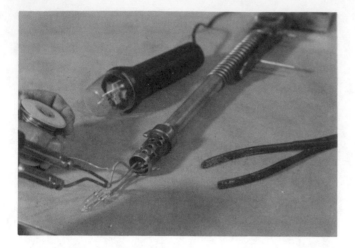

We housed the circuit board in the 1½″ square tube near the trigger. Three long wires were run up the length of the barrel, forming a sort of extension cord, so that the strobe tube could be placed at the barrel tip. The barrel tip had been perforated to allow the flashes to be seen. When we plugged the unit in (had you already guessed?) it wouldn't flash. Not once.

Packing up the strobe light pieces, we went to our resident electronics technician, whom we should have consulted in the first place. We told him of our problem, and left the ineffectual components for his scrutiny.

Three hours later he called to say that the strobe was working. The problem had been caused by a transformer that could not be located in a position remote from the flash tube. Move the tube, and the transformer must go with it.

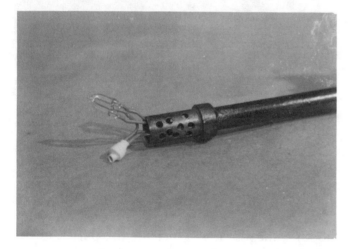

But the story doesn't end there. When we crammed the transformer and flash tube into the tip of the barrel, the strobe again would not work. We pulled the components out of the metal housing, and that allowed the unit to flash properly. Apparently the metal tip was acting as a core or shield or something, and that was preventing the transformer from functioning.

We decided to let the transformer remain exposed and pretend it would not be noticed.

The trigger was really two micro-switches ganged together to operate in unison. One switch activated the strobe light; the other allowed the signal from a tape recorder (which was running a continuous loop of tape) to reach the speakers. Pushing the two switches "triggered" the light pulses and the sound effect to operate in apparent synchronization.

We experienced two operating failures during the run of this production. One occurred because the metal band around the flash tube slid forward on the glass (the placement of this band is critical); the other was the result of the exposed trans-former being smashed in the handling of the gun. Fortunately we had two guns in operation during the scene, and there was never a time when both guns failed simultaneously.

Swords

Making a sword might appear to be a tough job, but it needn't be. The blade is easy enough; it can be made of ¾″ strap metal, either aluminum or iron. The grip is another matter. Sword handles can be intricate. Even a sword meant for business and not for show, such as a Roman broad sword, can have an imposing handle. If you are willing to accept some compromise, and especially if you have the benefit of a proscenium stage's aesthetic distance, you may surprise yourself with what you can do to construct a convincing rapier or saber.

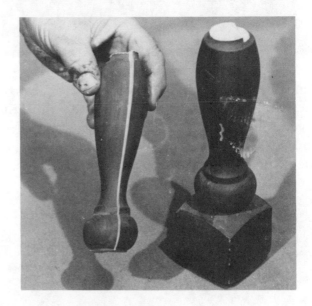

The grip of this sword was made from a portion of a railing baluster. The center of the spindle was removed by running the spindle through a band saw twice. If this does not yield a handle with a comfortable feel, it can be further dressed down with a disk sander.

This pair of swords were built for *Brigadoon*. They were made for the humble but necessary task of lying on the ground while a dancer performed a sword dance over them. These dress swords are characteristic of what can be turned out with found objects and a little imagination.

We found some drawer pulls to serve as the decorative hilt and hand guards. (The drawer pulls came from a garage sale a few months earlier, and we bought them with the intention of using them

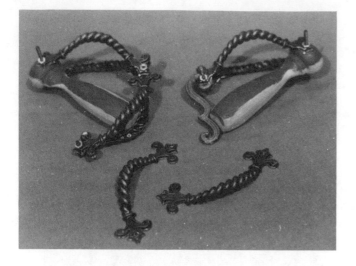

Sandwich your metal blade between the halves of the handle. Drill and bolt the blade and grip together. Shape the blade point on a grinder, and polish it with a wirewheel. You could spray the blade with silver paint.

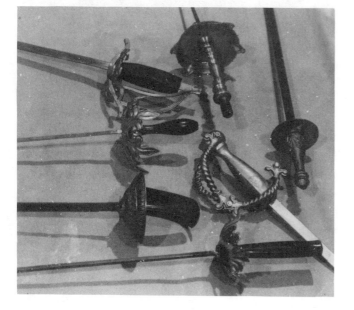

someday as drawer pulls. Even if you have to search for them at specialty hardware stores, it would be worth the cost of a few drawer pulls to have dress swords on hand for future use.)

The handles were styled after a picture of an authentic courtesan sword, with design compromises made along the way as we had decided from the beginning. The handle on the right is an alternate design; the decorative hilt piece was taken from a decorative wall sconce.

All of the exposed bolts in the photo above were clipped short, dressed on a grinder, and covered with epoxy putty. Finally the sword handles were painted with copper and brass aerosol paint.

These sword handles were made from lamp parts and assorted found objects.

WRITING MATERIALS

A Historical Overview

Practically every play ever written calls for some kind of scroll, note, sealed document, letter, or manuscript to be used in the actors' business. Many times "parchment" is what the playwright or the director specifies for the writing material.

There is a marked difference between what is thought of as parchment today, and what, in earlier times, this material really was.

Parchment

Animal skins were among the earliest of man's writing materials. For centuries these hides were designed to receive written inscriptions on one side only. About 160 B.C., a new process for dressing skins was developed whereby hair was removed from the hide and both sides could be written upon. This new writing material was called "parchment."

Parchment was made of sheepskin or goatskin. The process in which it was polished and prepared made it thin, flexible, and capable of receiving inks. The finer grade of parchment, made from newborn or stillborn calves, was known as "vellum."

Stationers today sell paper called "parchment" and "vellum," but their use of these names designates particular grades of typing paper. These papers have little application as props except in contemporary plays which call for a typewriter to be used on stage.

The paper that usually masquerades as parchment on stage is much thinner than animal skin could ever be, and much more nearly approximates rice paper.

Paper

Animal skins remained the most popular writing material until about A.D. 200 when paper as we know it made its appearance. Paper made from the bark of the mulberry tree was invented in China. During the next two or three hundred years, as the techniques of paper-making improved, parchment continued to be used, vying with paper for popularity.

Linen or flax paper was manufactured in Arabian countries in the ninth century, but its use was slow to spread into the European countries. The first European paper mills were set up in Spain and Italy in the mid-1300s. This paper was hand made in small batches from rag pulp, but the demand was not great. It took another hundred years and the invention of the printing press for paper to become generally available in England. In 1800 the first machine to make paper in continuous rolls was invented. Even after widespread acceptance of paper for literary purposes, vellum was still preferred for important documents because of its durability and prestigious appearance.

Simulating Parchment

If the script calls for a message to be written on parchment, the document should be composed of a thin, flexible hide. In some respects it would resemble the chamois skin available today that is popular for polishing cars. (A chamois is a European mountain goat.)

A real chamois skin is not prohibitively expensive. When you add an inscription and roll it up —well, what could be more realistic than the authentic item?

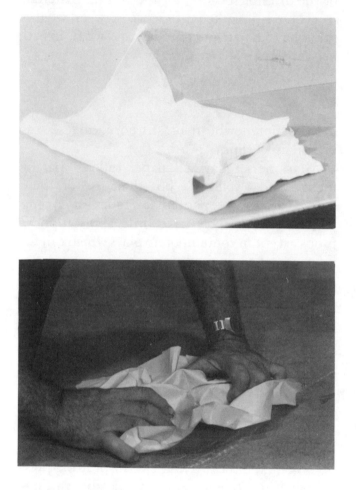

A manila folder that has been folded and abused will take on some of the qualities of antique parchment.

Make thin wash of raw umber by mixing 2 tablespoons of acrylic scene paint in a pint of water. Brush this onto the manila tagboard. The color collects in the wrinkles, accentuating them and giving the surface an uneven textured look.

Cut away a bit of the edge to get rid of the "factory-cut" look, and write your message on the manilla "skin" with a brown felt marking pen.

Simulating Early Hand-Made Paper

There are coarse textured papers available from stationery stores that will pass for early hand-made paper. Rice paper can be purchased or simulated as follows from tissue paper.

Spread a sheet of tissue paper (the kind sold for gift wrapping) on a large table. Use a sponge to wipe the paper with a wash of watered-down raw umber acrylic paint. Don't soak the tissue; just dampening it will cause it to wrinkle and give it the desired color. When the paper is dry, inscribe your message with a brown felt pen.

The job of transcribing "indifferent" messages on many sheets of paper gets boring, and the "scribes" sometimes succumb to the temptation of being clever or cutesy in an effort to relieve the boredom. This is unfair to the performers who handle the prop; the message should not distract the actors from doing their best work for the audience. The inscription should be either accurately within the context of the scene being played, or totally indifferent.

Pens

Several major changes have been evident in the evolution of techniques of transcribing words on parchment, papyrus, or paper. One of these revolutions has taken place within the past 40 years.

As a grade school student in the 1940s, the author was taught penmanship using fountain pens and blotting paper. Ballpoint pens were introduced in the middle of that decade, and they caused a revolution. The use of hand-dipped pens and inkstands had already given way to fountain pens with internal ink bladders, and suddenly the ballpoint eclipsed all pens of the split-nib variety. The metal nib is rarely used today except for calligraphy, but fountain pens (which enjoyed a revival in the 1960s with the introduction of disposable ink cartridges) can still be purchased in stationery stores. Obtaining these period writing tools is not difficult, though one must be wary of the contemporary look of some of the pens on the market.

The Chinese used ink with brushes three to four thousand years ago. Quill pens were developed much later, but the actual date seems to be vague. Quail, turkey, and crow feathers were widely used by both writers and artists. Another favorite quill was made of large goose feathers. These were tempered with heat and alum to make them flexible but durable.

The metal nib was introduced about 1820, and the quill pen was slowly replaced. A practical version of a self-contained fountain pen was introduced in 1885. Traditional quill pens were, however, still being used to sign formal documents at the turn of the century.

Pencils

The first pencils were actually sticks of lead used by the Egyptians and Romans. They left a rather faint impression. Graphite replaced lead around 1500. Graphite enclosed in a wooden shell (a crude version of the pencil we know today) first appeared in 1795. Faber opened the first pencil factory in the United States in 1856.

Making an Inkwell Set

This inkwell set would be acceptable in a play of any period from the 16th or 17th century to about 1930.

The parts are as follows: a piece of pine 4½" × 9", two pieces of 1½" diameter PVC water pipe, two drawer pull backing plates, two small cabinet hinges, and some lamp parts—two 2¼" ball shade holders, two pyramid knobs, two ¾" threaded pipe nipples, and two lock nuts.

Cut slight bevels, angling upwards as shown, on all four sides of the pine base.

Make a pen tray along one side of the base with a bull-nosed router bit. Drill two holes in the base large enough for the PVC "bottles."

Attach the pyramid knobs to the shade holders with the ¾" ⅛ IPS nipples and lock nuts.

Drill extra holes in the drawer pull backing plates: enlarge the center hole of one for the pen to dip into; put several small holes in the other, which will serve as the lid of the powder shaker.

Paint the base black, or give it a natural stain and varnish, or whatever finish suits your production.

Screw four small porcelain drawer pulls onto the base to serve as feet.

Solder a small cabinet hinge to the lower edge of each shade holder.

Attach the loose flap of each hinge to the appropriate place on the base to allow the lids to open and close. The finished inkwell would be equally at home with pens or feather quills. If your play is set before 1850, use a quill and eliminate the pen tray in the base.

APPENDIX

Glossary

Acetate ink. An ink or dye specifically formulated to color sheets of acetate or acrylic.

Acetate sheets. A transparent plastic, manufactured in a variety of film thicknesses from 2 mils (.002″) to 125 mils (⅛″).

Acrylic sheets. A clear plastic, used in the theater as a substitute for glass window panes. Common trade names: Plexiglas, Lucite, Acrylite.

Adhesive. The medium by which objects are held together—glue, paste, cement, etc. (*see also* **spray adhesive**)

Aluminum powder. A finely divided silvery powder, used as a coloring agent in mixing metallic paint.

Aluminum sheet. A soft metal sheet, easily cut, drilled, and riveted, recommended in this book for the construction of the gramophone horn and footlight housings, and as a template in sculpting urethane foam.

Aluminized Mylar. A Mylar film, surfaced on one side with an aluminum coating, providing a mirror finish.

Aviary wire. A version of chicken wire with a grid of very small holes, used for caging birds. Used by the prop builder to construct small frames to support and reinforce papier-mâché. The fine grid of wires allows you to sculpt details which are not possible with chicken wire.

Baluster. One of a series of spindles or small pillars supporting a handrail.

Balustrade. A complete set of balusters and the supported handrail.

Bead Foam. A rigid foam made of expanded polystyrene in bead form. Commercially produced as a flotation and packing material. (*see also* **Styrofoam** *and* **Falcon Foam**)

Bevel. An angle on the edge or end of a board other than 90°.

Binder. The bonding medium (varnish or glue) to which a coloring agent (dye or pigment) is added to make paint.

Board foot. A standardized unit of measuring lumber—equal to one square foot on the surface of a piece of wood which is one inch thick.

Bondo. A trade name of Dynatton / Bondo Corp. for a plastic body filler used in auto body and fender repair. (*see also* **polyester resin** *and* **plastic body filler**)

Brass sheet. A thin brass metal sheet, manufactured for shims, metal stampings, and crafts projects.

Brownline paper. An ozalid paper used in the blueprinting process which, instead of producing a blue image, makes a brown image.

Burlap. A coarse fabric made of jute, flax, or hemp, used for costumes, draperies, and some bags and sacks.

Cabosil. An agent used to thicken paints and plastic resin.

Casting. The reproduction which is formed in a mold.

Casting resin. A polyester resin formulated for casting solid objects. (*see also* **polyester resin**)

Chamois. A soft leather (originally from a mountain antelope, now made from sheep, goat, or deer skin) manufactured for use in cleaning and polishing automotive paint. Recommended in this book for use in constructing coin purses, parchment, and a heart.

Cheesecloth. A loose weave, lightweight cotton fabric.

Chicken wire. A wire netting manufactured for use in the construction of small animal pens. Used in prop building as a lightweight form to support and reinforce papier-mâché or glue cloth.

Cloth mache. A molding material (similar to papier-mâché) consisting of strips of muslin, saturated with glue, laminated on a chicken wire form.

Crystal Craze or **Crystaline.** Trade names of a particular glass stain which, on drying, forms colored translucent crystalline patterns.

Detergent. A cleaning agent. Used by the prop builder as a paint additive (and obviously for cleaning dishes). Small quantities of detergent added to paint reduce surface tension, allowing the color to flow. Larger quantities inhibit the adhering capability of paint, facilitating easier removal.

Distressing. A technique of aging new or bright properties to give them the appearance of having been used.

Dulling spray. A wax-based aerosol spray used by artists, photographers, and prop builders to remove the glare from shiny surfaces.

Durham's Rockhard Water Putty. The trade name of Donald Durham Co. for water-mixed putty largely used for filling wide voids in wood. The manufacturer also recommends this putty for use as a casting material.

Elvanol. The trade name of DuPont de Nemours & Co. for a water soluble synthetic resin adhesive made of polyvinyl alcohol. (*see also* **PVA**)

Epoxy Putty. A very tenacious, hard-drying putty. In industry, its uses range from mending pipes to model making. In prop building it is primarily used as a material for sculpting small items that must stand up under rough treatment.

Erosion cloth. An open-weave, oil-treated matting manufactured for the landscaping industry. Laid on hillsides, this fabric reduces the effects of water erosion while young ground cover vegetation is rooting through the open weave. The prop builder uses this product as a texturing material, often to simulate foliage.

Ethafoam. The trade name of Dow Chemical Co. for a firm but flexible polyethylene foam. Used in the theater to simulate wood molding on curved surfaces.

Falcon Foam. A trade name of Falcon Foam Plastics Inc. for expanded polystyrene. This product is produced commercially for insulation and packaging, and as a floatation material. Used in the theater to represent stonework and as a sculpting material. (*see also* **bead foam** *and* **Styrofoam**)

Fiberglass. A glass reinforcement, used with plastic resin (usually polyester resin) to make an exceedingly strong material having a weight-to-strength ratio greater than iron.

Fir. A medium-soft wood with a pronounced grain and a tendency to splinter, cut from fir trees. Widely used in the manufacture of plywood and beams for house construction — 2 × 4, 2 × 6, 4 × 4, etc. (*see* **lumber**)

Flameproofing. A chemical treatment applied to flammable materials (cloth, straw, foliage) to retard combustion.

Flex-glue. An adhesive made of polyvinyl acetate (PVA) that remains flexible when cured because of plasticizers added to the mixture. Used commercially in bookbinding. Used by the prop builder as a texturing medium as well as the intended use as an adhesive.

Florist's tape. A crepe, self-sticking tape, colored brown or green, used on arrangements of artificial flowers to bind the places where stems join the stalk.

Foliage flameproofing and preserving. A green paint based in neoprene rubber. Manufactured primarily as a flameproofing agent for the leaves of trees and bushes used in a stage setting. Secondarily, the coating forms an airtight envelope around each leaf, tending to preserve its freshness by retarding the effects of evaporation.

Fuller's earth. A fine powder manufactured to be used as a filtering agent. It is nontoxic, but is classified as a nuisance dust. The prop builder uses fuller's earth to simulate smoke or dust.

Gelatin glue. A glue made of animal gelatin (hoofs, hides, and bones). Formerly used as a paint binder for scene paint made of dry pigments, for applying glue cloth, and for bonding wood. This glue has been superseded by plastic adhesives.

Glass frosting. An aerosol spray formulated to frost transparent panes making them translucent.

Glue cloth. A molding technique wherein repeated coatings of muslin strips soaked in glue are laminated over a form (usually made of chicken wire). The process is identical to that of papier-mâché, except that cloth is used instead of paper as the laminating material. (*see also* **cloth mache**)

Gold metallic tape. An adhesive tape with a shiny gold finish. (*see* **matting tape**)

Graphite. A soft black variety of carbon having a slippery texture, manufactured for use as a lubricant. Used by prop builders as a coloring agent when mixing metallic paint.

Grass mat. A carpeting material manufactured to simulate grass at cemetery sites.

Hot glue. A thermoplastic glue which becomes highly tenacious when heated to its melting point and cures to maximum strength as soon as it cools. It can also be used as a casting material.

Invisible knot. A knot used to terminate the ends of a lashing in such a way that the knot and resultant loose ends are hidden deep inside the wraps of the lashing.

Latex rubber. A liquid rubber that cures on exposure to air to form a flexible skin. Used for making soft coatings on rigid forms, and for making flexible castings from a plaster mold.

Lumber sizes. Lumberyards stock precut boards and beams in stock sizes—1 × 3, 1 × 6, 1 × 12, 2 × 4, 2 × 6, 4 × 4, etc. But lumber always measures less than the designated size. Shrinkage accounts for some of the difference, planing for the rest. Planing is a process which smooths all four edges of a board and necessarily reduces their width and thickness. A so-called 1″ board (a 1 × 6, for example) has an actual thickness of only ¾″. The width of a 1″ board, and the width and thickness of construction beams, are reduced by a uniform ½″. Thus, a 2 × 4 has actual dimensions of 1½″ × 3½″ and a 1 × 12 is ¾″ × 11½″. Economy dictates that this convention be carried into the prop shop. A board 11½″ wide cannot yield two boards with actual width of 6″, so you must cut them 5½″ each. A 1 × 3 will be cut to an actual width of 2½″. This will be true whether the cut is made in the lumberyard or your own shop.

Lumber with these reduced measurements is acceptable for use on most construction projects; however, there are times when precision is called for. When a cutting list specifies 3¼″ it really means that the cut is to be made with a 3¼″ width. When the designer's plan says 3″ he means that the cut is to be made at 3″ exactly! The section in this book on making rehearsal furniture includes a cutting list which must be followed with care in order for the parts to fit.

The only time you can take liberties with lumber sizes is when you know that the shorthand notation is in effect:

1. When you are ordering lumber from a lumberyard.
2. When you are cutting stock lumber widths for purposes of general construction.
3. When you read a designer's notation which says "1 × 3," "2 × 4," etc.

Lumber types. Lumber is divided into two general types: hardwood, lumber sawn from deciduous trees (oak, birch, elm, maple, cherry, etc.); and soft wood, lumber sawn from coniferous trees (pine, fir, cedar, spruce, etc.). Most prop building makes use of the soft wood pine. It nails, cuts and sands easily; it resists splitting; and it is lightweight. Pine is too soft, however, for building furniture. It is very susceptible to scratching and marring. The grain is distinctive also, and stained pine always looks like "knotty pine." (*see also* **plywood**)

Masonite. A trade name for one of a variety of hardboards made by compressing wood fibers in a heated hydraulic press. Normally, hardboard comes with one side smooth, and the other textured to appear somewhat like the weave of cloth.

Matting tape. An adhesive tape, made in a variety of colors, used by the artist or the prop builder to apply clean straight lines to frame or decorate their work.

Miter. A joint made between two surfaces which have been cut on a bevel.

Muslin. An inexpensive cotton fabric used in the theater to make backdrops and as a utility cloth. The prop builder uses it to make patterns and as a fabric for working glue cloth.

Nail. A metal pin for fastening wood. Hundreds of types of nails, brads, and tacks are made, most of them for very specific purposes. The nails most useful to a scenery or property builder are these:

1. Box nails. Thin shank with a head. Used for most utility fastening.
2. Finish nails. Thin shank with a very small head. The nail is designed to be driven below the surface of the wood, puttied and painted to provide a "finished" surface.
3. Duplex nails. Double-headed nail with about ⅜ " between the two heads. The nail is designed for easy removal and is used for temporary fastening.

Nail length is designated by a number and "d," the British abbreviation for "penny." This designation is a reference to the original cost per hundred: at one time ten-penny (or 10d) nails cost ten cents for a hundred.

Nonwoven fabric. A material made of fibers under the effects of pressure and heat. Two well-known products made in this manner are felt and Kleenex tissue. A more recent product, sold as

Pellon and Vantex, is made from polyester fibers.

Nylon net. A fine weave netting with a hexagonal hole, made of nylon and available in many colors. This netting (usually colored black) is used by the prop builder to soften or dull objects on the stage which are distracting because of their brightness or glare.

Paraffin wax. A waxy petroleum byproduct manufactured for preserving jelly and for use in making candles. Used by the prop builder as a lubricant, or as a casting material.

Pellon. A trade name for polyester nonwoven fabric. This material can be purchased in a roll 12' wide and more than 500' long. (*see also* **nonwoven fabric**)

Pine. A strong, lightweight, soft wood, easily carved, and not subject to splitting or splintering, cut from pine trees. Widely used in the theater as the preferred lumber for scenery and property construction.

Pipe insulation. A rubber jacket used to protect water pipes from freezing in cold climates. Used in prop building for flexible molding and padding.

Plaster of Paris. A fast-setting plaster used in the making of molds. It is also useful as a casting material, to make multiple copies from a flexible rubber mold.

Plastic body filler. A polyester resin in paste form, used by auto repair shops for filling minor dents in car bodies. Used by the prop builder as a molding material, a putty for finishing fiberglass, or as a bonding agent.

Plasticine. A modeling clay based in oil (sometimes wax) used for sculpting objects of moderate size. The soft clay sculpture is frequently preserved by making a casting of the shape in plaster or some other molding material.

Plexiglas. A trade name of Rohm and Haas for transparent acrylic sheets. (*see also* **acrylic**)

Plywood. A laminate, made of three or more

thin veneers of wood (usually an odd number). They are glued together, with the grain of alternate layers running in opposite directions, producing a sheet of wood with exceptional strength. Plywood made of fir is most common, and is suitable for most prop building. However, plywood surfaced with a hardwood or fruitwood is used in cabinet making.

Construction plywood is graded with letters from A to D, referring to the appearance quality of the surface veneers—face and back. "AA" is top grade both sides. "AD" (generally acceptable for theater work) has top grade on its face with open defects and pitch pockets on the back.

Polyester. The polyester family is a large one. It can be extruded, stretched into filaments and woven into fabrics (Dacron), drawn into sheets (Mylar) or, most useful to the property builder, formulated as a resin which is used in laminating fiberglass and making clear castings.

Polyester resins. Polyester resins are available in many formulations, each for a special purpose. A catalyst (MEK Peroxide) is mixed into the resin, causing it to cure to a solid. Some polyester resins are compounded to be flexible when the cure is complete. The most likely resins to be found on a dealer's shelves, however, are these:

1. **Gel coat**, a fast-setting resin used to make a thin, smooth impression before the fiberglass is introduced to a casting.
2. **Laminating resin**, reinforced with fiberglass and used to make castings.
3. **Plastic body filler** (Bondo), formulated with fillers which facilitate sanding and finishing of the casting.
4. **Casting resin**, with a wax designed into the formula which rises to the surface of the casting as it cures to produce a smooth, non-tacky finish.

Polyethylene sheets. An inexpensive plastic film used in the manufacture of trash bags, temporary coverings for weather protection, and painters' drop cloths. Since polyethylene resists adhesives it is sometimes used as a working surface for projects that require the use of large amounts of glue.

PVA. A plastic (polyvinyl alcohol) that has been formulated into two forms useful to the property builder: (1) Elvanol, a fabric adhesive, and (2) a water soluble mold release used in molding and casting.

PVC water pipe. A strong, lightweight white plastic tubing made of polyvinyl chloride, used for sprinkler installations and home plumbing, or in larger diameters for sewers. The plastic pipe is used by the prop builder as a raw material for building rods and staffs, and for making the basic shape of many smaller properties.

Spray adhesive. A rubber contact cement packaged in an aerosol spray can. Used by the prop builder as an adhesive for bonding plastics, and as a priming coat when painting Ethafoam.

Styrofoam. A trade name of Dow Chemical for expanded styrene. The name has become used to refer generically to all products made of foamed styrene. Common usage has spread to the point of erroneously calling urethane foam by the name "Styrofoam."

Urethane foam. A foam product made of polyurethane which is formulated to be either flexible or rigid. It is available in very large pieces of $2' \times 4' \times 10'$ (logs) and sheets cut from the logs (planks). Rigid urethane foam is used by the prop builder as a sculpting material because it is so easy to carve. Flexible urethane foam is used in making pillows and for padding upholstery.

Zip cord. A colloquial name for parallel conductor lamp cord. This cord is designed with a weakened seam in the insulation between the twin conductors so the wires can be separated by ripping them down the center. Surface markings to identify polarity are another feature of zip cord. These markings (stripes, ridges, or grooves) are stamped onto one of the wires during manufacture. Another informal name for this product is "spit wire." The name refers to the catalog designation "SPT" which stands for "small parallel thermoplastic."

Where to Get Your Supplies

The following table lists 60 of the products and materials mentioned in the text of this book and suggests sources for obtaining them. Some of the materials (chicken wire, spray adhesive, paraffin wax, etc.) are so common they can be found at any hardware store. Some (dulling spray, acetate ink, flameproofing, etc.) can probably be found only in larger communities, where the population can support specialty stores. Others (Elvanol, Pellon, stage money, etc.) are so unique they must be ordered directly from the manufacturer or his distributor.

The sources listed are mostly businesses in Southern California, the area in which I work. Most of these vendors do mail order business on a regular basis and will ship on the strength of a purchase order number. Others, however, require prepayment, and you must allow time for your check to reach them by mail. A quick phone call will let you know the particulars.

Acetate ink. See "Crafts Supplies" or "Artists Materials & Supplies" in your phone book, or
> Kit Craft
> Studio City, California
> (818) 984-0780

Acetate sheets. See "Plastics—Rods, Tubes, Sheets" in your phone book, or
> Cadillac Plastics
> North Hollywood, California
> (818) 980-0840

Acrylic sheets. See "Plastics—Rods, Tubes, Sheets" in your phone book, or
> Gem-O-Lite Plastics
> North Hollywood, California
> (818) 766-9491

Adhesive (spray). See "Crafts Supplies," "Artists Materials & Supplies," or "Hardware" in your phone book.

Aluminum powder. See "Crafts Supplies" in your phone book, or
> Mann Brothers Paints
> Hollywood, California
> (213) 936-5168

Aluminum sheet. See "Metals" in your phone book.

Aluminized Mylar. See "Plastics—Rods, Tubes, Sheets" in your phone book, or
> Transparent Products Corp.
> Los Angeles, California
> (213) 938-3821

Aviary wire. See "Hardware" or "Pet Supplies" in your phone book.

Bead Foam. See "Plastics—Foam" in your phone book.

Brass Sheet. See "Metals" in your phone book.

Brownline Paper. See "Blueprinting Equipment & Supplies" in your phone book, or
> Continental Graphics
> West Los Angeles, California
> (213) 938-2511

Burlap. See "Fabrics" in your phone book, or
> Dazians
> Beverly Hills, California
> (213) 655-9691

or
> Gerriets International
> Allentown, New Jersey
> (609) 758-9121

Cabosil. See "Plastics—Raw Materials" in your phone book, or
> Mann Brothers Paints
> Los Angeles, California
> (213) 936-5168

Casting Resin. See ''Plastics—Raw Materials'' in your phone book, or
>Hastings Plastics
>Santa Monica, California
>(213) 829-3449

or
>Polyester Chemical Corp.
>Pacoima, California
>(818) 896-5208

Chamois. See ''Automobile Parts & Supplies'' in your phone book.

Cheesecloth. See ''Fabrics'' in your phone book.

Chicken wire. See ''Hardware'' in your phone book.

Crystal Craze or **Crystaline.** See ''Crafts Supplies'' or ''Artists Materials & Supplies'' in your phone book, or
>Kit Kraft
>Studio City, California
>(818) 984-0780

Dulling Spray. See ''Artists Materials & Supplies'' or ''Photographic Equipment & Supplies'' in your phone book, or
>Flax Art Store
>Westwood, California
>(213) 208-3529

Durham's Rockhard Water Putty. See ''Hardware'' in your phone book.

Elvanol.
>DuPont de Nemours
>(800) 441-7515

Epoxy Putty.
>Martin Carboni Co.
>Santa Barbara, California
>(805) 628-0465
>(Hand Workable Epoxy Putty)

Erosion Cloth. See ''Nurseries—Plants, Trees'' in your phone book.

Ethafoam.
>C. R. Laurence—West
>Los Angeles, California
>(213) 588-1281

Feathers. See ''Feathers'' in your phone book, or
>Rainbow Feather Dyeing
>Burbank, California
>(818) 842-3210

Fiberglass. See ''Plastics—Raw Materials'' in your phone book, or
>Hastings Plastics
>Santa Monica, California
>(213) 829-3449

Flameproofing.
>Flamemaster Corp.
>Sun Valley, California
>(818) 982-1650

or
>California Flameproofing
>Pasadena, California
>(213) 681-6773
>(foliage flameproofing ''No. 57 Green'')

Flex-glue.
>Swifts Adhesives
>Los Angeles, California
>(213) 726-2625
>(Glue #43917)

or
>Spectra Dynamics
>Albuquerque, New Mexico
>(505) 843-7202
>(Phlexglu)

Florist's tape. See ''Artificial Flowers'' in your phone book, or
>Stats Decorator and Crafts
>Pasadena, California
>(818) 795-9308

Fuller's earth.
>Mann Brothers Paints
>Hollywood, California
>(213) 936-5168

Gelatin glue.
The Olesen Co.
Hollywood, California
(213) 461-4631

Glass frosting. See "Paint" or "Artists Materials & Supplies" in your phone book, or
Mann Brothers Paints
Hollywood, California
(213) 936-5168

Gold metallic tape. See "Artists Materials & Supplies" in your phone book, or
H.G. Daniels Co.
Los Angeles, California
(213) 387-1211

Graphite.
Joseph Dixon Co.
Lakehurst, New Jersey
(201) 244-7110

Grass mat.
Pacific Cemetery Supply
Los Angeles, California
(213) 268-8121
(Raffia grass)

Hot glue. See "Hardware" in your phone book, or
Adhesive Machinery
Seabrook, New Hampshire
(603) 474-5541
(Hysol glue guns)

Lamp parts.
Crystal Lamp Parts
Los Angeles, California
(213) 746-2520

Latex rubber. See "Hobby & Model Construction Supplies" in your phone book, or
Don Post Studios
North Hollywood, California
(818) 768-0811

Matting tape. See "Artists Materials & Supplies" in your phone book, or
H.G. Daniels
Los Angeles, California
(213) 387-1211

Muslin. See "Fabrics" in your phone book, or
Dazians
Beverly Hills, California
(213) 655-9691
(9′ wide)
or
Gerriets International
Allentown, New Jersey
(609) 758-9121
(Seamless widths of 30′ and over)

Nonwoven fabric.
Mark Textile Corp.
Los Angeles, California
(213) 680-0860

Nylon net. See "Fabrics" in your phone book.

Paraffin wax. See "Candle Supply" or "Grocers" in your phone book.

Pipe insulation. See "Plumbing Fixtures & Supplies" in your phone book.

Plaster of Paris. See "Hobby & Model Construction Supplies," "Paint," or "Lumber" in your phone book.

Plastic body filler. See "Automobile Parts & Supplies" in your phone book.

Plasticine. See "Crafts Supplies," "Hobby & Model Construction Supplies," or "Artists Materials & Supplies" in your phone book, or
Westwood Ceramics
City of Industry, California
(818) 330-0631

Polyester resin. See "Plastics—Raw Materials" in your phone book, or

> Polyester Chemical Corp.
> Pacoima, California
> (818) 896-5208

or

> Plastic Mart
> Santa Monica, California
> (213) 451-1701

Polyethylene sheets. See "Plastics—Rods, Tubes, Sheets" in your phone book, or

> Plastic Sales, Inc.
> Los Angeles, California
> (213) 728-8309

PVC water pipe. See "Building Materials" or "Plumbing Fixtures & Supplies" in your phone book.

Spray adhesive. See "Artists Materials & Supplies" or "Hardware" in your phone book.

Stage money.

> Earl Hayes Press
> Sun Valley, California
> (818) 765-0700

Urethane foam. See "Plastics—Foam" in your phone book. For small pieces, see "Crafts Supplies."

Water pumps.

> Calvert Engineering, Inc.
> Van Nuys, California
> (818) 781-6029
> (Manufacturer of pumps for small fountains)

Zip cord. See "Hardware" or "Electric Equipment & Supplies" in your phone book.

INDEX

A

Acetate ink, 259
Acetate sheets, 259
Acrylic sheets, 259
Adhesive, 259
    spray, 263
Alfalfa/straw, bales of, 188-9
Aluminized mylar, 259
Aluminum powder, 259
Aluminum sheet, 259
Animal forms, 1-25
Animal glue, 141
Archaeological relics, 26-7
Arrowheads, 26
Artificial foodstuffs, 121-140
Atomizer, perfume, 175
Aviary wire, 259

B

Baluster, 259
Balusters, sculpting foam, 71-2
Balustrade, 259
Barbecue grill, 118
Barbecued lamb, 18-21
Barbed wire, 28-9
Batteries, lamp conversion to, 95-6
Bead foam, 259
Beehive, sculpting foam, 72-3
Beer can label, fake, 78-9
Bench, rehearsal, 208-9
Bevel, 259
Beverages, 121
Binder, 259
Binocular replicas, 99-100
Blood, 30-1
Bloody knife, 33-4
Blueprinter, for processing old-time photos, 178-9
Board foot, 259

Bondo (plastic filler putty), 162, 259
Bone tools, 26
Book covers, 37-9
Bookbinder's glue (see Flex-Glue)
Books, 35-45
    antique replicas, 36-7
    character, 40-1
    dust jackets, 44-5
    familiar, 36
    lightweight, 42-4
Brass and copper relic jewelry, 27
Brass bed headboard, 177
Brass sheet, 259
Bread, 121-2
Brownline paper, 178-180, 259
Burlap, 259
Bushes, topiary, 184-6
Butter churn, 53-8
Butterflies and moths, 2-3

C

Cabosil, 259
Camp fire, 112-3
Candy, 123-5
    chocolates, 123-4
    peppermint sticks, 124-5
Casting, 259
Casting resin, 259
Casting with hot glue, 157-8
Cauliflower, 126-7
Chair, rehearsal, 198-204
Chamois, 259
Cheese, 127
Cheeseburger, 130-1
Cheesecloth, 259
Cheetah, 11-2
Chicken drumstick, 128
Chicken wire, 260
Chocolates, 123-4

Churn, butter, 53-8
Cloth mache, 260
Coins, stage money, 214-5
Confetti, 46
Construction techniques, 47-77
Containers, 78-86
Crystal Craze, 260
Crystal Lamp Parts, 173
Crystaline, 260
Cube, rehearsal, 205-7
Cuts, fabric, 75-6

D

Detergent, 260
Distressing, 260
    wood, 226-9
Dog, urethane, sculpting, 65-6
Doughnuts and Danish, glazed, 156
Drapery table, 73-5
Drumstick, chicken, 128
Dulling Spray, 260
Dummy figures, 1
Durhams's Rockhard Water Putty, 260
Dust jackets, books, 44-5

E

Ear trumpet, 175
Edible prop food, 120
Electric pump, recirculating, 211-2
Electrical hardware, 169
Electricity
    battery connections, 88-91
    low voltage lamps, 87-97
    physics of, 87-94
    power supply package, 92-4
Elvanol (polyvinyl alcohol), 141-3, 260

Embedding material, 149-151
Epoxy putty, 47-9, 260
    bonding with, 49
Erosion cloth, 260
Ethafoam, 260
Eyeglasses, 99-106
    granny glasses, 102-3
    history of, 101
    lorgnette, 105-6
    monocle, 103-4

F

Fabric, nonwoven, 262
Fabric cuts, 75-6
Falcon Foam, 260
FEV (French Enamel Varnish),
    143-4
Fiberglass, 260
Filler, plastic body, 262
Fir, 260
Fire
    camp, 112-3
    flickering log, 110-2
Fire/flames, 107-119
Firearms, 236-242
Fireplace, smoldering, 114-5
Flameproofing and preserving
    foliage, 186-7
Flash pot substitute, 119
Flameproofing, 260
Flashlight, dimmer-controlled, 97
Flex-Glue, 144-5, 260
Flickering log fire, 110-2
Florist's tape, 260
Foam
    polyethylene, 50-1
    urethane, 263
Foliage, flameproofing and
    preserving, 186-7, 260
Food, 120-140
    artificial, 121-140
Foreign currency, stage money,
    218
Forms, animal, 1-25
Found objects, use of, 169-172
French Enamel Varnish (FEV),
    143-4
Fruit cocktail, 136-7

Fruits and vegetables, 132-3
Fuller's earth, 260
Furniture
    light-colored, 233
    rehearsal, 196-209

G

Garden, patio, 182-3
Gelatin glue, 141, 260
Glare reduction, 232-5
    softening with nylon net, 234
Glass, stained, 219-225
Glass frosting, 260
Glasses, Russian tea, 82-3
Glazed doughnuts, 156
Glossary, 259-263
Glue, hot, 152-6
Glue cloth, 260
Glues and adhesives, 141-158
    hot, variety available, 155
Goblet, 174
Gold metallic tape, 260
Goose eggs, urethane foam, 67-9
Gramophone, 159-164
Granny glasses, 102-3
Graphite, 260
Grass mat, 260
Greens, definition of, iv
Grill, barbecue, 118
Gun-metal finish, painting, 247-8

H

Hamburger, with the "works" 128
Hand props, definition of, iv
Hand-made paper, 255
Hay cart, dressing and
    flameproofing, 189-192
Heart, human, 31-2
Hedge, 182-3
Hookah, 174
Hot glue, 152-6, 260
    casting, 157-8
    non-adhesive applications,
        156
    ornamentation, 156
Hourglass, 171

I

Ice Cubes, 165-7
Ink, acetate, 259
Inkwell set, 256-7
Inkwells, 176
Insulation, pipe, 262
Invisible knot, 52-3, 260

J

Jugs, rustic, from wine bottles, 83-
    6
Junk art, 168-172

K

Knife, 174
    bloody, 33-4
Knot, invisible, 52-3, 260

L

Lamb, barbecued, 18-21
Lamp parts, various applications
    of, 173-7
Latex rubber, 260
Leather texture, 145-8
Lettuce, 132-3
Lorgnette, 105-6
Low voltage lamps, 87-97
Lumber sizes, 260
Lumber types, 260

M

Machine gun fire, simulating with
    strobe light, 249-251
Machine tooling urethane foam,
    67-70
Manual sound effects, definition
    of, v
Marbleizing, 229-232
Masonite, 262
Matting tape, 262
Miter, 262
Money, stage, 214-8
Monocle, 103-4
Morgue, picture, viii
Moths and butterflies, 2-3
Muslin, 262

N

Nails, 262
Net, nylon, 262
Nonwoven fabric, 262
Nylon net, 262

O

Oil lamp, dimmer-controlled, 98
Ornamentation with hot glue, 156
Owl, 3-7

P

Paint binder, 151
Paper, 253
    brownline, 259
    hand-made, 255
    stage money, 216
Paraffin wax, 262
Parchment, 253-4
Patio garden, 182-3
Peacock, 8-11
Pellon, 262
Pelt, building a, 11-4
Pencils, 256
Pens, 256
Peppermint sticks, 124-5
Perfume atomizer, 175
Personal props, definition of, iv
Photos, old-time, 178-181
Picture morgue, vi-viii
Pie, blueberry, 134-5
Pine, 262
Pipe, PVC, 59
Pipe insulation, 262
Pistols, 236
Plant foliage, stylized, 192-4
Plant forms, 182-195
Plaster of Paris, 262
Plastic body filler, 262
Plasticine, 262
Plexiglas, 262
Plumbing, 169
Plywood, 262
Polyester resins, 263
Polyester window pane, 224-5
Polyethylene
    foam, 50-1
    sheets, 263

Pottery urn, 27
Powder, aluminum, 259
Prop food, edible, 120
Prop man, definition of, v
Properties, definition of, ii
Properties Master, definition of, v
Putty, Durham's Rockhard Water,
    260
Putty, epoxy, 47-9
PVA, 263
PVC pipe, 59, 263

R

Rain effects, 213
Rapier, 173
Recirculating electric pump, 211-
    2
Rehearsal
    bench, 208-9
    chair, 198-204
    cube, 205-7
    furniture, 196-209
    sofa, 204-5
Relics, archaeological, 26-7
Resins, polyester, 263
Rough textures, 152
Rubber, latex, 260
Running water, 210-3
Russian tea glasses, 82-3

S

Sandwich, 131
Sapling tree, 195
Sausage, 135-6
Scarecrow, 14-7
Scroll, 175
Sculpting urethane foam, 61-6
Set dressings, definition of, iv
Set props, definition of, iv
Sewing techniques, 73-7
Shatter-resistant skin, 152
Sheep, 13-4
Sheets
    aluminum, 259
    acetate, 259
    acrylic, 259
    polyethylene, 263
Shepherd's Crook, 59-60
Shotgun, 236-241

Simulating fires, 109
Skin
    membranes, and tissue, 148-9
    shatter-resistant, 152
Smoke effects, 118-9
Smoldering fireplace, 114-5
Sofa, rehearsal, 204-5
Spray adhesive, 263
Stage money, 214-8
    coins, 214-5
    do-it-yourself, 217
    foreign currency, 218
    paper, 216
Stained glass, 219-225
Straight hems, sewing, 77
Straw/alfalfa, bales of, 188-9
Strawberries, 137-8
Stylized plant foliage, 192-4
Styrofoam, 263
Sub-machine gun, Thompson,
    242-6
Supplies, sources of, 264-7
Swords, 251-2

T

Tape, matting, 262
Techniques, construction, 47-77
Telephones, antique, 176
Textures, 226-236
    rough, 152
Tissue, membranes, and skin,
    148-9
Topiary bushes, 184-6
Torch and brush weathering
    technique, 227-9
Torch/firebrand, 116-8
Tree, sapling, 195
Trim props, definition of, iv
Turtle, 21-5

U

Urethane foam, 263
    machine tooling, 67-70
    sculpting, 61-6

V

Vegetables and fruits, 132-3
Vial, 79-81

W

Water, running, 210-3
   under pressure, 211
Water supply, gravity-fed, 210
Wax, paraffin, 262
Weapons, 236-252

White glue (polyvinyl acetate),
   141
Window pane, polyester, 224-5
Wire
   aviary, 259
   barbed, 28-9
   chicken, 260

Wood, distressing, 226-9
Writing materials, 253-7

Z

Zip cord, 263

About the Author

Thurston James has been active in educational theater for the last 28 years. For seven years, he served on the faculty of Immaculate Heart College in Hollywood, acting as technical director and teaching courses in theater crafts.

Mr. James has been with the UCLA Theater Arts Department for nineteen years, serving as shop carpenter, scenic artist, lighting designer, and most recently, as its properties master for the last twelve years.

Concurrently with his responsibilities at UCLA, Mr. James serves as a free-lance property builder for motion picture and television studios.